Skill-Building for the Beginner Artist

How to Draw the Portrait in Pencil

by Jacquelyn Descanso

Skill-Building for the Beginner Artist: How to Draw the Portrait in Pencil

by Jacquelyn Descanso

ISBN-13: 978-1517632311

ISBN-10: 1517632315

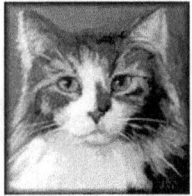

Lumpy & Stinky Press

lumpyandstinky.com

Dedication:

To my family and loved ones—my eternal gratitude for your support and understanding.

Table of Contents

INTRODUCTION

A lot of people look upon drawing as some mysterious thing that only "talented" people can do. They believe that if you're not born with that talent, you're out of luck.

This book will help convince you that this is not true. The fact is, anyone can learn how to draw. Why have we all been brainwashed into thinking that we must have "talent" in order to draw?

Part of the problem is that our brains have stored these symbolically-styled "formulas" of how to draw certain things. Every time we try to draw something like a person, a house, or a car, we don't even think past the formulas that we were taught as children. As we grow older, we're never taught how to move past that. As a result of this, our drawings continue to turn out looking awkward and childlike, even when we are adults. So, we throw up our hands, proclaim that we don't have any artistic "talent," and that's all there is to it!

But, it's not about a lack of talent, it's about being taught to truly "see"!

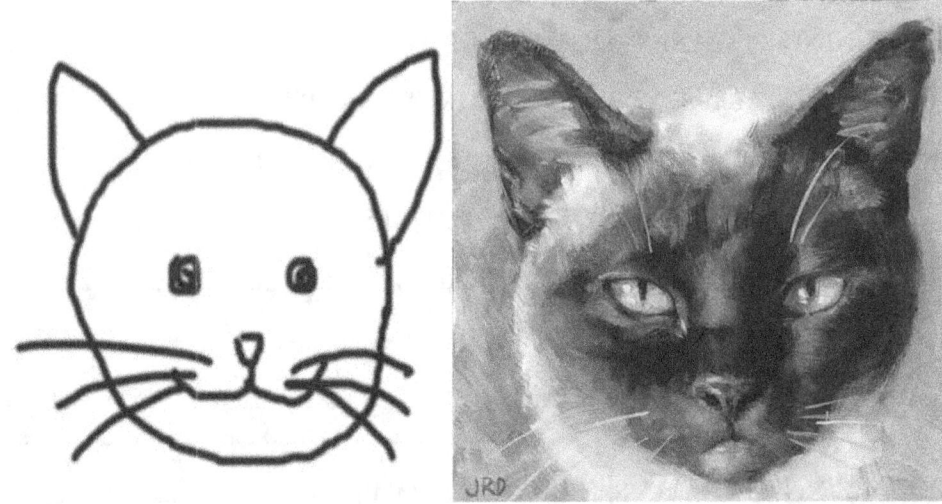

The picture on the left is what a lot of us get when we are thinking with symbols. The more analytical, unartistic side of our brain says: "Draw a cat? Right. Make pointy ears, three lines on each side for whiskers, triangle nose, round head, dots for eyes, DONE!" But the result is far from realistic. When we ignore the stereotypical "symbolism" method of drawing a cat and start to really SEE, we are able to create something that looks far more like the picture on the right.

I've had the art bug since childhood. While I had an aptitude for drawing, what also happened was that I stumbled upon a way to "see" more correctly. I remember one time puzzling out how to draw some difficult pose of my cat and for a moment I looked at a cat—I mean, really LOOKED at it—and "saw" the actual shape of its head, its nose, its eyes. I had moved past my "symbolic" understanding, at least for a moment, to draw what I actually saw. My drawing was still a childish rendition but was starting to lean more towards realism.

What I discovered by happenstance can be given to anyone. Some people start to figure it out on their own (like many artists do), but everyone else can be taught. The end result will be the same either way. Learn how to "see", and you can learn how to draw.

WHAT'S IN THIS BOOK:

The first chapters contain an introduction to some drawing basics. Since this book is for "beginner artists," it's necessary to include these fundamentals. If you already have some drawing experience, some of these lessons may seem redundant. If that is the case, you may review them briefly and move on. However, if you have little experience with drawing, you may also want to pick up a book which is devoted to the general subject of beginning drawing. I have listed several beginning book recommendations at the end of this book. (My motto is that you can never have enough art books!)

There are several portrait projects that you will be expected to complete. These projects are sometimes followed with a chapter which covers some new technique, which you will then apply to the next portrait projects. Each chapter should introduce you to new insights and methods. You'll be naturally acquiring new skills as you go along.

Even though there are some step-by-step lessons included in some of the chapters, often you will be also guided with tips and advice to help you complete the assigned project.

While the first part of the book introduces the grid method as part of the process, later chapters move on to other techniques. These other methods give artists more freedom and flexibility in their drawing. In this book, we'll be using the grid as a sort of artistic "training wheels". Helpful for beginners, but not something to be used indefinitely.

The last portion of the book contains some "FAQs" (Frequently Asked Questions) about being an artist, and answers questions like "When can I call myself an artist?" and "When can I start selling my work?"

HOW TO GET THE MOST OUT OF THIS BOOK:

Start with the first chapter. Please don't read the book out of order. I gradually add new techniques and skill-building concepts as we go along. If you skip around, you may end up being confused, as I sometimes refer to something that was taught in a previous chapter.

PEARLS OF WISDOM FOR THE BEGINNER ARTIST:

If you want to enjoy rapid improvement and exciting results, then you should be determined and focused.

There are a lot of ways to make time for drawing. It's easier than you think. Try doodling while in waiting rooms and in line at the DMV. Spend less time on your mobile phone and work more at drawing. It can be done!

You should practice regularly. It doesn't have to be every day or for long stretches at a time. But, try to make a habit of it. Think of it this way: it's better to practice for one hour twice a week (though, ideally it would be great if you could do more than that) than to go on an eight-hour drawing marathon once a month.

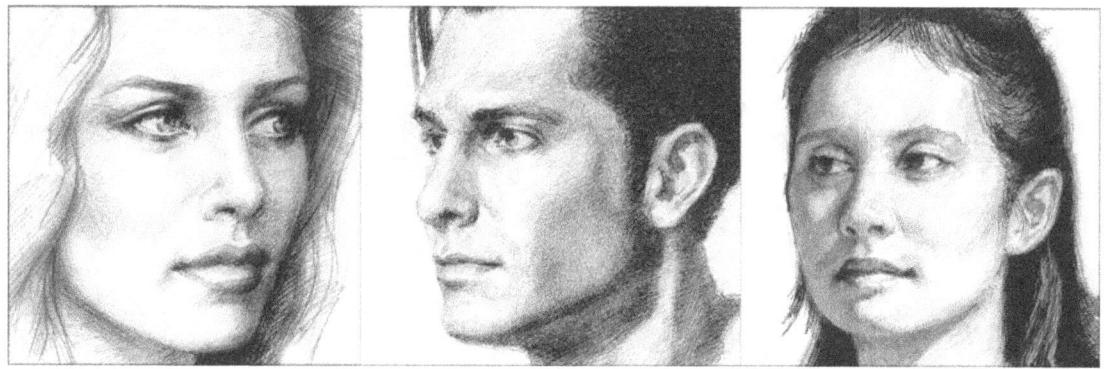

Some example drawings seen in the chapters of this book.

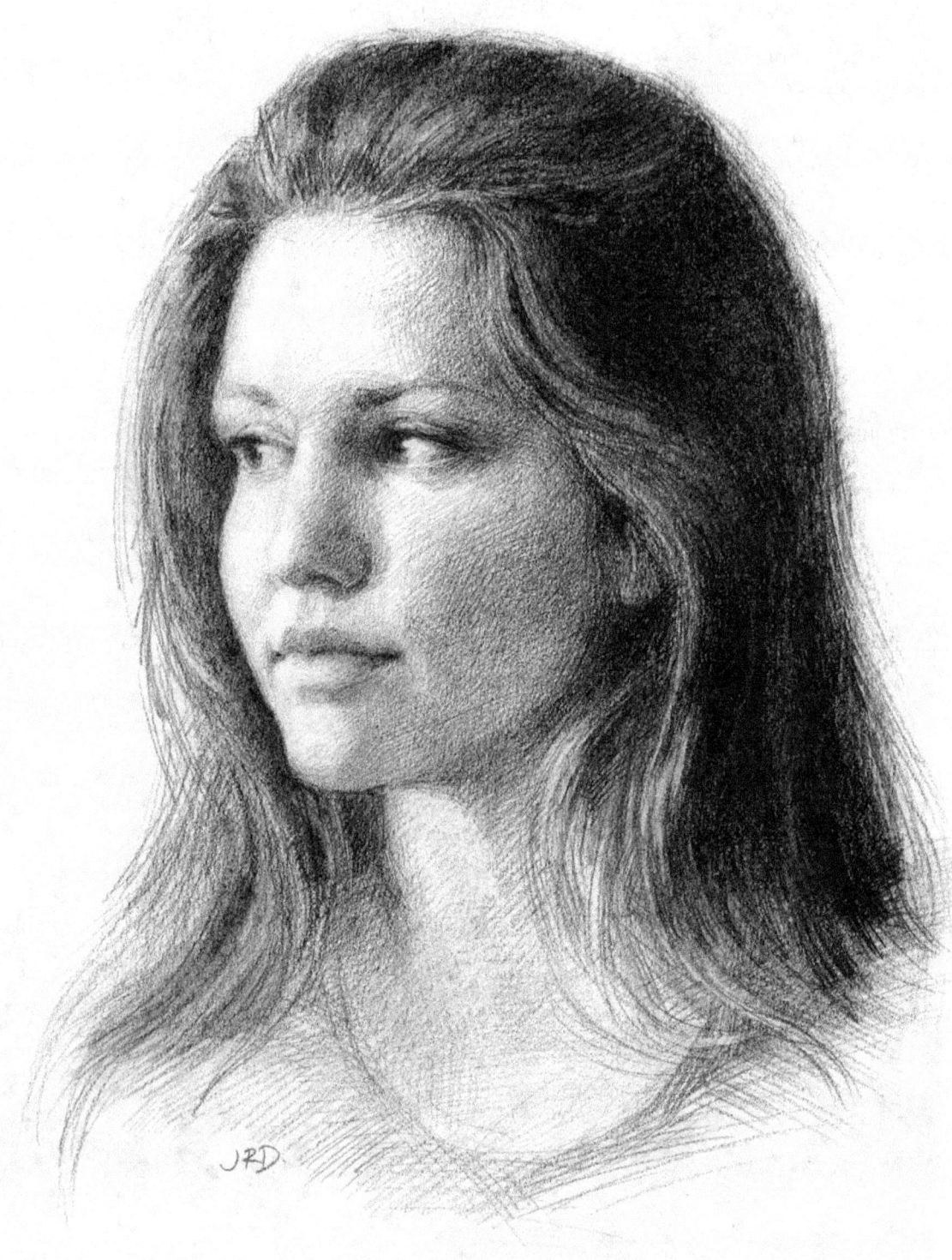

Portrait, graphite on toned paper, 2016

CHAPTER ONE: BEGINNING TECHNIQUES AND A DRAWING OVERVIEW

THE NECESSARY MATERIALS:

You cannot begin to draw unless you have some art materials! Fortunately, the necessary supplies are easy to find, affordable, and definitely not exotic. You can buy some of the supplies at your local grocery or drug store. Other supplies should be available at the local hobby or craft store, or in the art/craft department of a Walmart-type store.

SUPPLY LIST:

- Sketch or drawing paper, acid-free. (Do NOT get newsprint or any art paper that does not specify "acid-free." If the paper is not acid-free, it will deteriorate and turn brown over time.) You can usually find sketch pads at a larger supermarket, most craft stores, and of course art stores. You don't want paper that is excessively thin, but for practice sketches, it's not required to have the most expensive paper either. Try for something with a smoother texture. (What constitutes "smooth" texture is open to interpretation. You may want to experiment with various textures of paper as you go along.)

- Regular #2 pencil (yellow wooden pencil is most common) and pencil sharpener, OR

- Mechanical "clicky" type pencil, with either 0.7mm or 0.5mm leads. "HB" or "B" lead preferred. HB , also known as "#2," is the most common. (The "B" rating refers to "Black," meaning that the lead is softer and therefore makes a darker (black) line. The higher the number, the softer (and blacker) the pencil lead will be. Therefore, a 4B is darker than a 2B, and a 6B is darker (and smudgier) than a 4B. Pencils with an HB or 2H (4H, etc.) designation have a harder lead, which means they make lighter (less black) lines. (HB is as "hard" as I like to go.) I used a mechanical pencil with 0.5mm HB leads for most of the artwork seen in this book. If you prefer a regular wood pencil that can be sharpened, that works great, too. Don't forget a sharpener if you go with wood pencils.

- While it will not be needed immediately, a pencil with at least a 2B lead is also a wonderful thing. This softer pencil lead makes a stronger mark and will be perfect for getting the darkest shades in your drawings.

- Plastic (vinyl) white eraser. Found in craft or art stores; excellent for erasing graphite on paper.

- Kneaded rubber eraser. You'll have to go to a craft or art store for this, though some Walmarts may have them in the craft section. You'll find that it's very flexible, and in fact can be stretched and molded into any shape you like. It's perfect for erasing small, delicate areas. (If you absolutely cannot locate a kneaded rubber eraser right now, just use the erasers you have and keep on the lookout for a kneaded rubber eraser.)

- Ball point pen (Bic or other mainstream brand). Don't get the super-cheap kind, as the ink will blob and leak. (Granted, Bic brand pens may do this too, just not as badly.)

- Cheap note paper for sketching technique practice.

- A simple school ruler (12 inches or more). This book uses inches as the unit of measurement, but it is easy to estimate proper measurements in centimeters. (Approximate 3 centimeters for each unit of measurement. It doesn't have to be exact as long as the measurements are consistent within themselves.)

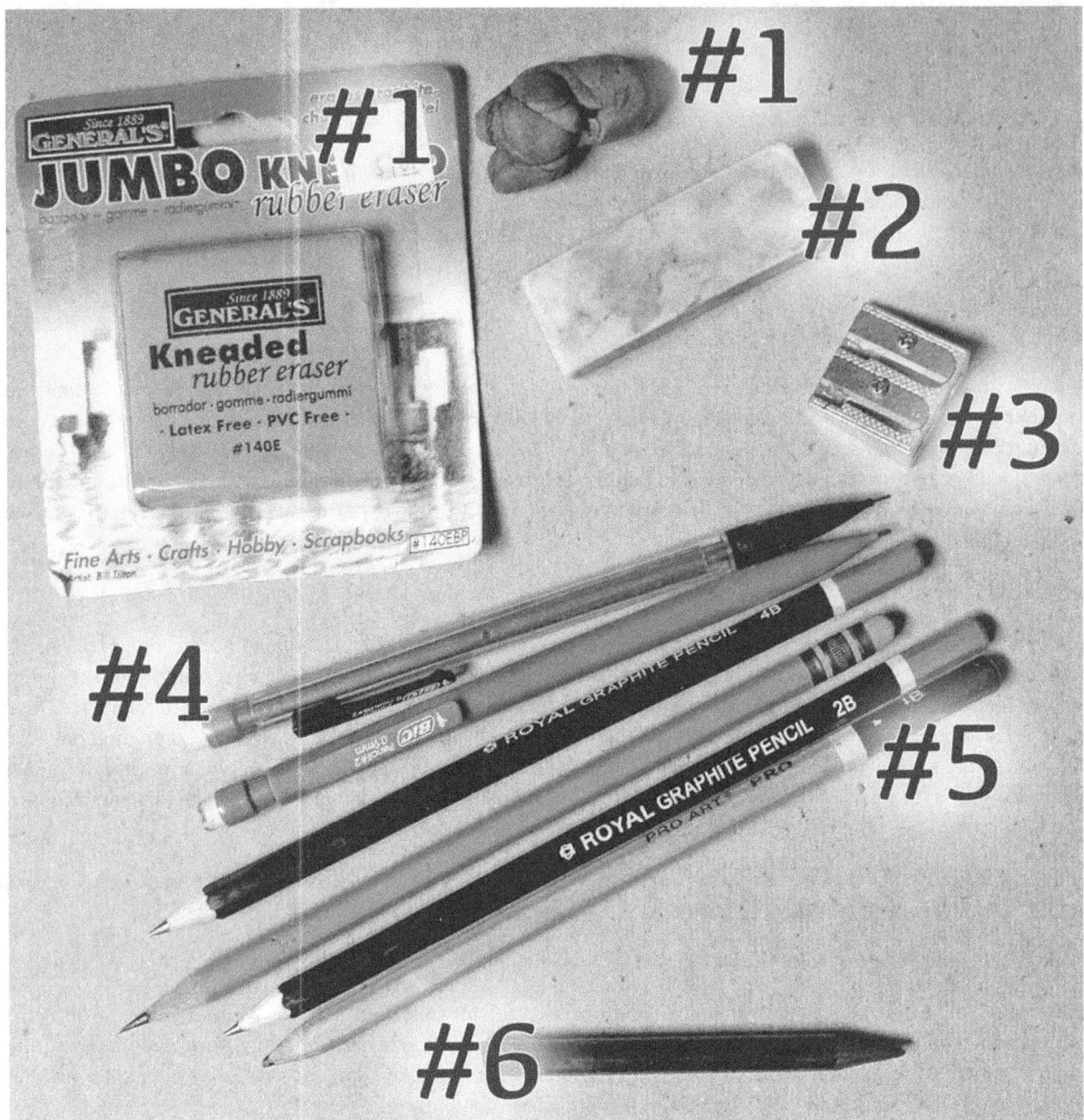

1. Kneaded rubber eraser (both packaged and unpackaged shown). There are many brands to choose from. They are usually sold as grey squares, but you will knead them into whatever shape you want. They'll end up resembling a wad of putty. They occasionally will be blue instead of grey.

2. White vinyl eraser. The one in the picture has been well-loved, so it is no longer pristine and white.

3. Simple pencil sharpener. If you use wooden pencils, you'll need one of these too. You can get a fancier electric one if you prefer.

4. Mechanical pencils. These are what I use probably 90% of the time. I end up getting BIC brand a lot, but most brands will suffice. It doesn't matter if they are the refillable kind or the disposable. Both work.

5. If you prefer wooden pencils, there are all types and brands. Note the softness rating on the pencil (2B).

6. (OPTIONAL) All-lead pencil. No wood, just pencil lead, which you can sharpen like an ordinary wood pencil. These come in handy when covering large dark areas in your drawing.

If you prefer, you can buy a drawing set at a local store or online. I recently purchased a set made by Royal & Langnickel. They sell several different sets with varying prices. As long as the set contains pencils, a kneaded rubber eraser, a vinyl eraser, and a pencil sharpener, it's good to go. The extra supplies often present in these kits are nice, but not required. While there are many companies which sell these kits, I am most familiar with General's and Royal & Langnickel brands and find them acceptable.

YOUR FIRST STEPS: CROSSHATCHING, AN OVERVIEW

Before we get started, you should learn about the primary pencil technique that we'll be using in this book. Many contemporary fine artists, as well as masters from generations past, have used the crosshatching technique, which is simply the use of pencil strokes crossing over each other to create tones and shadow in your drawing.

There are other popular methods used with graphite pencil, including blending. But in my opinion, crosshatching has many unique advantages, including the potential to be crisp, elegant, and versatile. It can be used for a more finished, detailed, "tight" work that takes hours to complete, but it's also perfect for very fast 5-minute sketches.

Once you learn how to crosshatch, the world is your oyster (artistically speaking), because you can use it in so many different ways!

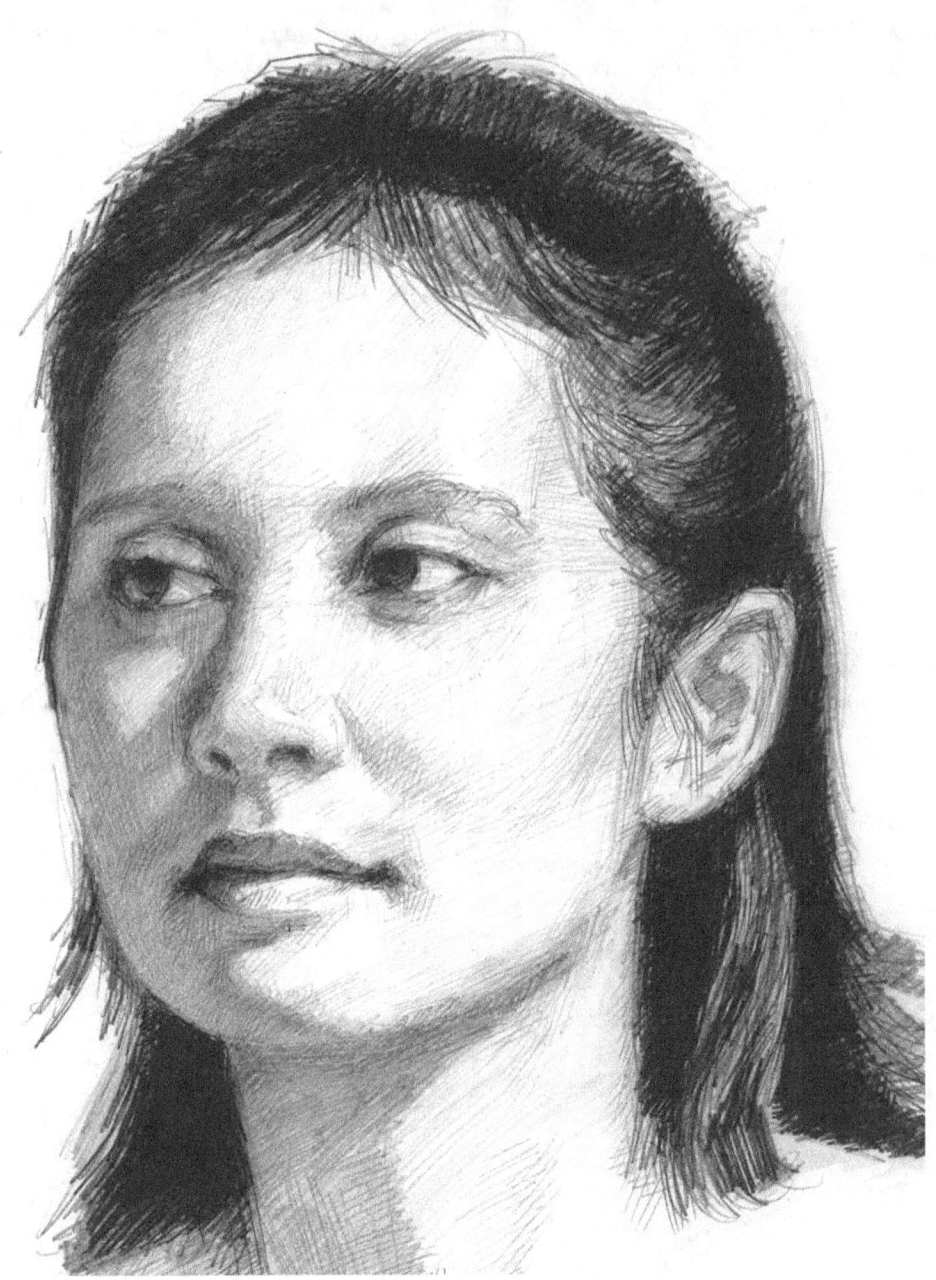

This is what I call a "value study," in which I was exploring the wonderful lights and darks (values) in this woman's portrait. I use a variety of lines, shadings, and strokes to capture the shadows and lights in her face.

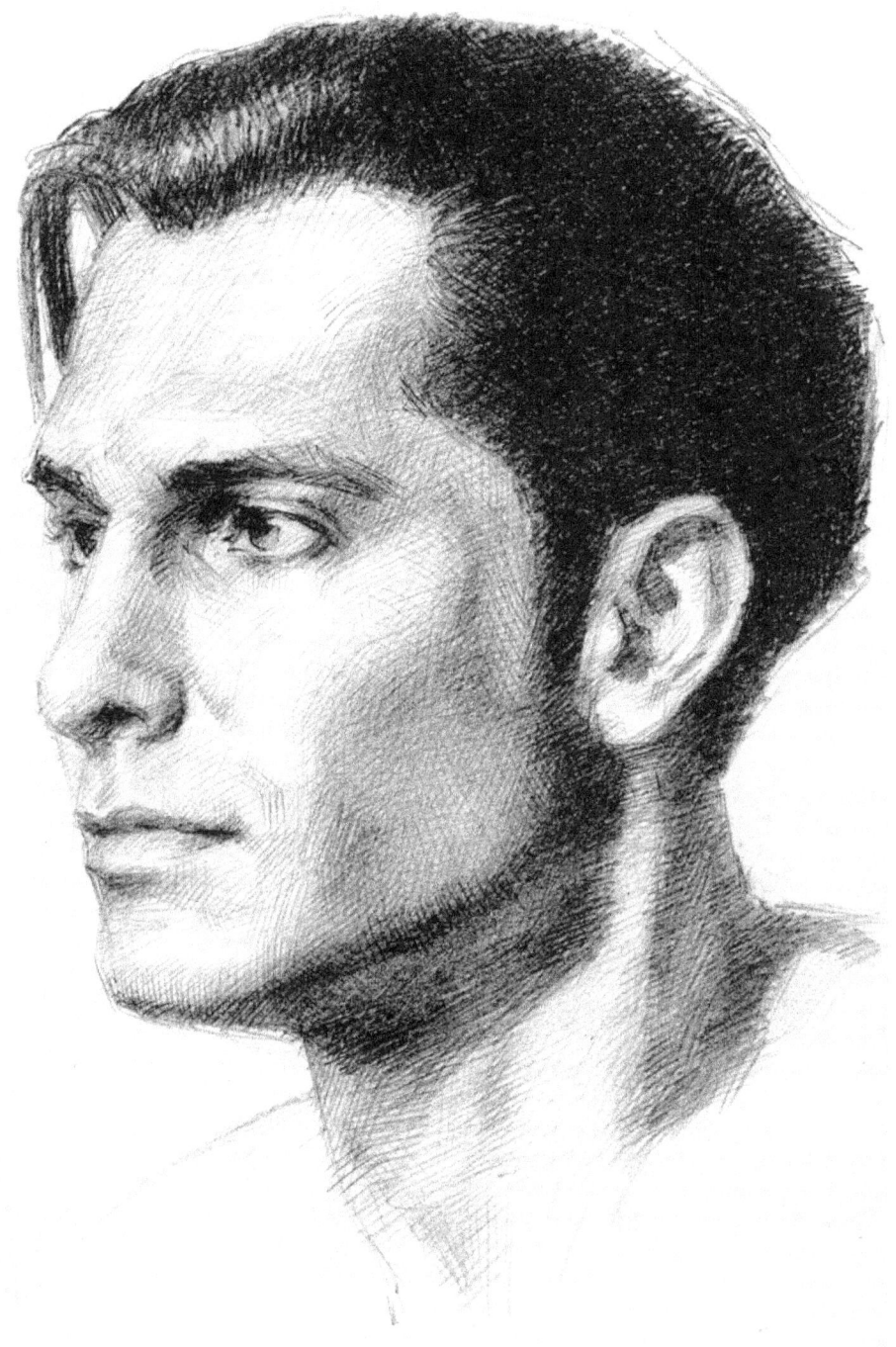

This portrait of "Miguel" is an example of more detailed crosshatching. It's not photorealistic, but is a little tighter and more carefully rendered than some of the other sketches in this book.

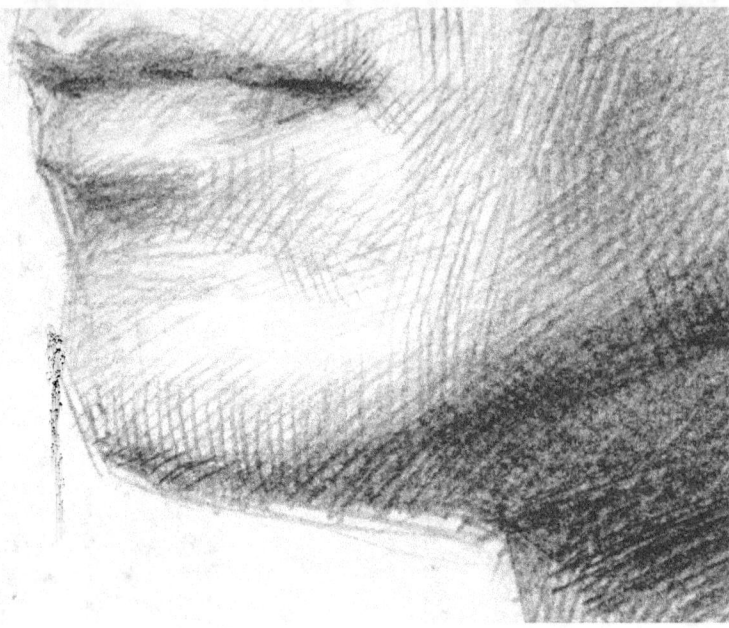

In this extreme close-up of Miguel's chin, you'll see that all the lights and darks, all the details, are created through cross-hatching-- hatching, hatching, hatching everywhere!

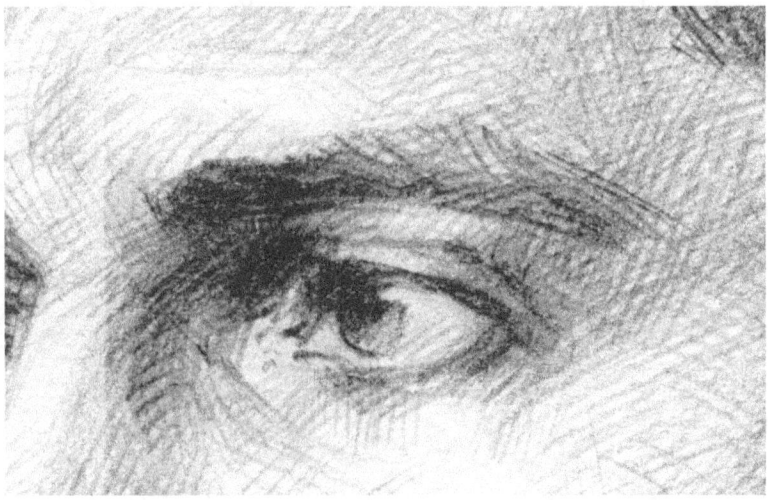

When seen at a distance, the portrait of Miguel doesn't look gratuitously "sketchy", but as you can see in this detail, it's all just more hatching and crosshatching!

GETTING ACQUAINTED WITH HATCHING

Now you should familiarize yourself with making these same kind of crosshatching lines. The best way to start is with simple practice of the crosshatching strokes themselves, without having to worry about applying them to an actual drawing.

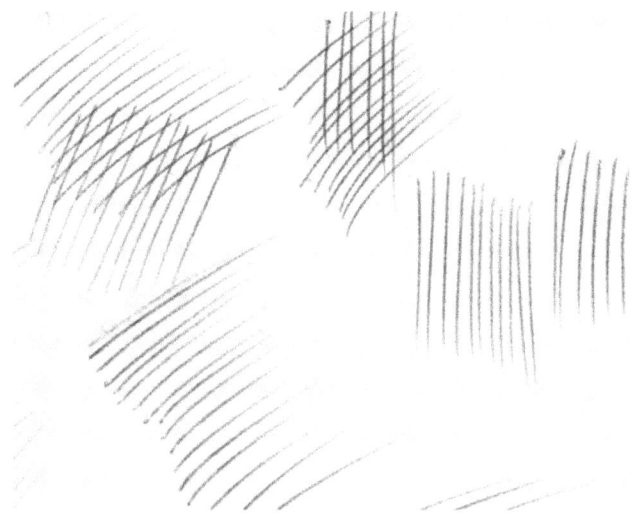

Using either a pencil or a ballpoint pen, start trying to make evenly-spaced lines on some note paper. Doodle these lines on the backs of envelopes, note pads, school papers—whatever you find in front of you!

You may have to do dozens, even hundreds, of these doodles before they start looking more polished. That's okay, because some of the best times to do these doodles is when you're bored, on the phone, waiting for an appointment, or don't have anything better to do. Working on these doodles is a completely worthwhile way to spend your time!

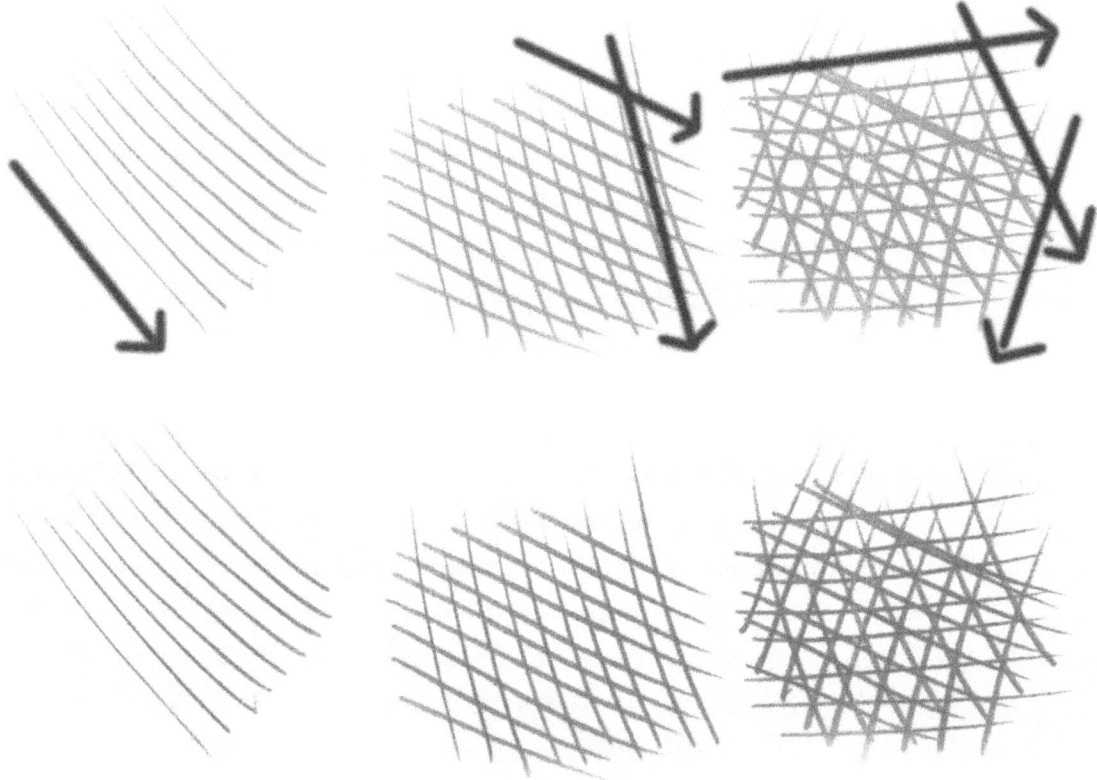

You can also start experimenting with a criss-cross pattern, which is basically what crosshatching is—lines crossing over each other. Try to make the lines more or less evenly spaced. (You'll see in the above illustrations they are not perfect, but still have a consistency to them.)

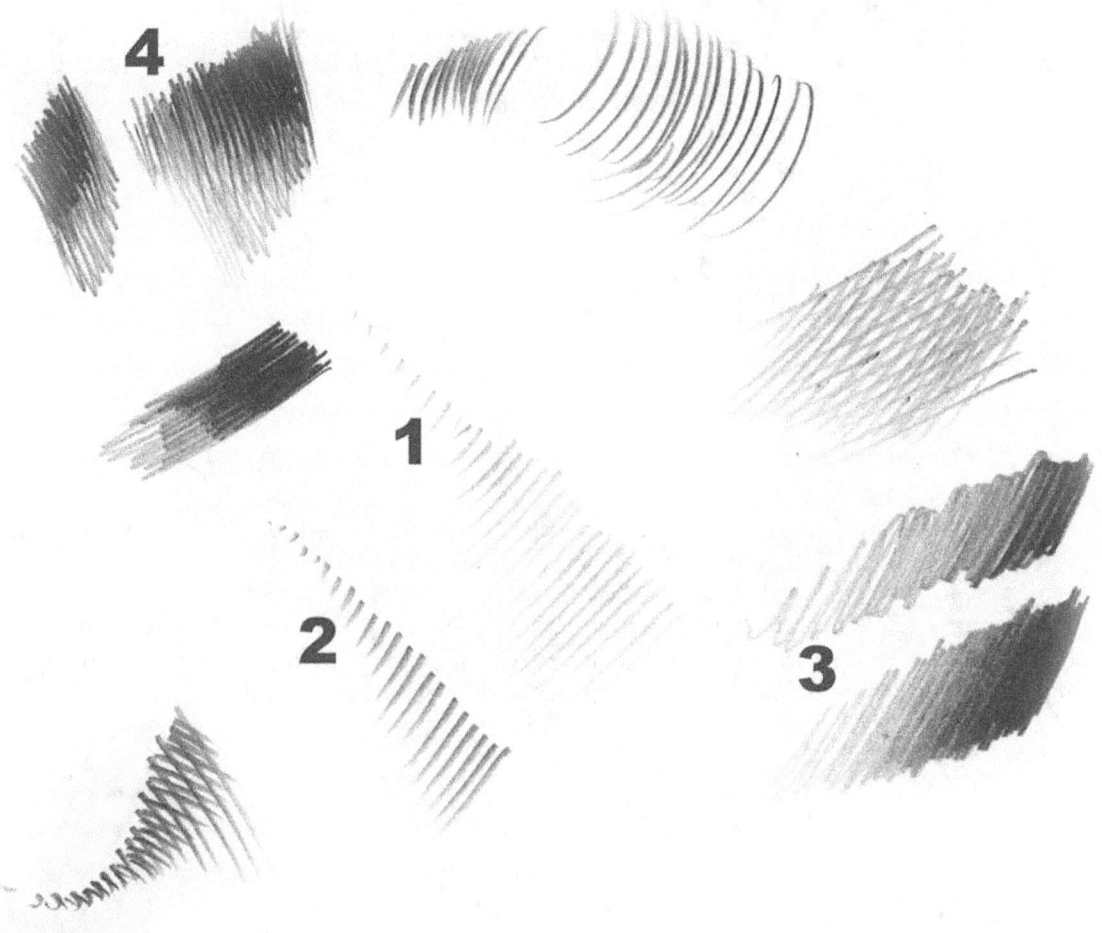

(These exercises are better suited for pencil, though you can experiment with pen, too!)

Make a series of light, delicate marks where your pencil barely grazes over the paper (example #1). Then make another series of marks where you put more pressure on the pencil to make the lines darker (#2). Learn how to control the darkness or lightness of the marks by using more or less pressure with your pencil.

Create darker, denser marks by leaving very little room between the hatch lines. Keep working over an area again and again until you have it almost completely black! (See example #4, where areas have been made black by heavy overlapping of pencil strokes.)

Then, try doing "gradient" doodles, where one half of the doodle is very dark, but tapers off to become gradually lighter. (#3).

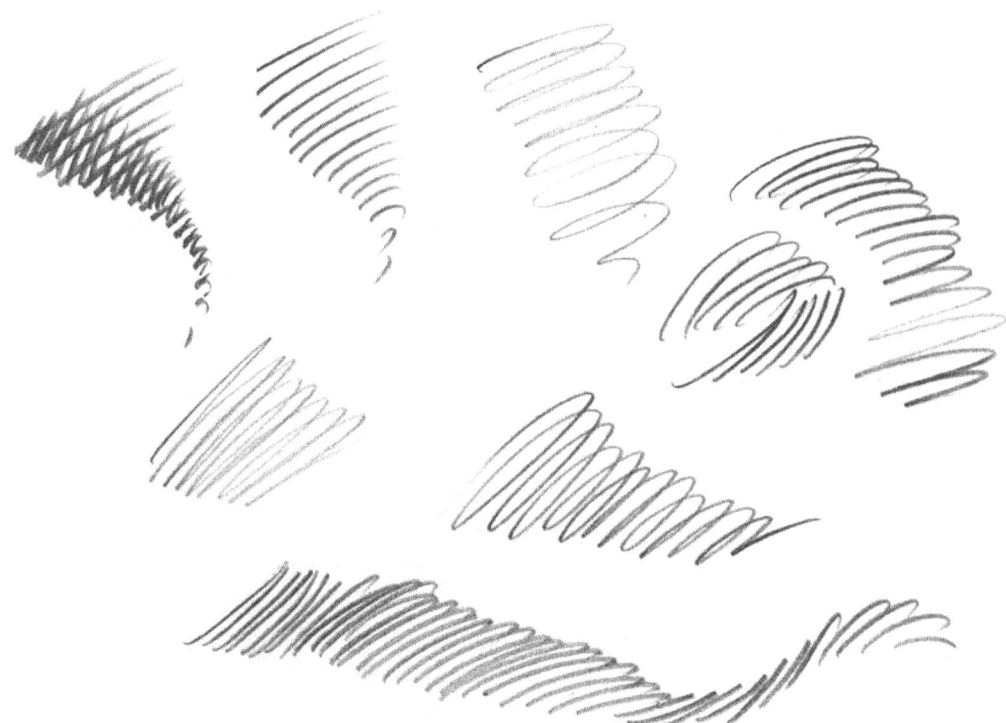

These doodles are what I call "cyclone doodles"; the ones which are one continuous loop are "slinky" doodles. Have fun making your pencil lines twist and turn and move in interesting directions.

If you find the crosshatching awkward or unnatural at first, don't worry, this is normal. Just keep doing it and your strokes will gradually become more even and controlled. It takes time for some people, so don't give up. Just keep doodling, doodling, doodling!

SKILL BUILDING LESSONS FROM CHAPTER ONE:

You have learned about the necessary tools needed for pencil drawing, and you've started to hone your crosshatching skills. You will keep practicing doodling in your spare time in the days and weeks to come. You are also learning how to control how light or how dark your crosshatching lines can be—skimming over the paper gently will make a light grey, while bearing down on your pencil (or pen) and repeatedly working over the same spot will make a very dark (or black) area.

CHAPTER TWO: GETTING STARTED WITH YOUR FIRST PORTRAIT

If you haven't ever drawn a face before, don't worry. I'll walk you through the whole process.

Remember, this is practice, so perfection is *not* required. If you only knew how many drawing pads full of horrible drawings I've collected over the years! Every artist I know has experienced the same thing. The purpose of this exercise is for you to gain new knowledge and skills, NOT to make the "perfect" portrait drawing.

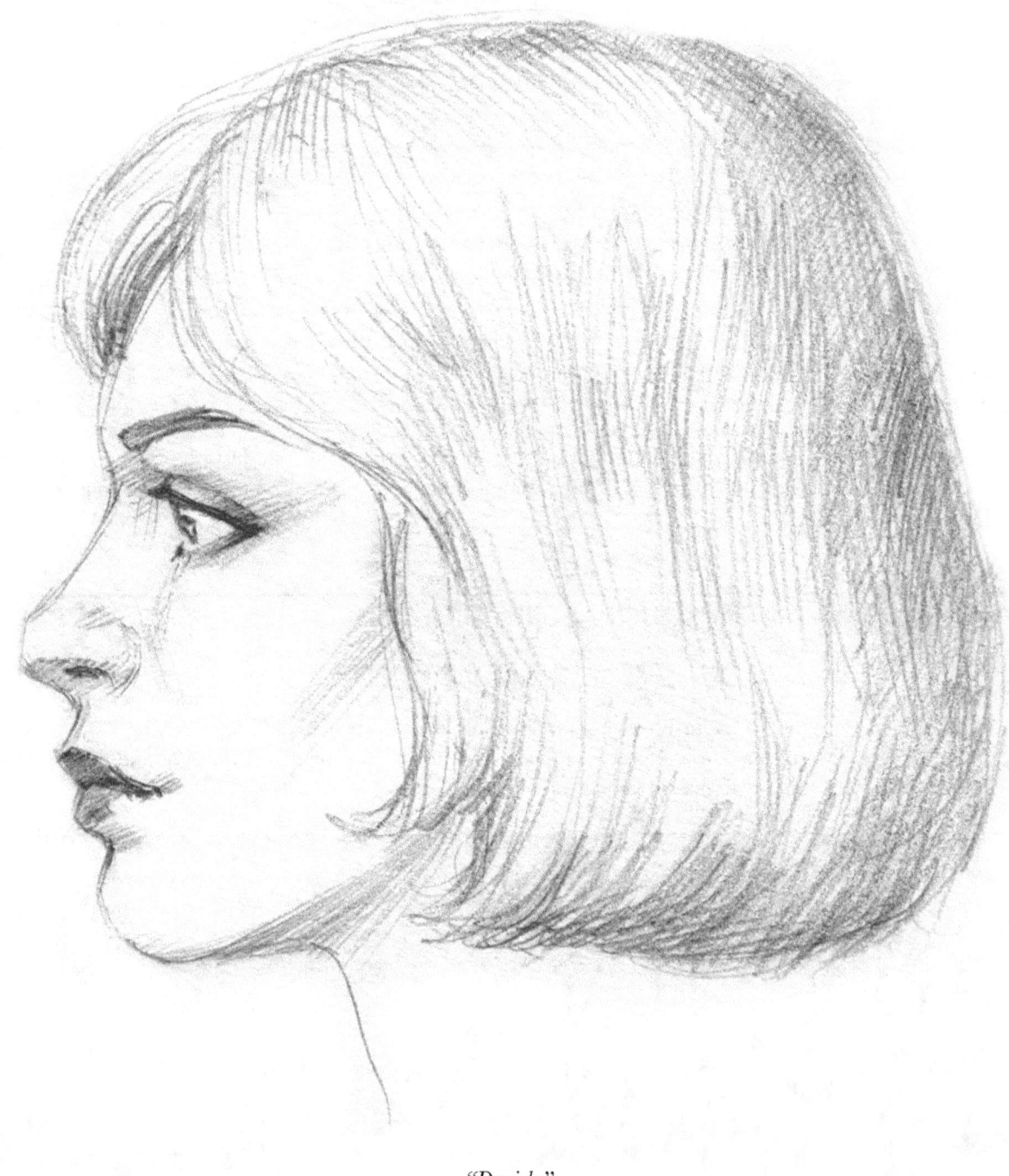

"Daniela"

In this project, you're going to learn how to use a grid. The grid will give you extra guidance, so you can position your lines in the correct place and your portrait looks in proportion.

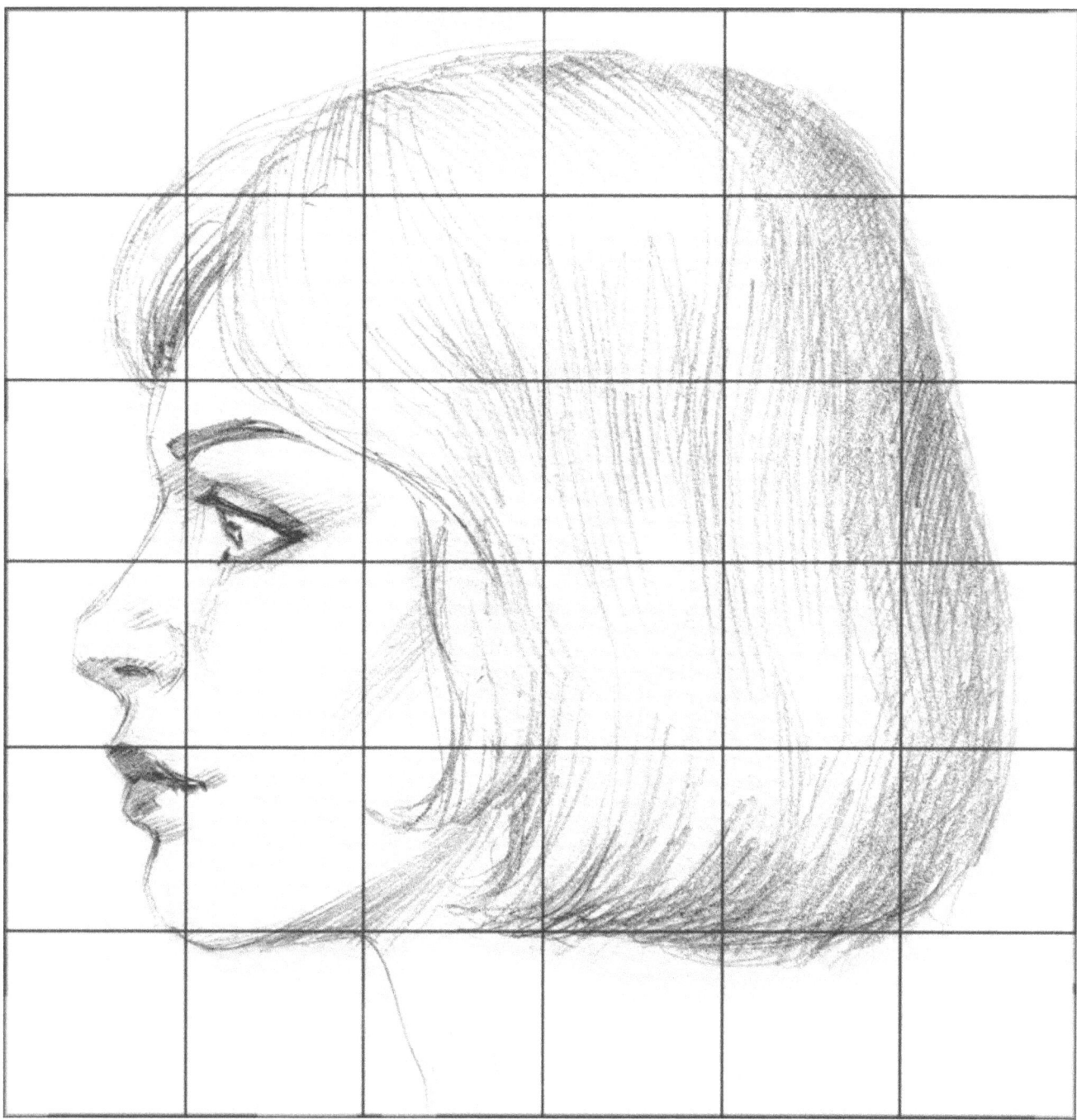

What I've done here is placed Daniela in a 6x6 inch square, and then marked off each inch, side to side, top to bottom. Then, with the help of a ruler, I've drawn one-inch squares over the whole drawing. (Well, it's not literally drawn on the drawing; I "cheated" and added the lines in Photoshop!)

For all the grids you will be making in this book, please remember that you can use whatever size you want, as long as all the squares are a consistent size. If your sketch paper size allows, you can go up to 12x12" (which, for the purposes of this particular portrait, would mean a grid consisting of two-inch squares). Or you can make 1-1/2-inch squares, for a total of 9x9". If you're using centimeters, aim for at least 3-centimeter squares or larger.

THE GRID

The grid is a tried-and-true method for aiding an artist with accuracy. It was used centuries ago, when the old masters would put grid squares over their preliminary drawings, and then transfer the outlines of these drawings onto a larger canvas to be painted. Nowadays, this method is often taught in art classes and in instructional books.

I think the grid is a wonderful tool, especially for beginners. It would be unfortunate, however, to have to always use a grid in order to achieve any accuracy in drawing. For one thing, that would not work well when you have only 25 minutes to draw a model! The grid has its uses, but it would be unwise to assume that you'll be able to rely on it every time you create artwork.

But we'll discuss those things later. All that matters for the moment is that as a beginner artist, this is the perfect time for you to use a grid.

MAKING THE GRID AND GETTING YOUR INITIAL OUTLINE

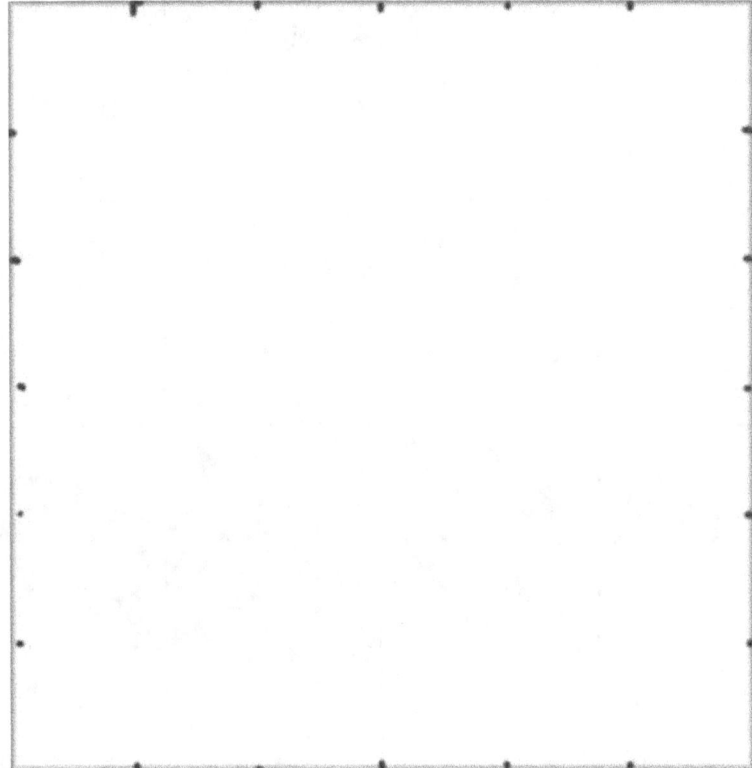

First, make a 6-inch square (or, it can be 9 or 12 inches if you prefer). Make marks every one inch (or every 1-1/2 inches for a 9-inch square, or every 2 inches for a 12-inch square—you get the idea) on each side of the square.

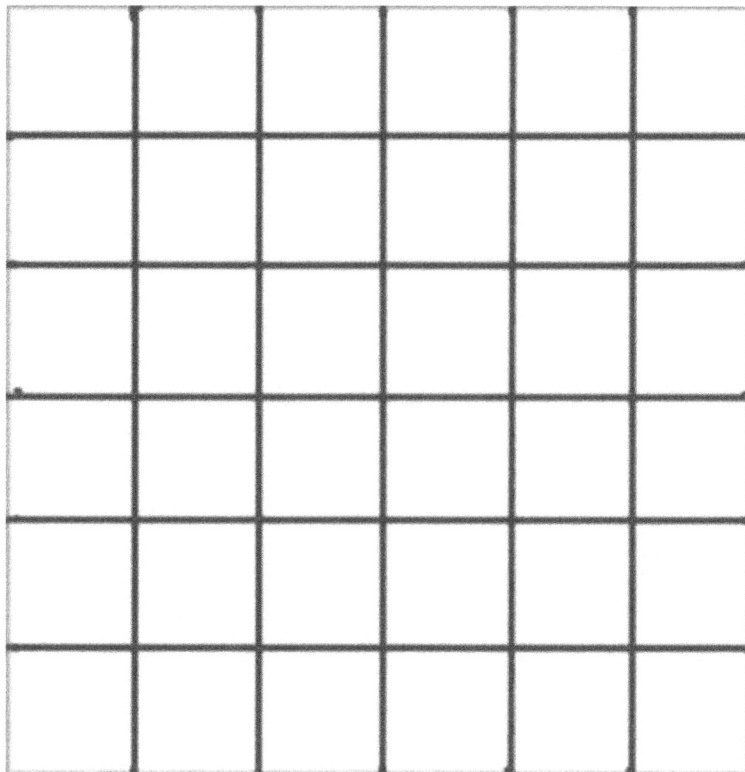

Using your ruler, connect all your marks, so you have a nice grid with six boxes going vertically and horizontally. This means there will be a total of 36 boxes. For illustrative purposes, I've made the grid lines dark and thick here, but ideally, your grid lines should be narrower (a single pencil line) and not too heavy or dark. You need to be able to erase all these grid lines later!

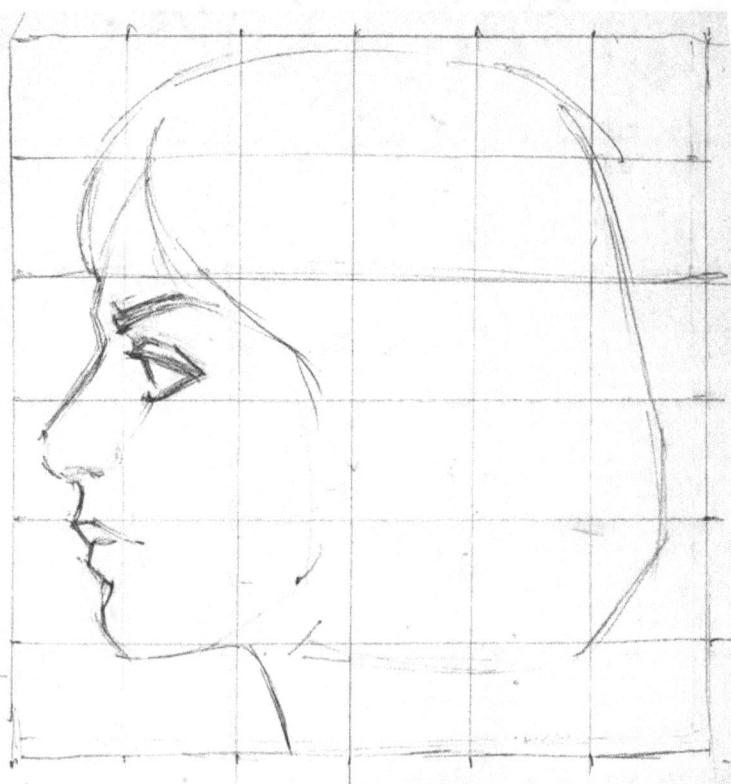

For demonstration purposes, I did a hasty little grid drawing and am copying my own sketch of Daniela. I increased the contrast in this picture to make the grid lines more obvious. However, your drawing should use lighter pencil strokes, so they're easier to erase in case you make a mistake. (I know I sure did some erasing!)

Refer to the portrait of Daniela (shown at the beginning of this chapter) with the grid squares over it. On the bottom row, the third square from the left, there is a line which indicates her neck. Draw that in on your own paper, trying to approximate the contour and placement of this line in the appropriate one-inch square. Then you will go on to copy what's in a neighboring square, and so on, and so on.

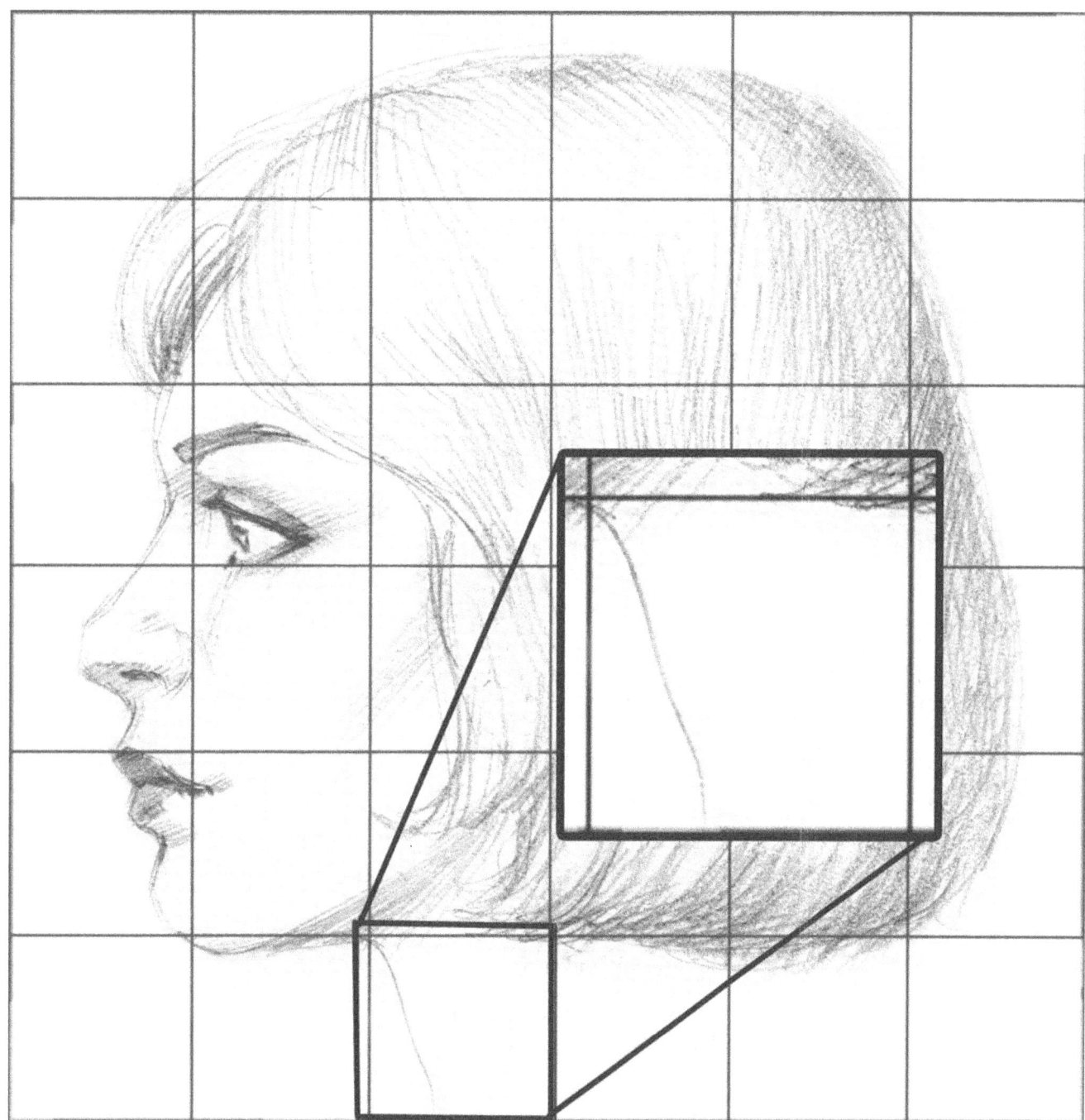

Here I've enlarged the individual grid square which has the line for her neck. Look at the placement of this line within that square—note where it starts (near the top left corner of the square) and where it ends, at the bottom of the square. It tapers over gradually, with a slight curve to the line. Replicate this line to the best of your ability in the appropriate square on your own grid.

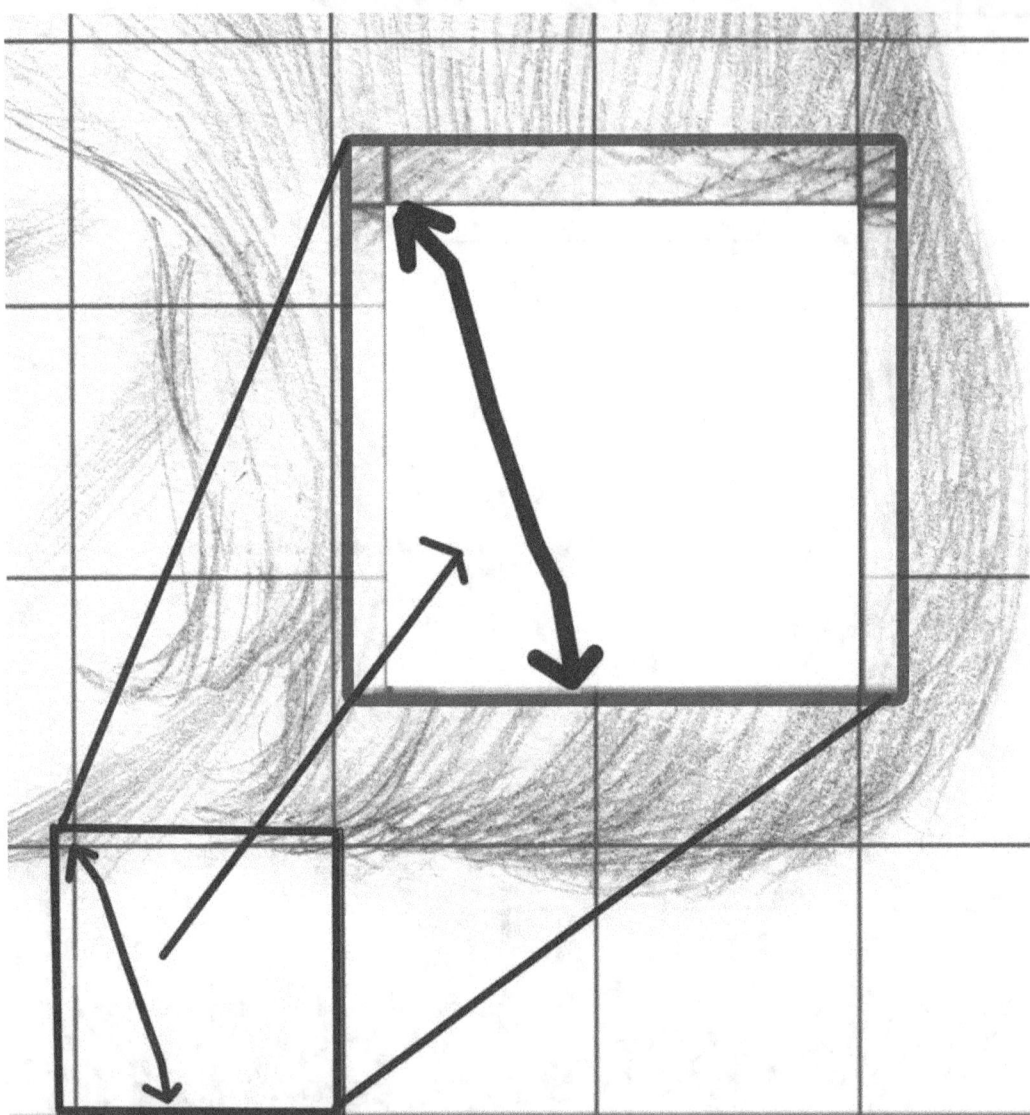

A closer look! Remember, it's not just a "line", it slants and curves a little as it goes down the length of the square.

You can simplify your shapes and angles first, and return to refine them later. The most important thing is that their general angle and placement match up with what you see in the gridded picture you are copying.

To finish the drawing, you will methodically copy the "contents" of each of these grid squares. You'll discover that if you focus on just what's in an individual square, your brain can view the lines and shapes more abstractly, and this, in turn, will help you draw with more accuracy.

To get a clearer idea of this concept, let's look at another grid square:

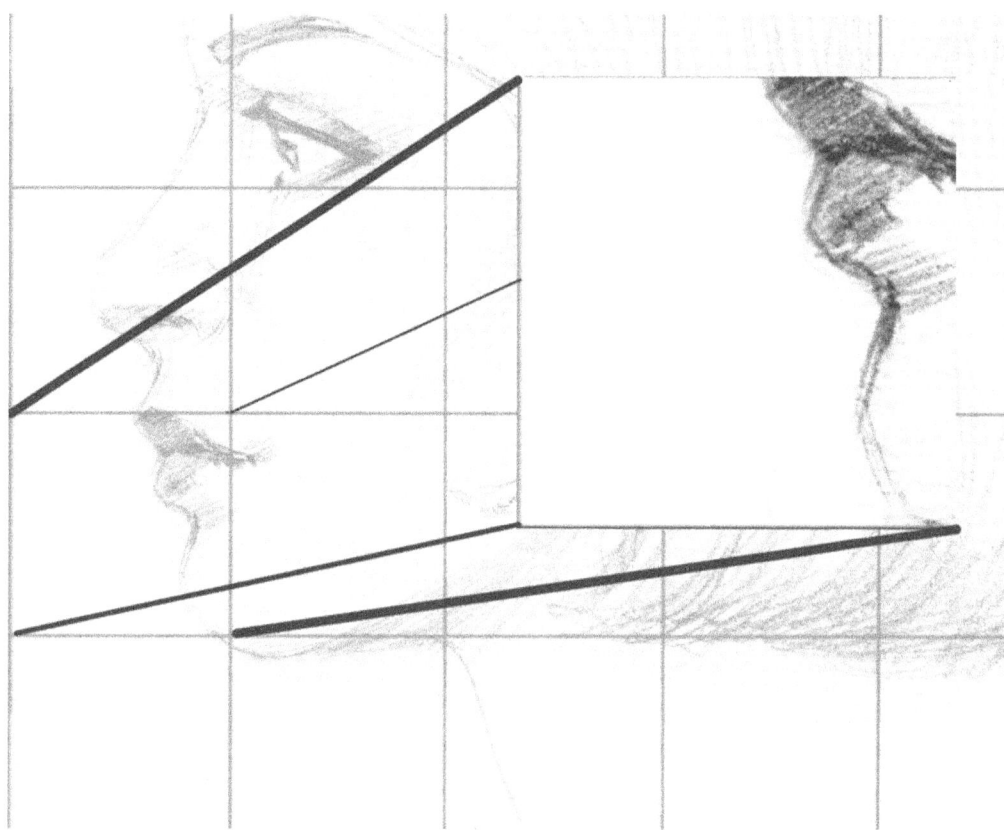

This time, it's the square which contains most of Daniela's mouth. We see that the majority of this square is just blank background space (to the left), and the lips are farther to the right. Analyze what you see—where are the lines that you will need to copy? Which lines are nearer to the corners? The middle? The right or left edges? The bottom or top of the square?

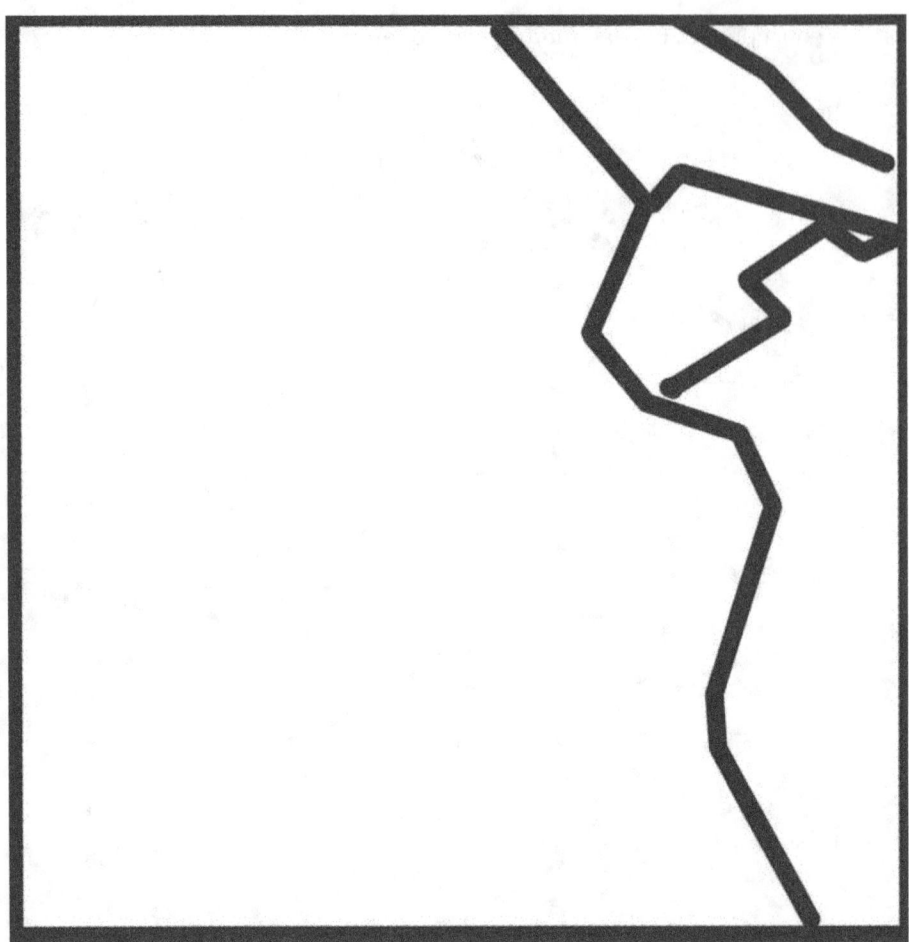

While I don't recommend your making your lines as thick and as dark as what I have done here, this is similar to what you should be getting when you start filling in all your grid squares.

As you work, look at the white areas around your lines. Are these blank areas as big or as small as what you see in the original grid square? Are the angles and location accurate? If the white shapes aren't matching up correctly, this means that somewhere, your drawing has become misaligned.

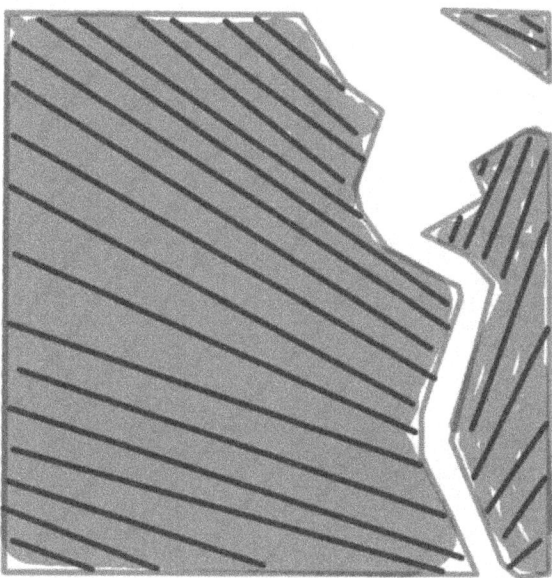

Here I've added grey shading and patterned lines to the former "white areas" (the blank areas) in the grid square which contains her lips. These blank areas are also known as "negative space." Take a moment and really look at them. For instance, see the little triangle-like shape in the very top right corner? Make sure that when you copy this grid square, that you have a triangle shape that looks just like the one you see here.

After you copy what's in one square and move on to neighboring squares, see how everything matches up (like pieces of a puzzle!). When all the squares are filled in, your drawing outline is ready to go!

Getting the outline of Daniela (with the help of the grid) should be your main objective for now. But, it will be good experience for you to try to do some shading as well. As you do this, be easy on yourself and remember that you don't have to get everything perfect just yet.

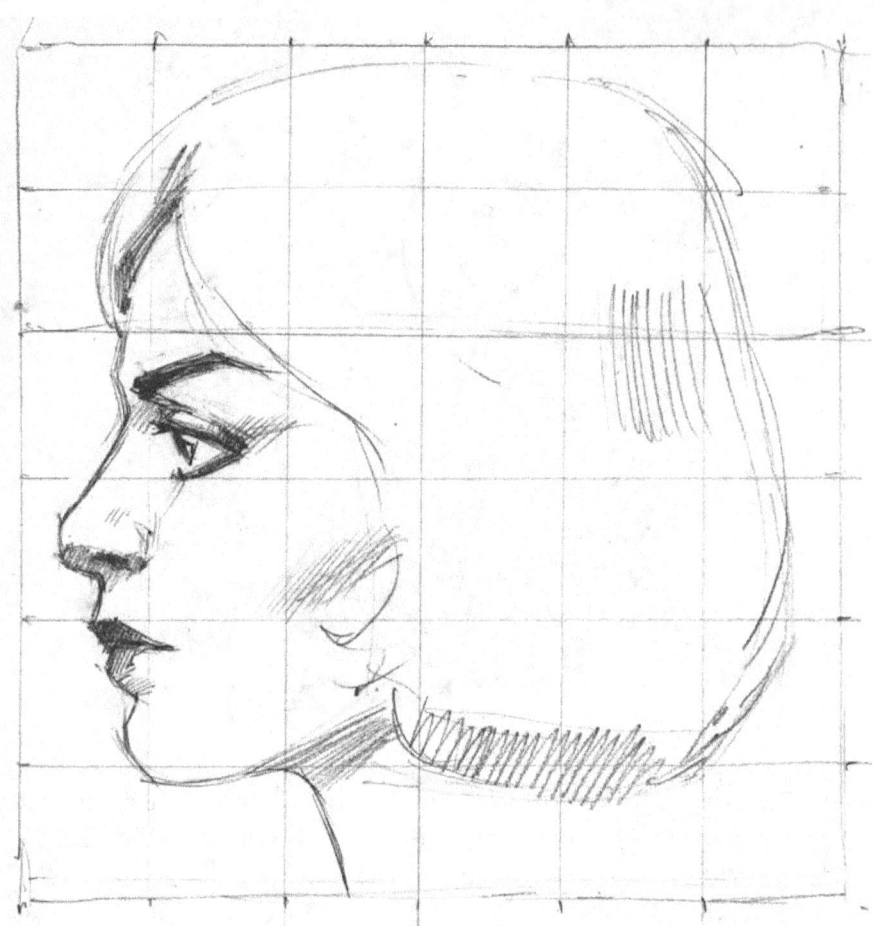

Here's what Daniela could look like when her portrait is about 1/3 completed.

Look at some of the interesting angles of Daniela's features:

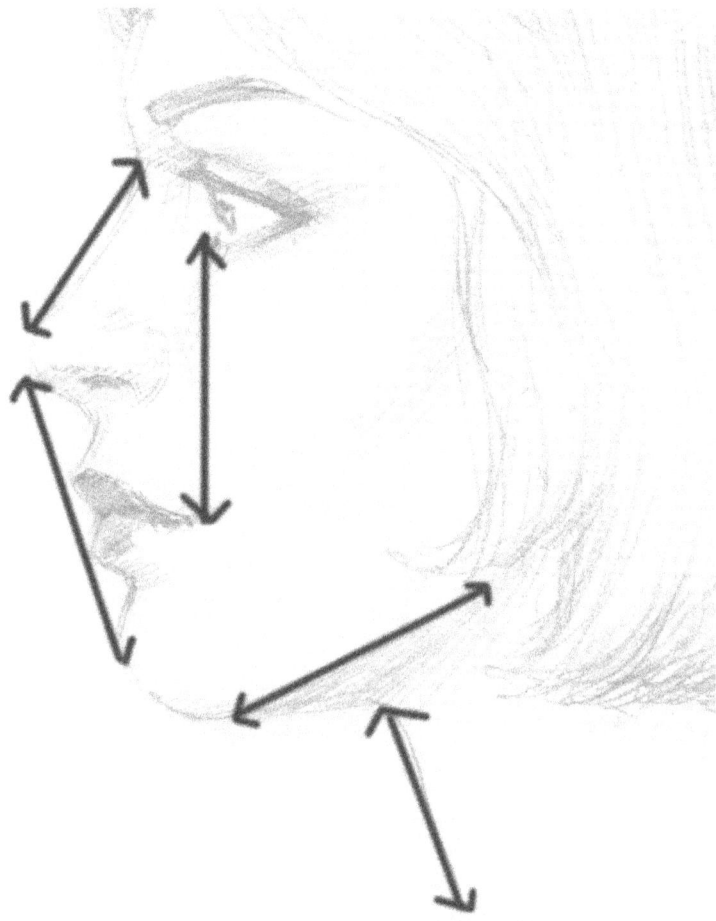

The nose tilts outwards from the brow. Take care to not make the angle of the nose too shallow. You won't make her nose look too big when you accurately draw what you see.

From the tip of the nose down to the chin, the angle definitely tips in.

The outer edge of the eye almost lines up with the edge of the mouth (see arrows in illustration). The angle of the jaw tips up towards the ear.

The angle of the neck is not straight up and down but slants inward.

These angles should be easier to capture accurately because you have your grid lines in place. However, I wanted to point these particular angles out now, because they are commonly seen in most people's faces, and you'll continue to see these angles show up in many of the faces you will draw in the future.

ADDING DETAILS AND SIMPLE SHADING

Now it's time to work on some details in this portrait of Daniela. This is where you will start to use some of the crosshatching doodle practice that you learned about in the previous chapter.

As you start drawing, keep a scrap piece of paper under your hand, so the side of your hand doesn't constantly rub against the paper and smear the drawing.

Let's look at the details in this drawing:

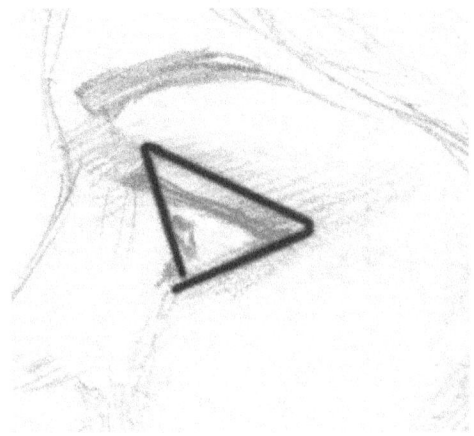

First, notice how Daniela's eye is triangle-shaped, tipped at an angle.

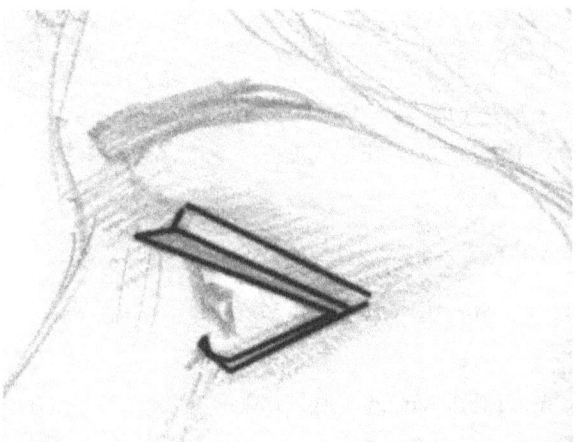

You must refine that triangle shape. The outer edges of her triangle-shaped eye extend past where the edge of the eyeball is located. You must allow for the thickness of the upper and lower eyelids. You are also drawing a thick "stripe" of black that suggests her eyelashes.

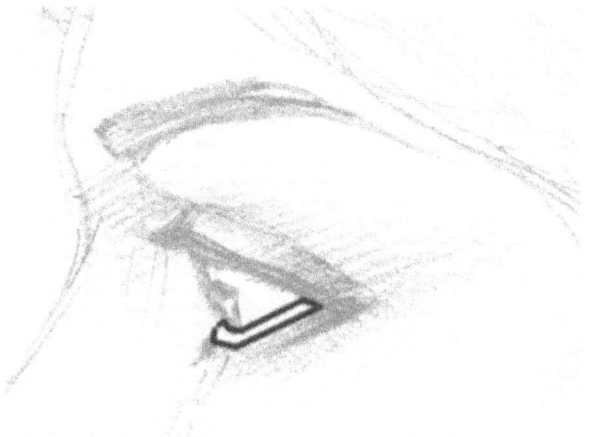

It's very important that you draw in the lower eyelid thickness!

For this simple sketch, we're going to leave the interior area of the lower eyelid blank. In this picture I've outlined where the lower eyelid thickness would be, if we were to draw it. But we DO NOT want to draw that lower eyelid in this particular exercise. It would make her look like she's got red-rimmed eyes. So, imagine that there is this space where the lower eyelid is supposed to be, and leave that area blank. You'll notice that I do this in many of my other drawings.

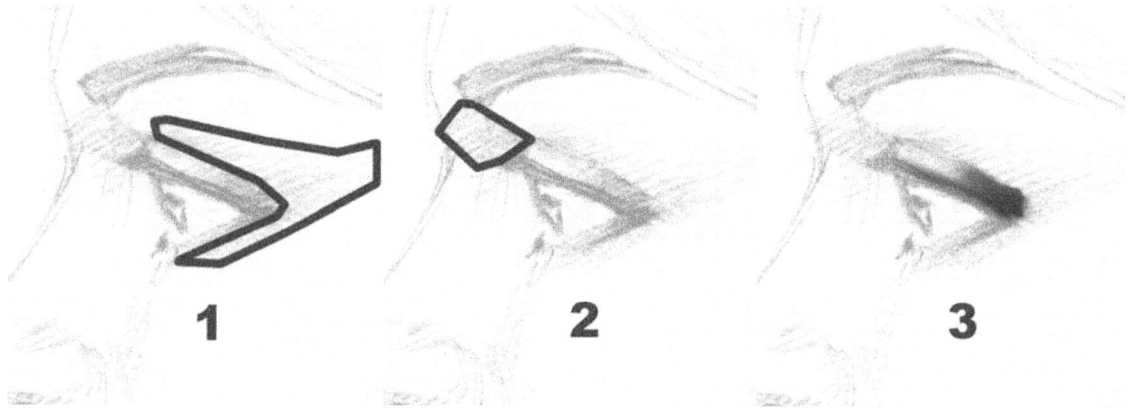

The shadows around the eye are a little more complicated, but, if you follow each step carefully, it will all fall into place!

1) There are large areas of simple shading around the outer edge (right side) of the eye. This shading is there because eyeball is set in its socket. It is similar to eyeshadow—eyeshadow makes the eyes look more deep-set. The shading you will be giving this eye will do the same.

2) There's a shadow running from the inner edge of the eye up to the eyebrow. It spreads to the edge of the brow.

3) Make the shading gradually get darker as it approaches the outer edge of her eyelid (the edge to our right). This is also due to her eye being set in its socket. (And eyeshadow often is darker in that area, too!)

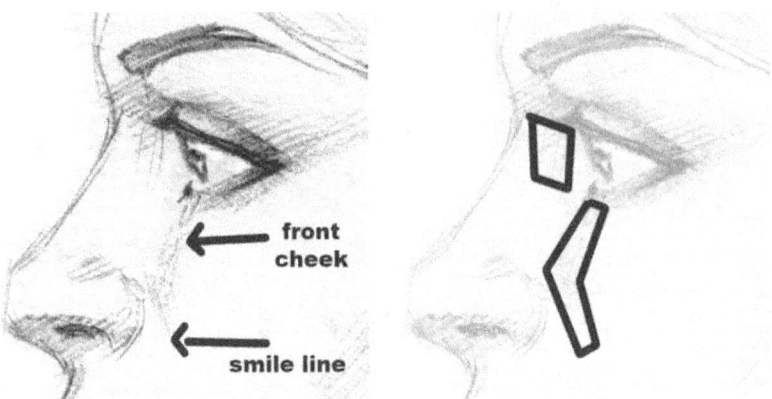

Add lighter shading along the upper bridge of the nose, the upper part of the cheek, and the "smile line" that is by the side of the nose. Don't make the shading here too dark; Daniela will look old and haggard if you do!

Adding all these little details may seem complicated at first, but with practice, it will soon become second nature to you.

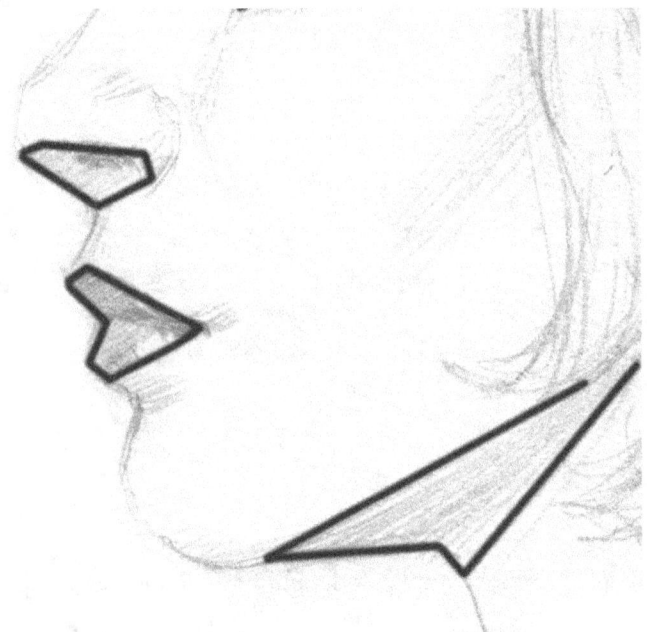

The shadow under her nose is like a triangle, but with a notch taken out of it at the lower right side.

The lips look like a side-ways heart shape.

The shadow for the jawline is also reminiscent of a triangle.

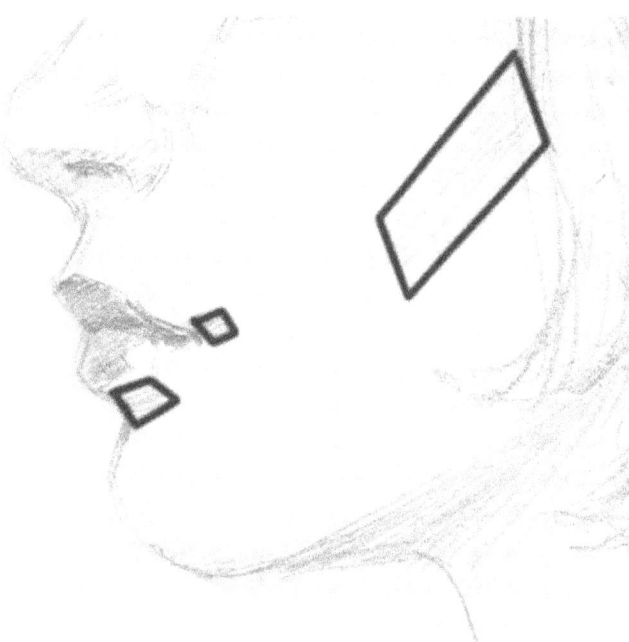

While these shadows are a little lighter than the others, you don't want to leave them out. The shading at the corner of her mouth gives her face more expression. Also, add subtle (but not too light) tones under her bottom lip and cheekbones.

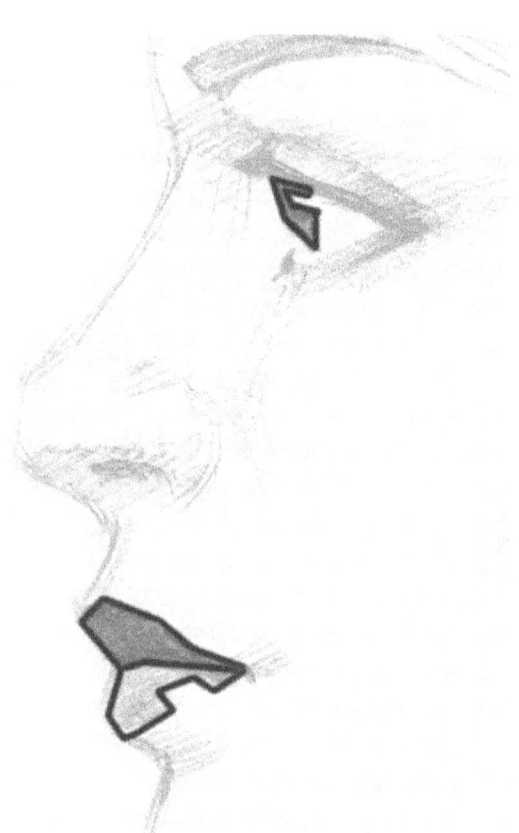

Make note of the highlights in her eye and in her lipstick. Look at the shape of her iris (the colored part of the eye) and see how the highlight "cuts in" to the iris shape.

I left a highlight in her lipstick. So, instead of her lips being a sideways heart shape, there's this chunk cut out of the heart shape which is left white for the highlight.

Notice how the upper lip is slightly darker than the lower lip. That's because the upper lip faces away from the light, and is more in shadow.

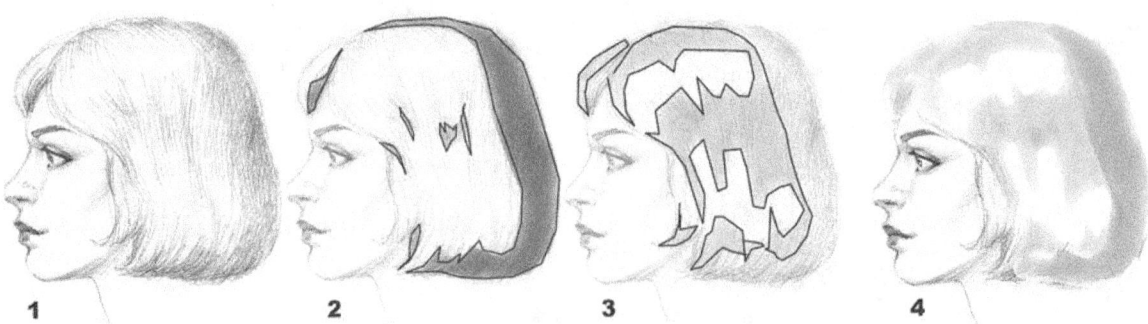

The secret to drawing hair is to simplify, simplify, simplify!

In this illustration, I've broken down the hair into three values: dark grey (#2 in the picture above), medium grey (#3 above) and white (also seen in #3 above). I've outlined the approximate boundaries of where the dark greys and light greys are located. What is left (what you don't shade in) are the highlights.

To make darker values you can crosshatch (make some hatching lines that go against the "grain" of the hair), but you should also include lines that follow the direction of the hair strands.

Picture #4 above has most of the sketching lines in the hair removed, so what is left are the blocks of darker and lighter grey (and white). Even with a lot of the detail gone, it still looks more or less like hair. It's the overall shading and values that create the illusion of realism, not drawing in a million little hair strands.

Don't agonize too much over the shading in this exercise. You'll be learning more about shading in upcoming chapters. Attempt to make your hatch marks as even as you can and look for areas that are lighter and darker. Do your best to recreate what you see. If it's a darker spot, bear down on your pencil and overlap your strokes until you get the darker shade. If there is a lighter area, lightly skim your pencil over the paper to make softer, lighter lines. If you mess up a little, that's okay. Erase and try again, but don't go over the same area again and again. Relax and accept that maybe everything won't be perfect yet. The main focus of this first project is to work on the outlines and angles of the drawing.

At the point when you believe you're finished with your drawing, carefully erase any stray grid lines. Now you're done!

NOTE: There's some additional information and advice on how to use crosshatching strokes on Daniela's face and hair in the next chapter. You can add extra tweaks to this project then if you like.

BONUS EXERCISE: VANESA

For extra practice, try copying this portrait of "Vanesa".

Make an 8-inch square, and mark off squares every 2 inches. (You can make your square larger, as long as its proportions match, meaning four rows of squares going both vertically and horizontally.)

Yes, the squares are bigger in this one and there are fewer of them. But that will be good practice! Remember the techniques you learned in the first lesson, and try again with Vanesa. Remember, don't worry about perfection. Try to get the outlines and angles as close as you can.

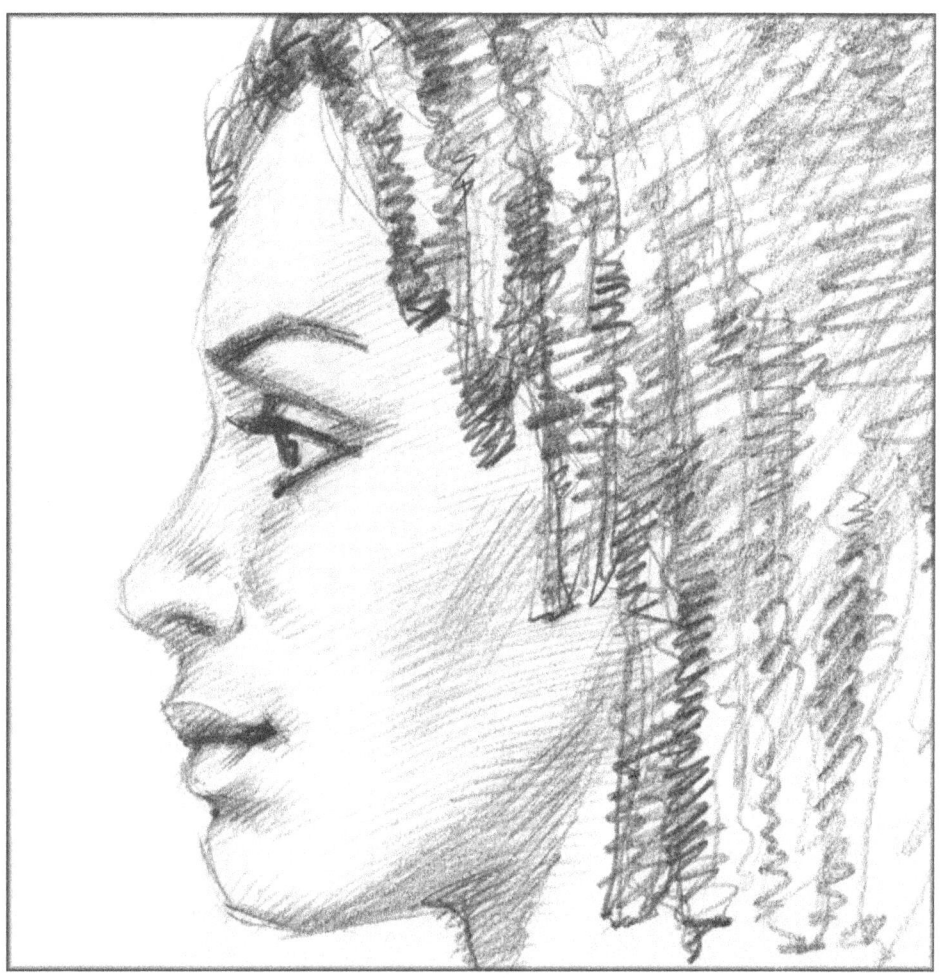

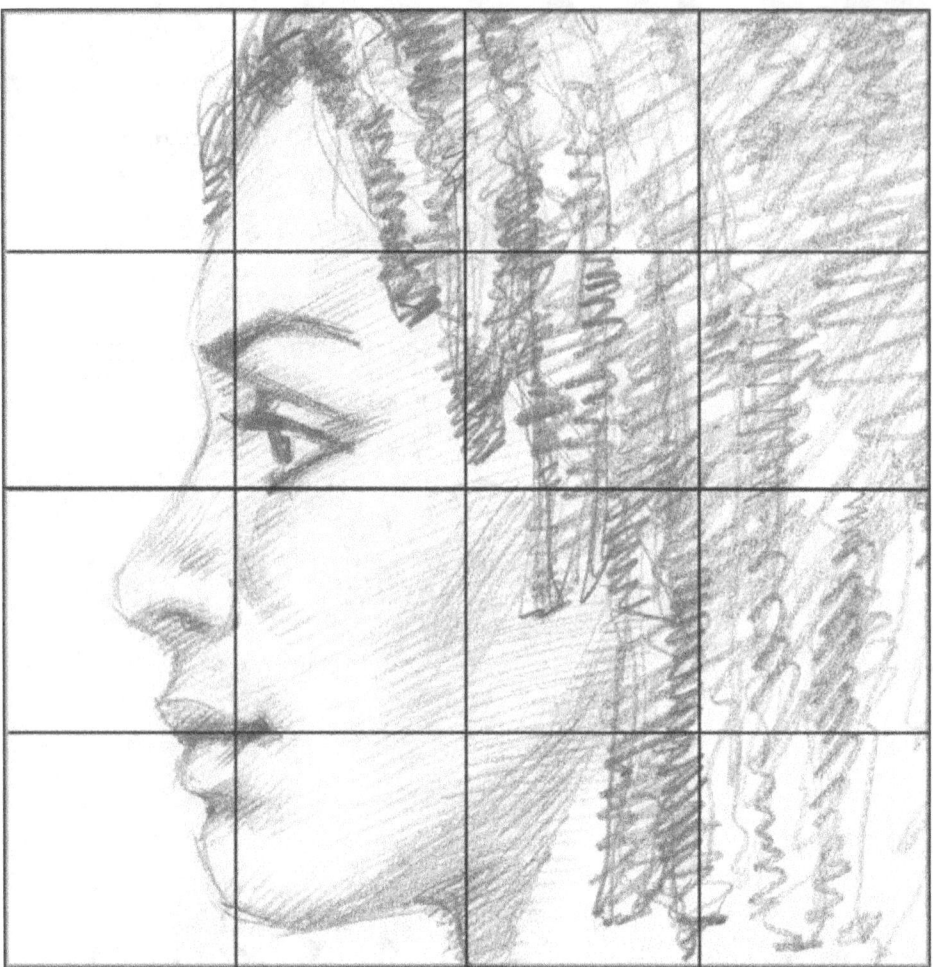

I've made the drawing of Vanesa lighter in this gridded version so you can see where the grid lines are. Use the first drawing (without the grid lines) as your reference when finishing up your copied drawing of Vanesa, as it has better contrast (lights and darks).

In this extra project, follow the same steps as you did with Daniela. Carefully draw in your outlines, look for angles, notice the shapes of the eyes, nose, and mouth, and erase your grid lines when you have your outlines correct.

This picture of Vanesa gives you a perfect opportunity to work more with negative space. You were introduced to negative space earlier in this chapter. It's the area around the thing you're trying to draw.

Look at the white area on the left side, which borders her profile. Focus on the outlines and contours of this shape and try to draw it, instead of worrying about the outline of Vanesa's features.

When we look at negative space only, we are no longer thinking consciously about drawing a person's profile (which might trigger all sorts of assumptions about what a person's profile is supposed to look like). Instead, we are just drawing some abstract angles and blobs. This helps us draw that shape more accurately because we are not working with any preconceived notions.

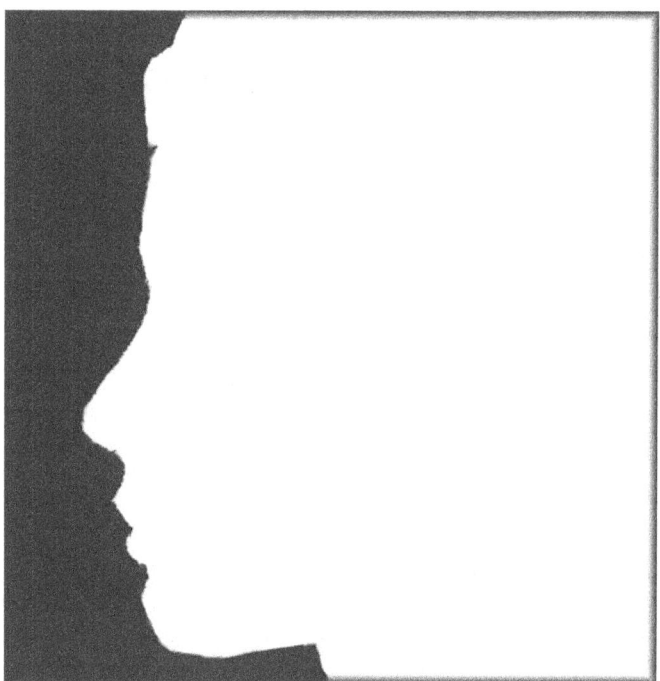

Vanesa's negative space!

When you have your outlines and angles properly placed in Vanesa's face, then you can start to shade the features and add detail to the hair. Once again, do not worry about perfection! This is mainly an exercise to give you more experience with getting your lines and angles in the proper place.

SKILL BUILDING LESSONS FROM CHAPTER TWO:

You've been introduced to the grid and have copied a drawing of a face by using the grid squares to get your outlines accurate and lined up correctly. You've learned more about the angles and unusual shapes seen in a person's profile. You've also learned a few tricks for helping you view an image objectively, like focusing on its "negative space."

CHAPTER THREE: SOME NEW TECHNIQUES—SHADING LIGHTS AND DARKS

Your art will look rather drab if you don't give it some dimension and depth, and that requires capturing the lights and darks. We call these lights and darks "values".

First, you're going to make some value strips. You may need to make several of these to get the hang of them. You can draw them with pencil as well as ballpoint pen.

Draw a long strip (you can use your ruler if you like) on your sketch paper, about 1-1/2 inches tall, and approximately 5 or 6 inches wide. Separate this long strip into five sections. You'll have five squares in your strip.

Leave the far left square blank. That will be your lightest shade. You can't get it any lighter than the value of the white paper!

Move to the far right square. With your ballpoint pen (or your pencil) start to make very closely-spaced hatch lines in this square. Press down on your pencil or pen; you want these lines to be dark. When you've covered the whole far right square with hatch lines, put a new layer of hatching at a 45 or 90-degree angle to your original lines. Keep on doing this until the box is as black as you can get it.

Now, you have established your lightest and darkest values. You can't get any lighter than the white box, nor can you go any darker than the black box.

Shade in the three boxes in the middle. Skim your pencil over the surface of the paper and make faint, feathery marks on the square next to the white square. (If you feel you made your marks too dark, use your eraser to remove the lines or lighten them.) The middle square will be a little darker. You can do two or more "passes" with your pencil strokes, one set of marks going in one direction, and the next series of hatching crossing over at a 45- degree angle. The square closest to the black box will probably need several layers of hatching marks, and you'll have to apply more pressure to your pencil so the marks are thicker and darker, but yet not black.

Your finished value strip will look something like this:

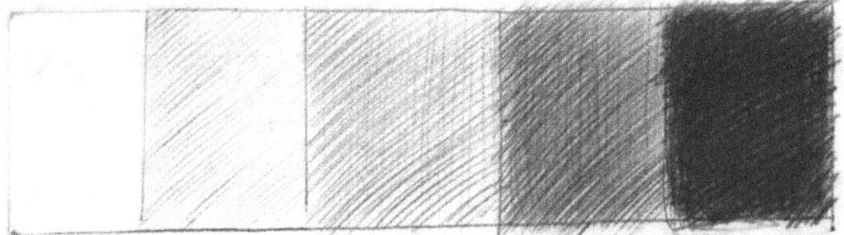

Your value strip doesn't have to look super-pretty (this one sure doesn't) but it's going to help you understand how to create different levels of light and dark with your pencil.

Your next exercise is to make a sphere. You'll create the illusion of depth from how you draw your shadows—the lights and darks. For this exercise, draw with your pencil, because you will probably need to do some erasing along the way.

Draw a simple circle. (It doesn't have to be perfectly round!) Follow this step-by-step illustration:

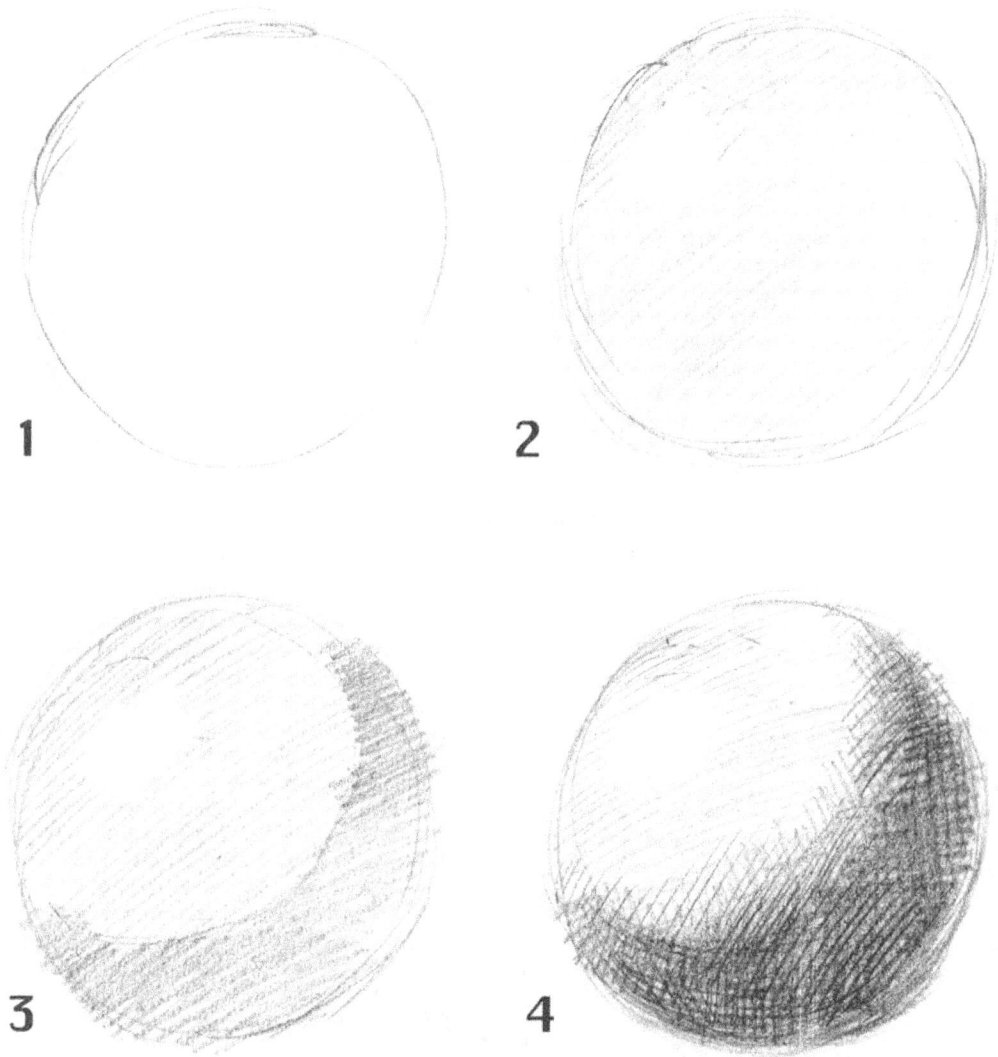

Lightly sketch a circle shape.

Sketch a very light grey shade over the whole sphere except for the big circle on the upper left (which is the highlight of the sphere). The highlight's location tells us where the light source is coming from—in this case, it's coming from our left.

Add a medium grey shadow, in a sort of crescent moon shape, around the lower bottom right side of the circle (as seen in the illustration).

Create a black crescent moon shape for the deepest shadow at the lower right rim of the sphere. Add some dark grey (not black) shadows above the deepest shadow at the bottom of the sphere. The shadows are on the side of the sphere that faces away from the light source.

The final step is to make sure there's a rim of a slightly lighter value on the shadowed edge of the sphere, and then to add a cast shadow to the sphere. You will learn more about that rim of lighter value next.

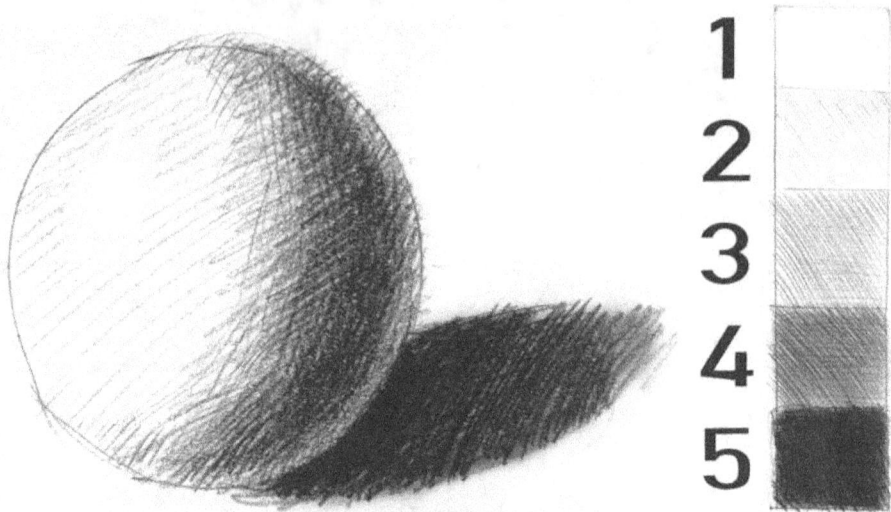

This is what the sphere should look like when you're finished. Compare the shadows and lights to the value strip on the right. I've numbered the values, 1 for white, 5 for black. Can you match up where the blacks, whites, and in-betweens go on the sphere?

Here's an idea of where the values belong on the sphere drawing:

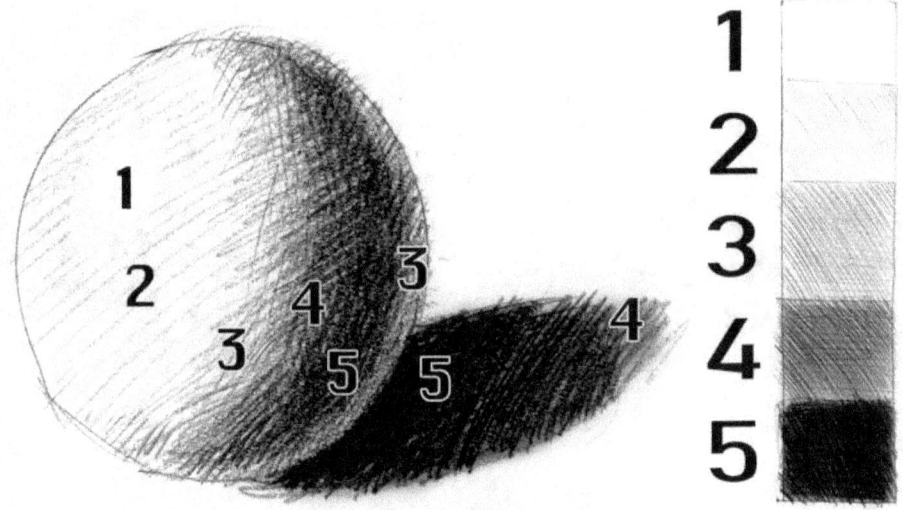

The highlight (#1) is the blank paper.

The #2 grey is the value of the sphere when it is facing the light source.

When we get to #3, this is where the roundness of sphere is starting to curve away from the light source. The shadowed area begins here, and the lighted (facing the light source) area ends.

Areas #4 and #5 get darker and darker as the body of the sphere turns farther away from the light source and deeper into shadow.

We get a slim strip of #3 or #4 (in the illustration I list it as #3) as a little bit of light from the pale-colored table reflected back up on the edge of the sphere. (This is called "reflected light".)

Then the shadow is #5 (which is always the most dark right underneath the sphere).

Then the shadow fades off a bit and becomes a #4 grey at the farthest edge of the shadow.

Next up, a cube!

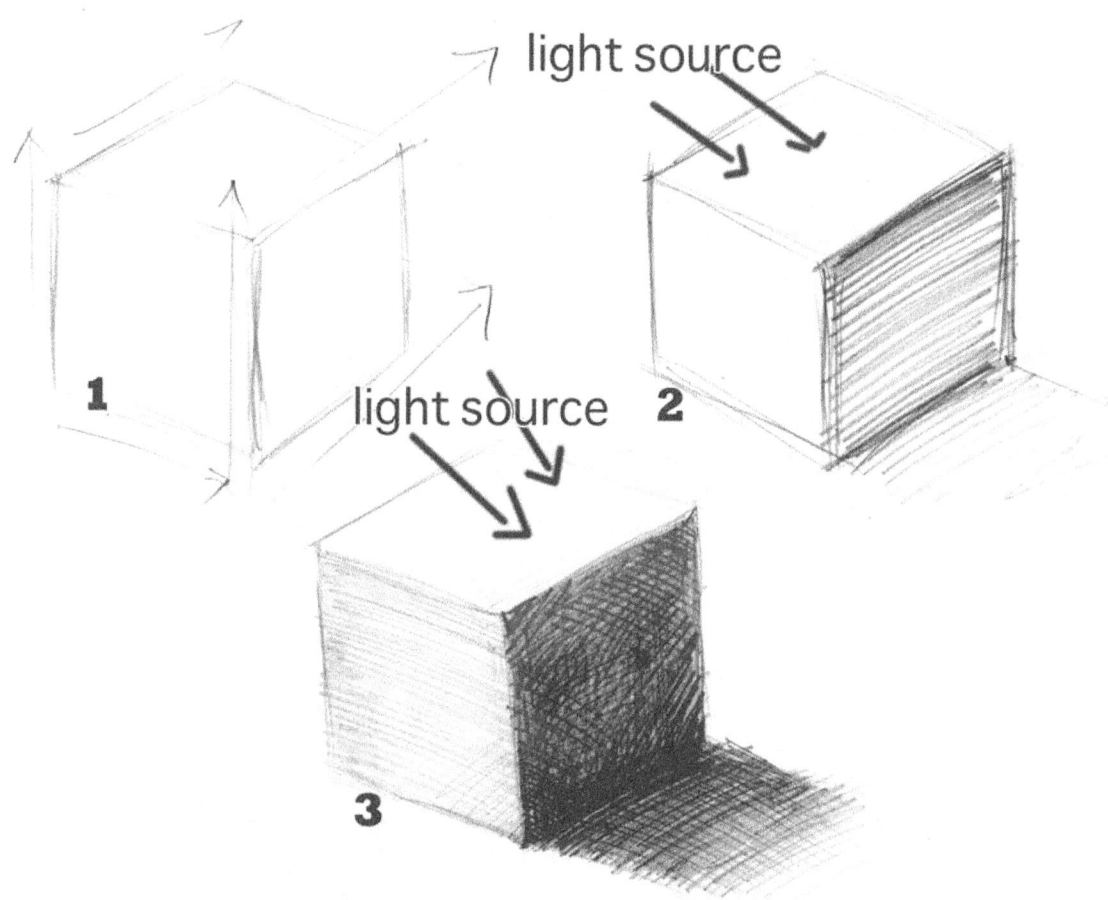

light source

light source

1

2

3

Make your cube outline shape. (See arrows on #1).

The light source for this cube is coming from the top and to our left, so the top side of the cube is the lightest and will need no shading, whereas the darkest side of the cube will face away from the light, or to our right.

Start to shade the side of the cube to the right (as seen in #2).

Lightly shade the edge of the cube angling more towards the left. It will not be shaded as darkly as the side to the right since it gets a little bit of light from the light source. Then, a shadow on the surface behind the right side of the cube (#3).

If you have difficulty figuring out how to draw the cube outline, this may help you:

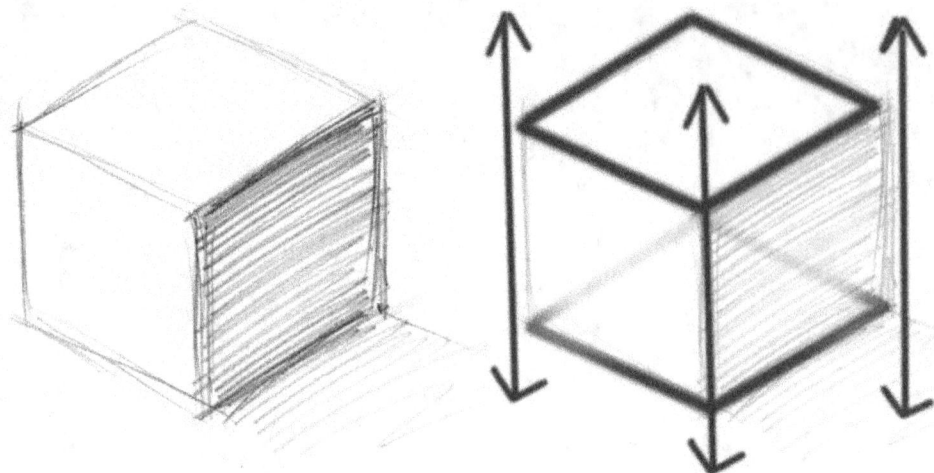

Think of the top surface of the cube as a sideways diamond. The bottom of the cube is also an identical diamond shape. The vertical edges go straight up and down (see the three double-sided arrows). Put these shapes all together, and you magically have a cube!

Here are some crosshatching techniques that could help you shade your cube or box. (These are just a suggestion, as there is no one "right" way to do it!)

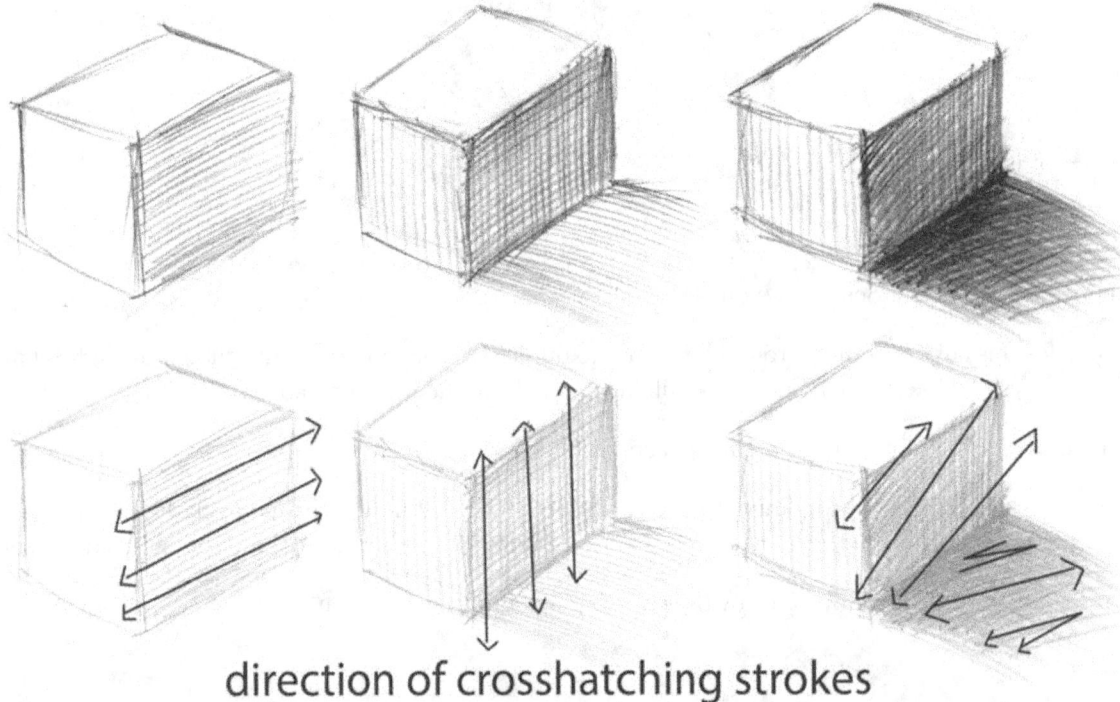

direction of crosshatching strokes

First, start shading the right side of the cube sideways (horizontally). Then go back over with vertical (up and down) lines, to make the shadowed side of the cube (or box) darker. Go back again for a third time (or more!) by angling your strokes. Do the same with the cast shadow on the cube. Lightly shade the left side of the cube with vertical strokes.

CUBE AND SPHERE PRACTICE IS ESSENTIAL!

Now you can doodle many cubes and spheres on sketch paper, note paper, in ballpoint pen and pencil. Whenever you have some spare time, practice, practice, practice! This practice is necessary and will help you prepare for the exercises in the upcoming chapters.

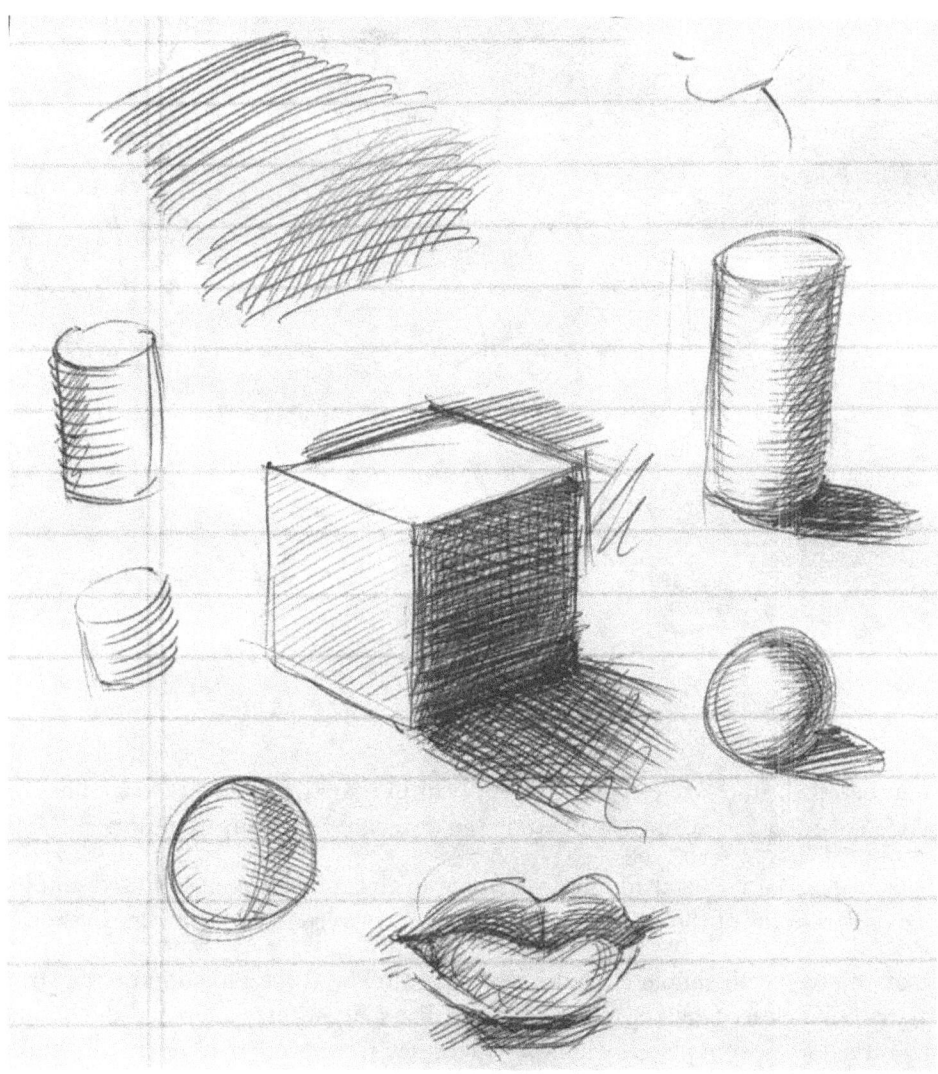

Here's a page from a cheap yellow notepad. I used a ballpoint pen and made a bunch of disjointed, messy doodles. You should do the same. You can use pencil, pen, even markers or crayons and make a mess! "Waste" paper! It's all helping you improve your drawing skills.

MORE ABOUT CROSSHATCHING

There are no hard and fast rules to crosshatching. Each artist will have to develop their own 'feel' for it, and it'll come naturally with practice.

With that said, it might be a good idea to examine one possible way to approach shading and crosshatching a drawing. I'm going to return to the portrait you just completed, of Daniela, to analyze some of the pencil strokes I used. However, please remember: This is just ONE way to use crosshatching. Many other ways will look just as good (or better)!

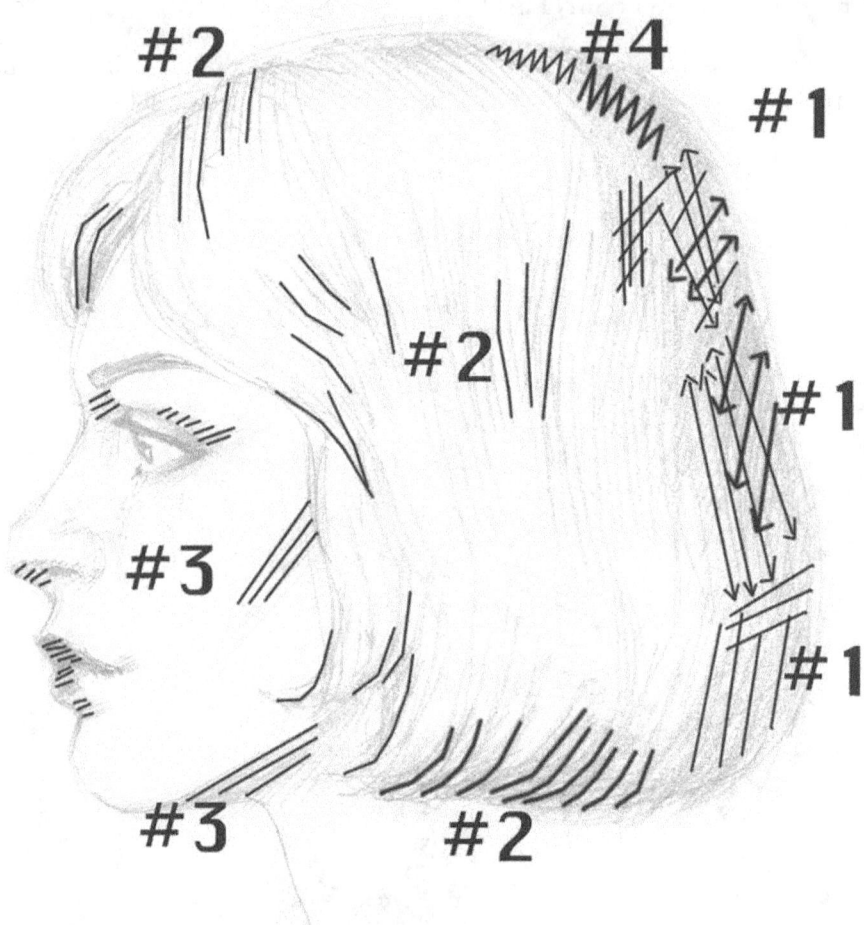

Each area has been numbered, for the sake of clarity. Please bear in mind that the dark black lines in this illustration are used to give a general idea of what I'm talking about, and aren't executed with any elegance!

1. The hair in the back of her head needed additional shading to give it dimension, so I used simple criss-cross hatching lines to get the area darker. Some of the crosshatching was in longer vertical strokes, some in shorter horizontal strokes.

2. I shaded the rest of the hair with simple curved lines, which followed the direction of the strands of hair. I made the curved lines darker and closer together to indicate a darker shadow (like you see at the bottom edge of her hair). Scattered random curved lines were placed whenever I felt they were needed, to create the look of the hair. I didn't try to draw every strand of hair on her head. That would have looked way too busy and overworked. Sometimes, less is more!

3. For adding the shadows on most of her features, I kept with simple hatching lines, all heading in approximately the same direction. Shorter, darker lines were used for her lips. Longer lines (going mostly in the same direction) to show the shadow under her jaw. Same with the shadow under her nose, her cheekbones, and the area around her eyes.

4. There are a few "slinky" lines (back and forth, back and forth) at the top of her hair. Slinky lines can be used in many places and I usually add them whenever the mood strikes me.

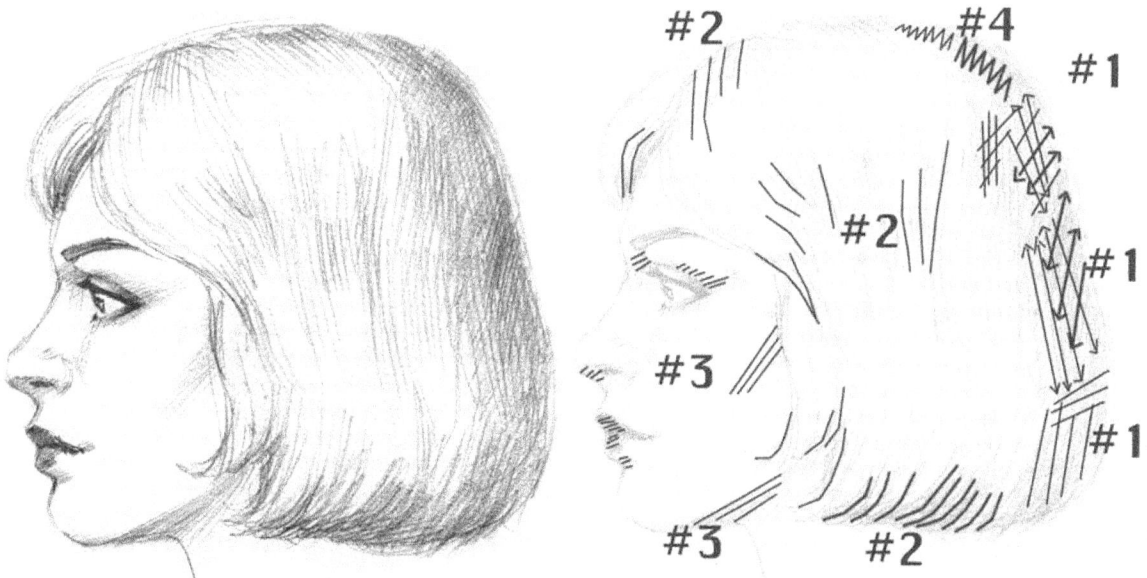

It's easier to understand the crosshatching strokes being discussed if you can see the original drawing side-by-side with the diagramed drawing.

In many of my example drawings, I tend to make a lot of shading lines that are about a 45-degree angle. But you don't have to do that if you don't want to. Here are two other ways that will work just as well:

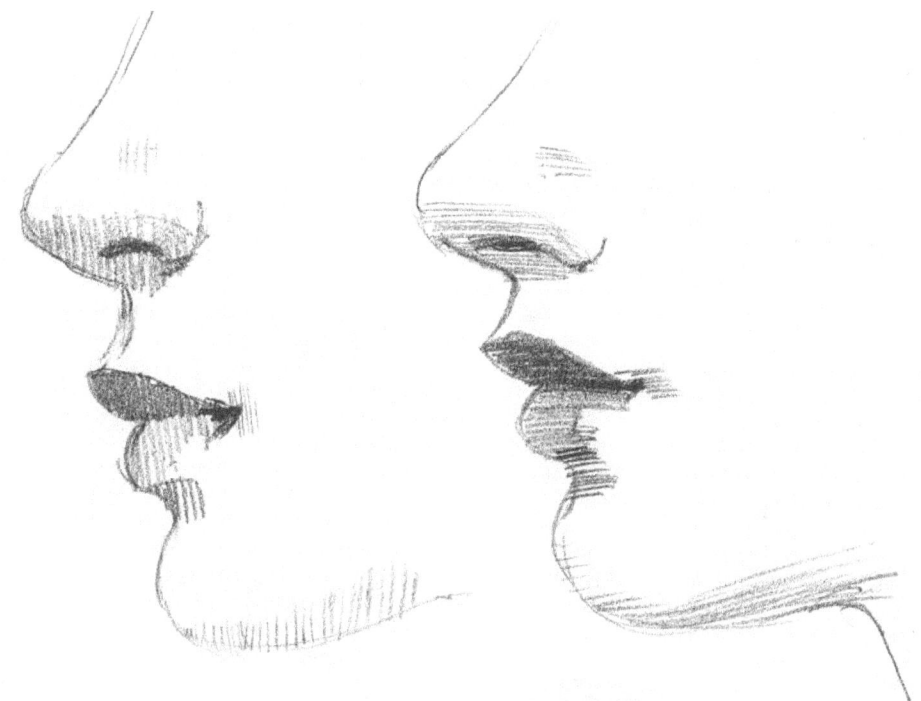

If you want to make many of your hatching lines straight up and down (like the example on the left), that looks fine, too! Or, you can draw the hatching lines horizontally. Both these examples look okay. Each artist has his or her own tastes.

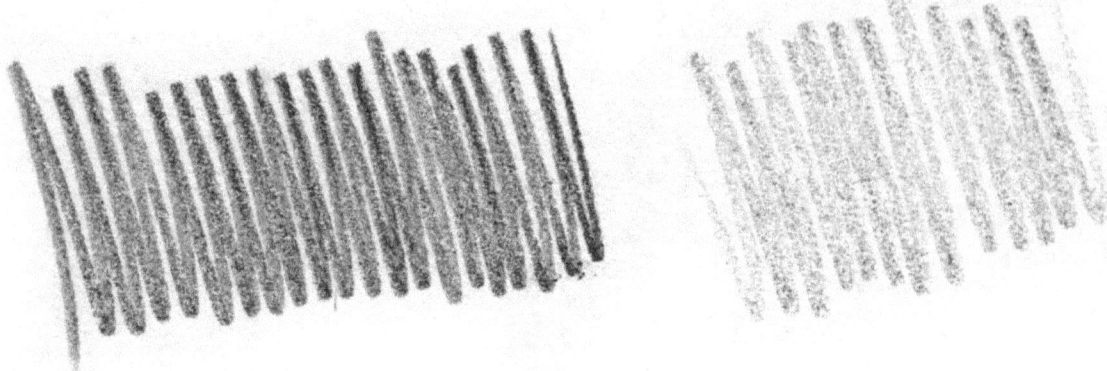

Here is a close-up of some slinky lines. The darker lines were made only by bearing down harder on the pencil. The lighter lines were created with a softer, more delicate touch. It's that simple.

I usually make a quick decision about which kinds of pencil strokes I'll use, with no planning ahead of time. I could have easily done them a different way. I'll repeat again, there are no hard and fast rules to this! Try different approaches and see what you like best. You will probably find that you'll change methods many times before you find a consistent style that you use frequently.

CONTOUR CROSSHATCHING

There's another thing to learn about using crosshatching lines, and it can be extremely powerful! I call them "contour crosshatching" lines. Contour crosshatching is one of those things that is a unique and beautiful feature that you can only do with this drawing technique. You can't get this effect when you blend all your pencil strokes away. This is another reason why I'm such an enthusiastic fan of crosshatching!

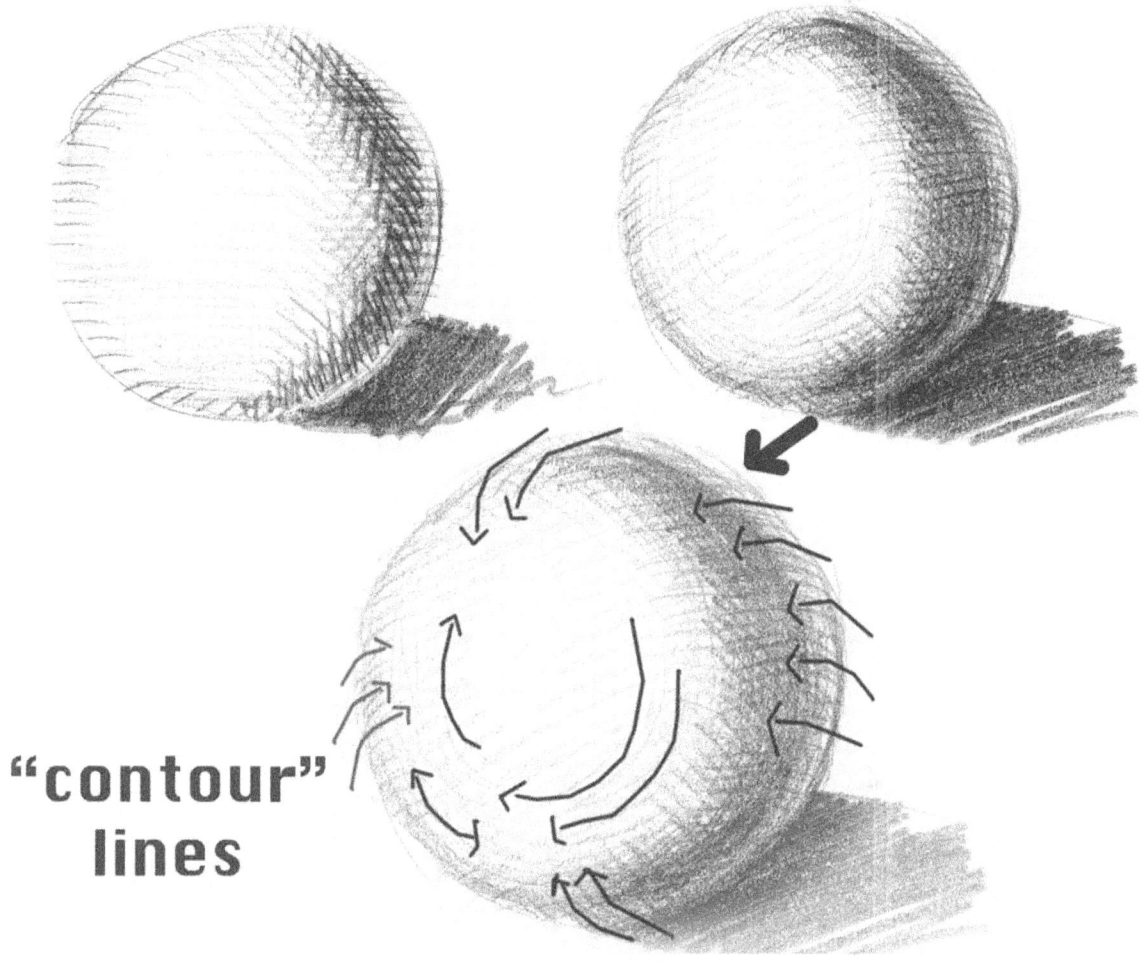

"contour" lines

Hatching lines don't always have to be just hatching lines. They can pull double duty! As you see in the picture here, there are two balls at the top. The ball on the left uses straight horizontal lines for most of the shading, with some vertical lines and a few 45-degree angle crosshatching lines. It looks okay, *but...*

The ball on the right has some lines that follow the shape of the ball. (See the enlarged detail of the ball, with arrowed lines showing the location and direction of the contoured strokes.) Do you see how using a contoured line can help make the object you're drawing look more three-dimensional? You don't have to do it with every single pencil stroke you make, but throw in some contouring lines now and then to spice things up.

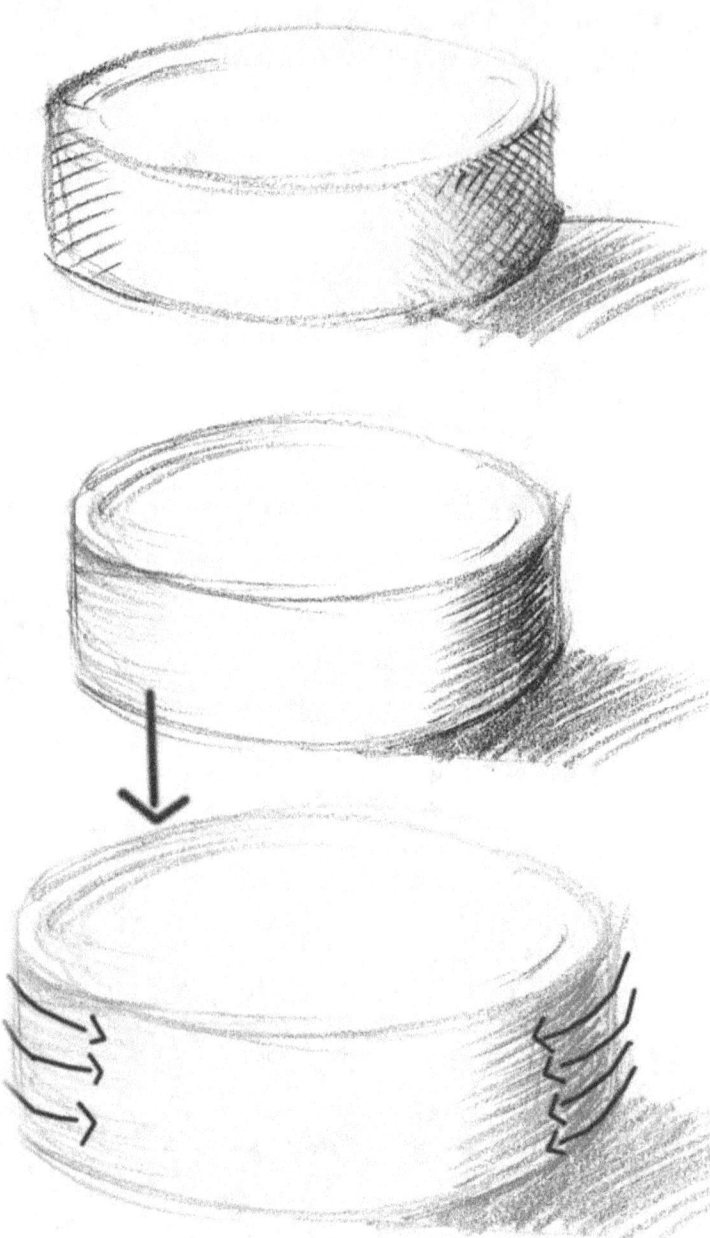

Here's another example, with some tuna cans. The first can is acceptable, but the second can looks so much more round!

Let's see how these contour lines look when applied to a portrait:

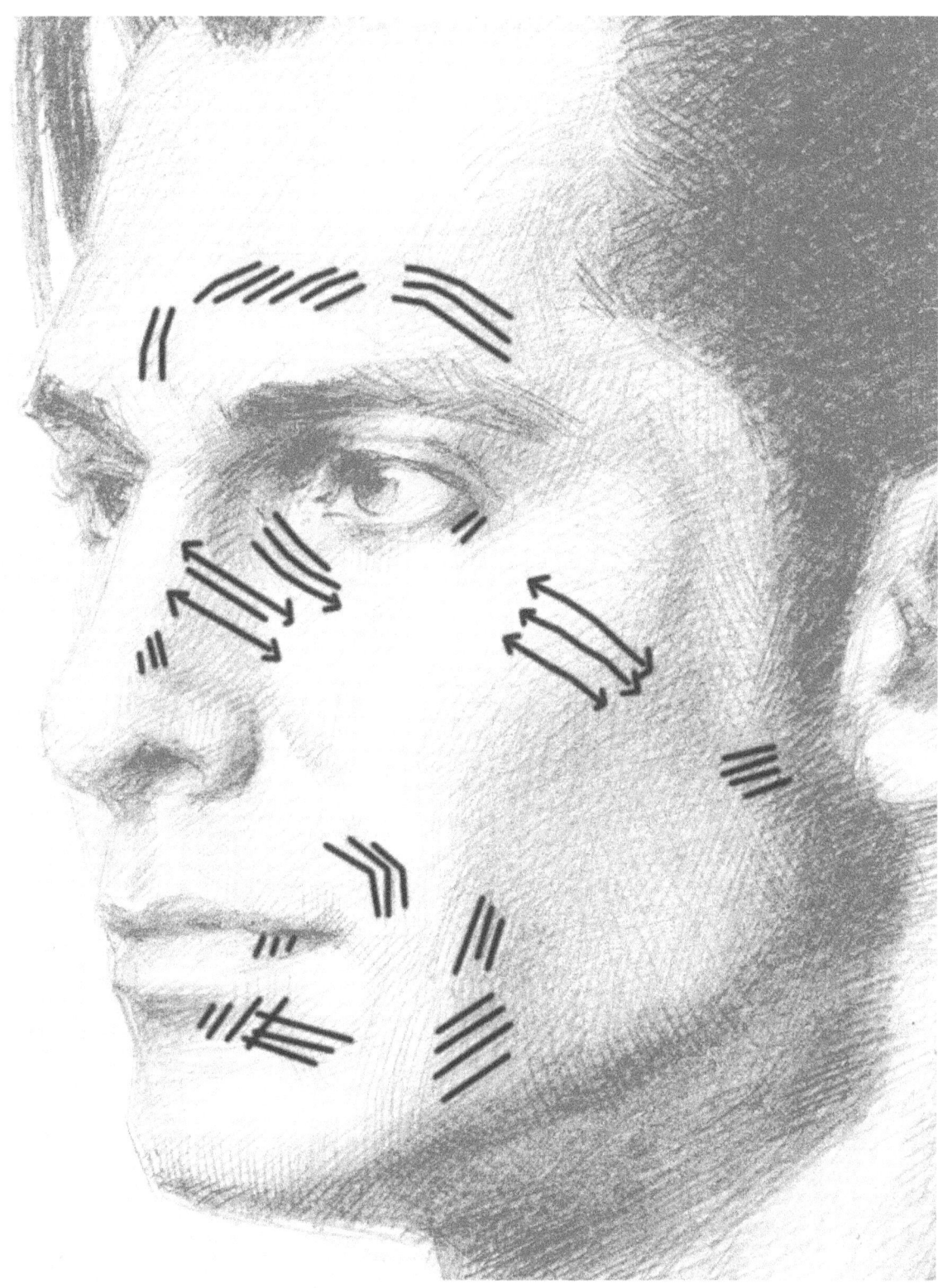

Here's a close-up of my sketch of Miguel, with the black arrowed lines showing the direction of a few of the pencil strokes.

As you can see, some of these lines follow the contour and structure of his face. The most obvious example is how the lines follow the angle of the side of the nose, starting under the eye and going down the length of the nose. More lines indicate the plane of the side of the head (short arrows near the ear and at the edge of the cheek). The temple area of his forehead has a few simple descriptive contour lines. Some pencil strokes follow around the edge of the eye socket.

You don't have to use these descriptive contour lines everywhere, but placing them here and there will enhance your drawing.

Again I remind you that the hatching examples in these drawings are by no means the only way or the best way. You will intuitively find your own style as you continue to draw and practice. I hope what I've shown you here will give you some different ideas of how to approach the shading of the face. Experiment and enjoy being creative!

> SKILL BUILDING LESSONS FROM CHAPTER THREE:
>
> You have done some exercises with making a realistic-looking sphere and cube, and in addition have been exposed to some new shading and some crosshatching techniques. You have learned how to identify the light, medium, and dark values in a picture. The concept of "contour cross-hatching" has been introduced to you, and you have seen how using these descriptive types of hatching lines can lend dimension to a drawing.

CHAPTER FOUR: MORE ABOUT VALUES AND LOST EDGES

Now, armed with newfound knowledge about shadows, highlights, value strips, and hatching, let's tackle Rogelio.

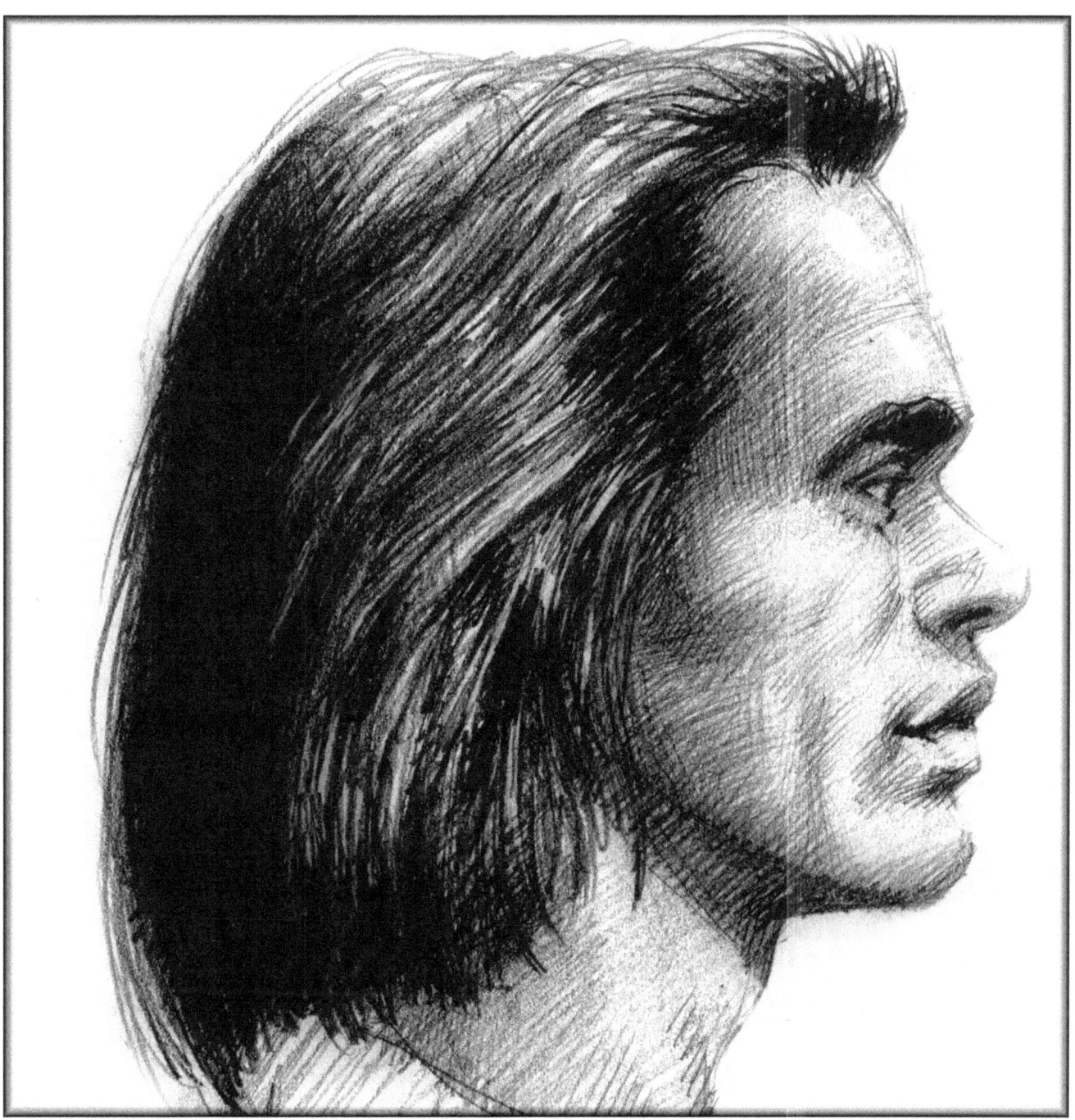

For Rogelio, we're going to have another 6 inch square. (Or, use any other size that you can easily manage, just as long as it has the same amount of grid squares as shown here.)

Measure off a mark every inch, like you did with the drawing of Daniela.

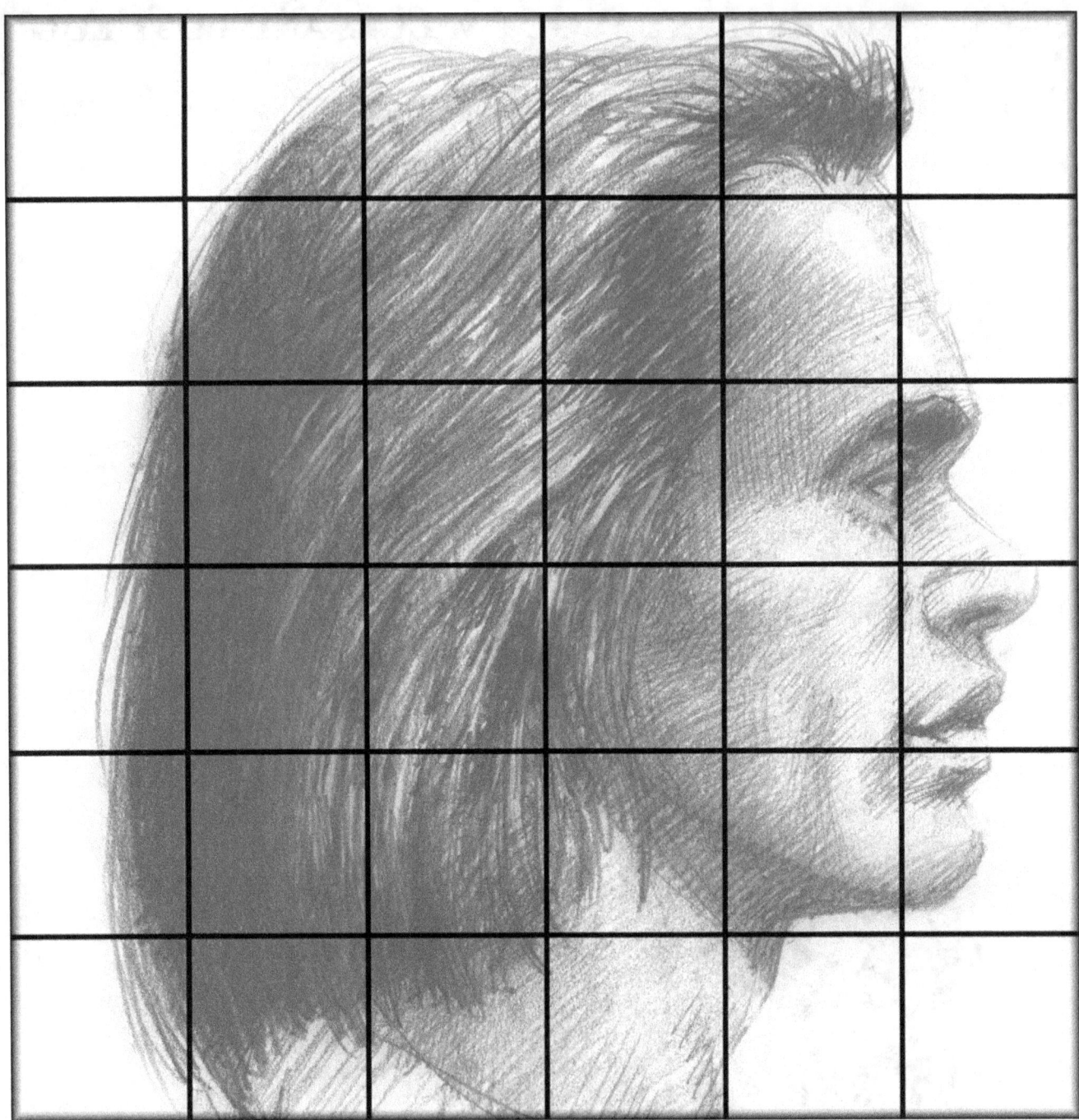

You'll notice again that I've lightened the picture of Rogelio a tiny bit just so you can see the grid lines clearly. Refer to the non-gridded picture of Rogelio when you are shading and selecting your values.

Let's return to the value strip, and see how we can apply our five values to the areas of light and shadow on Rogelio's face:

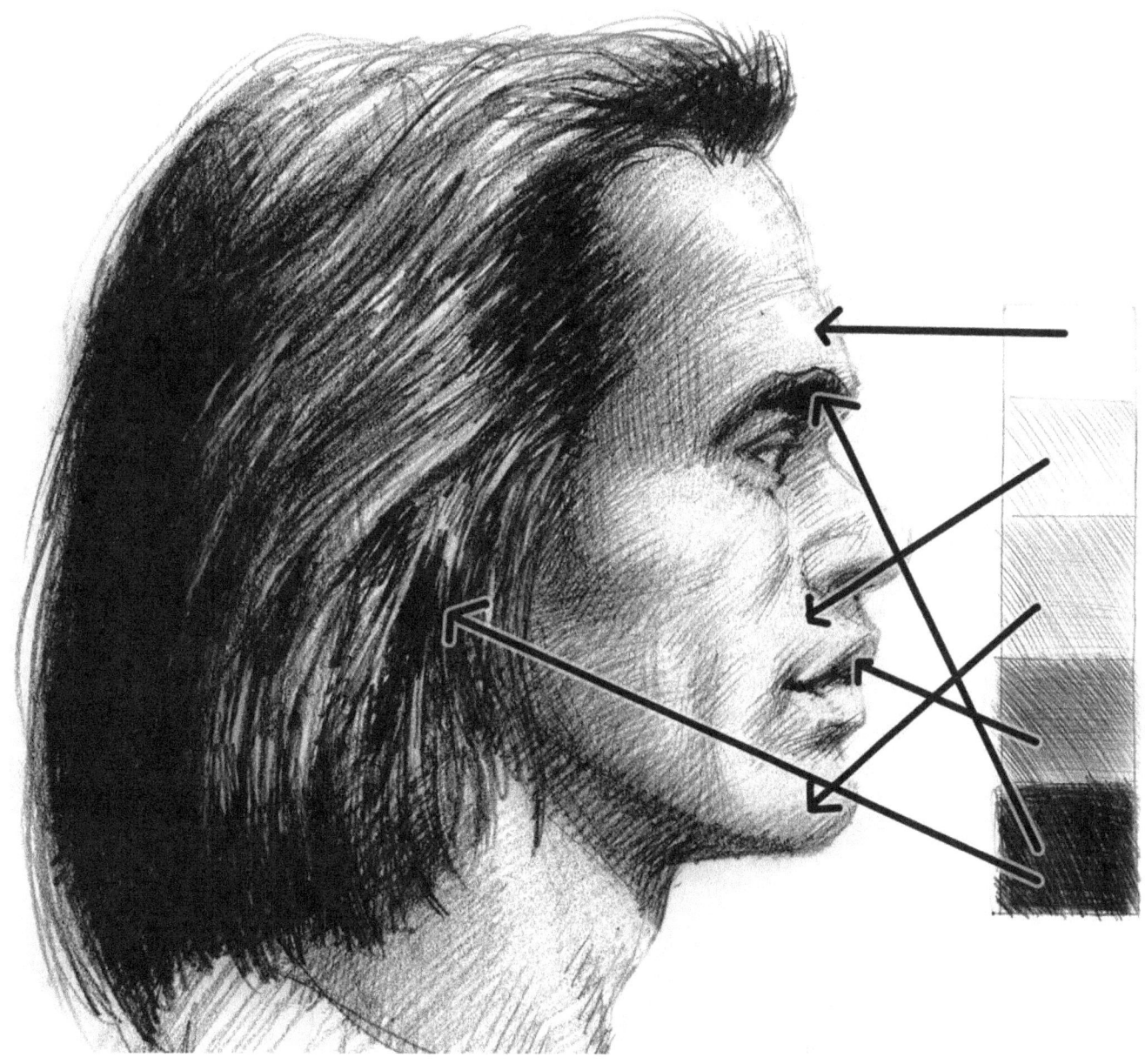

The shadows in Rogelio's hair (including a large area of hair at the back of his head) are mostly black or very dark. The shadowed part of his eyebrows are also black or almost black. Eyelashes, and the area at the edge of his mouth, are also very dark.

His upper lip (which is tipped away from the light source) is a dark grey. There are shadowy areas around his jaw area and his forehead, and under his nose.

A lighter grey is the general tone of his skin. It'll also be used in some highlighted areas of his hair.

The white (blank paper) will be used for some highlights on his forehead, the highlighted area of his lower lip, the tip of his nose, and a few areas of his hair. The whole forehead had been made a lighter grey area at first, then I went in later and erased the highlighted area to bring it back to the white of the paper.

I add a word of caution for when you're drawing in your values: It's common for beginner artists to be timid when it comes to making the blacks and dark greys. To combat this, I suggest you use a pencil with a B or 2B lead (which has a softer lead and will make darker marks compared to the standard #2 pencil). Make strong, dense pencil strokes in your black and dark grey areas. Don't be hasty—make sure that you are happy with your outlines and angles first. (You don't want to have to go back and erase these dark lines later, because of some unnoticed mistake!) But, once you're confident that everything is in its proper place, work on making those shadows nice and dark. Don't wimp out!

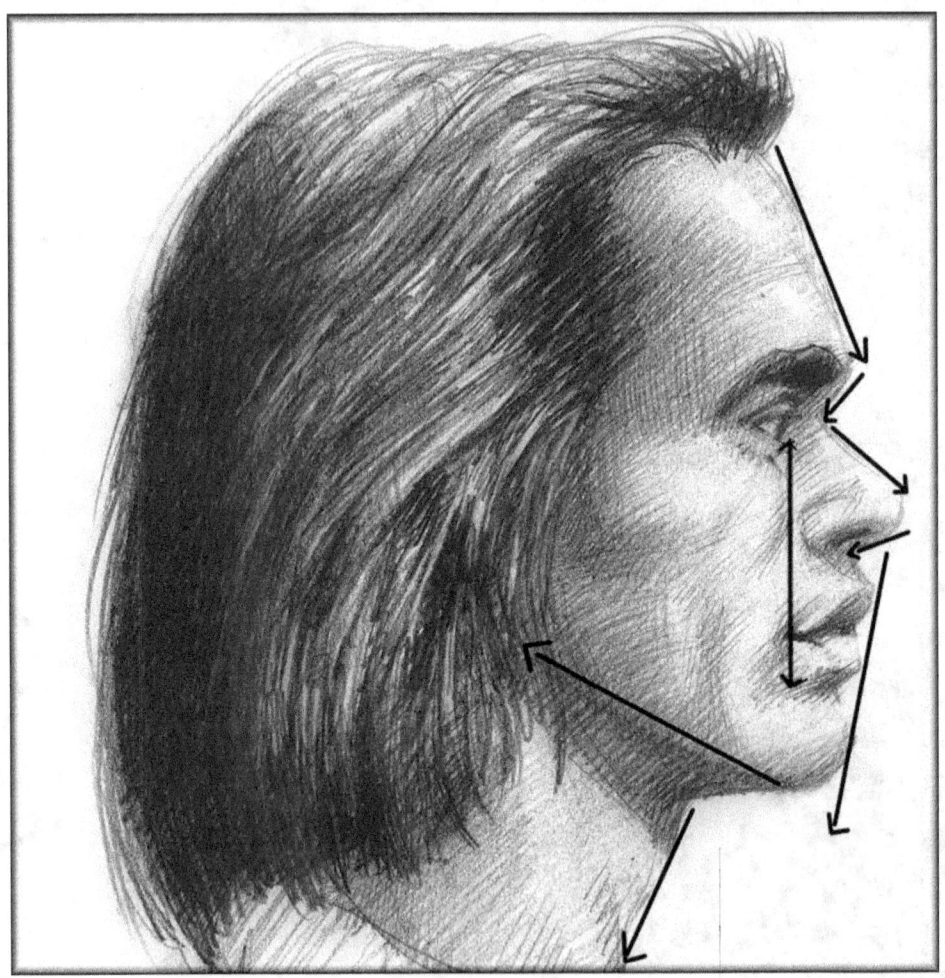

Here are some angles of Rogelio's face. (I've lightened this picture a bit so we can see the arrows better.) Notice how his forehead slopes back (is not straight up and down). His brow dips in at a sharp angle. Men often have more pronounced brows than women.

Just like with the portrait of Daniela, notice how the inner edge of his eye (seen from the side) lines up pretty much with the outer edge of the mouth. This is common.

And, like with the portrait of Daniela, his chin area slopes in a little. The upper lip juts out slightly more than his lower lip.

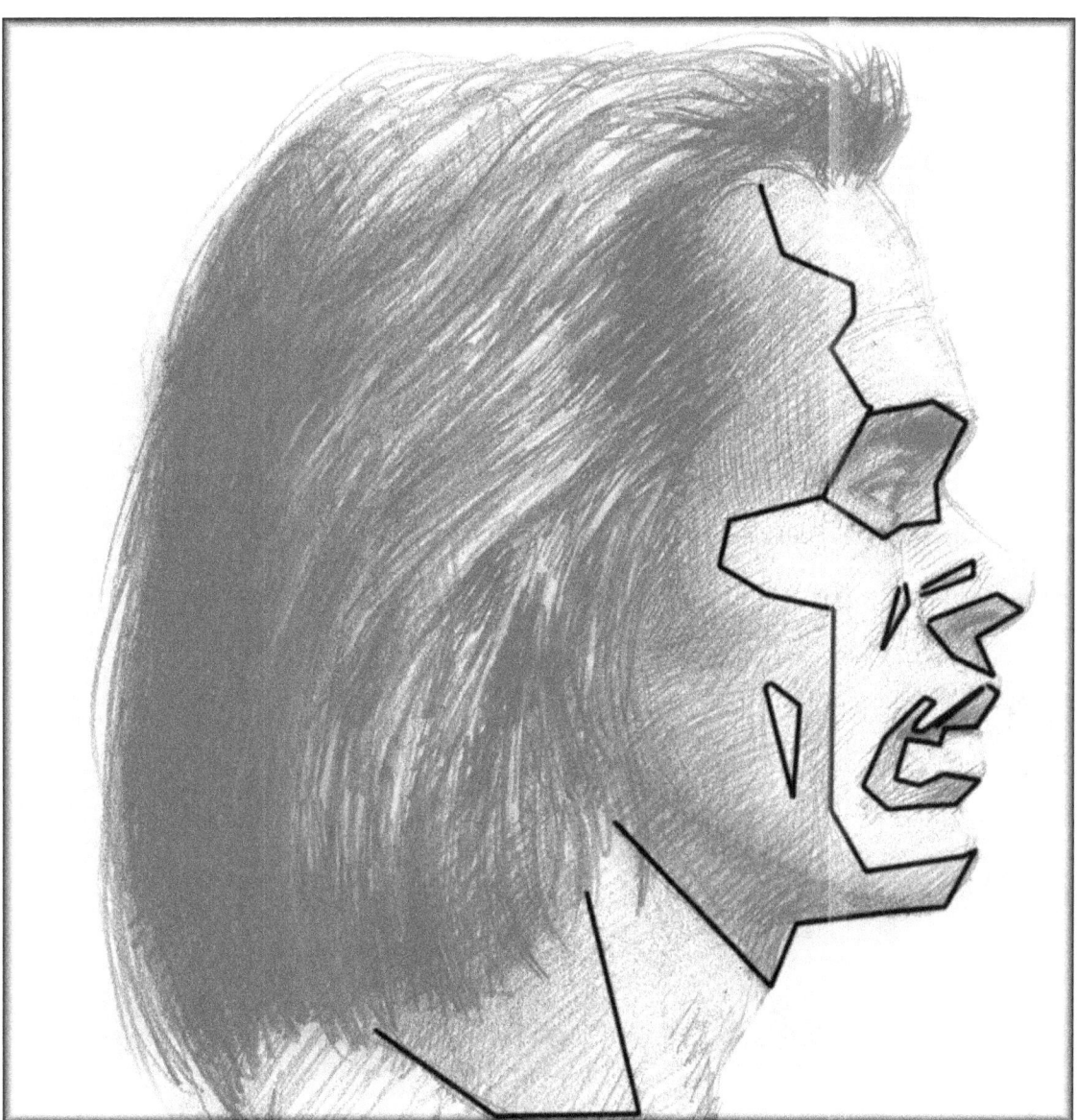

Here are the shadow patterns of Rogelio's face. The areas I've outlined are going to be either a medium grey or darker grey (with some accents of black here and there). Take note in particular of the shadow around his lower lip. We all have this same type of shadow surrounding our mouth, and with Rogelio, it is more pronounced because his lips are full.

A look at the features in more detail:

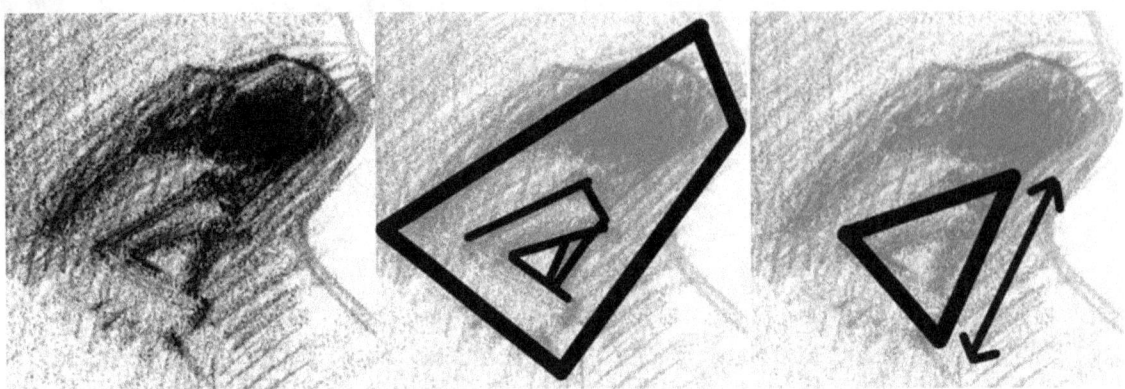

Rogelio's brow hangs over his eyes (and his eyes are deep-set), which puts a shadow over the whole eye socket (see center picture above). Notice also the angle of his eye—the bottom lid is set farther in than the top lid (see far right picture). We saw the same tilt in the portrait of Daniela (Chapter Two).

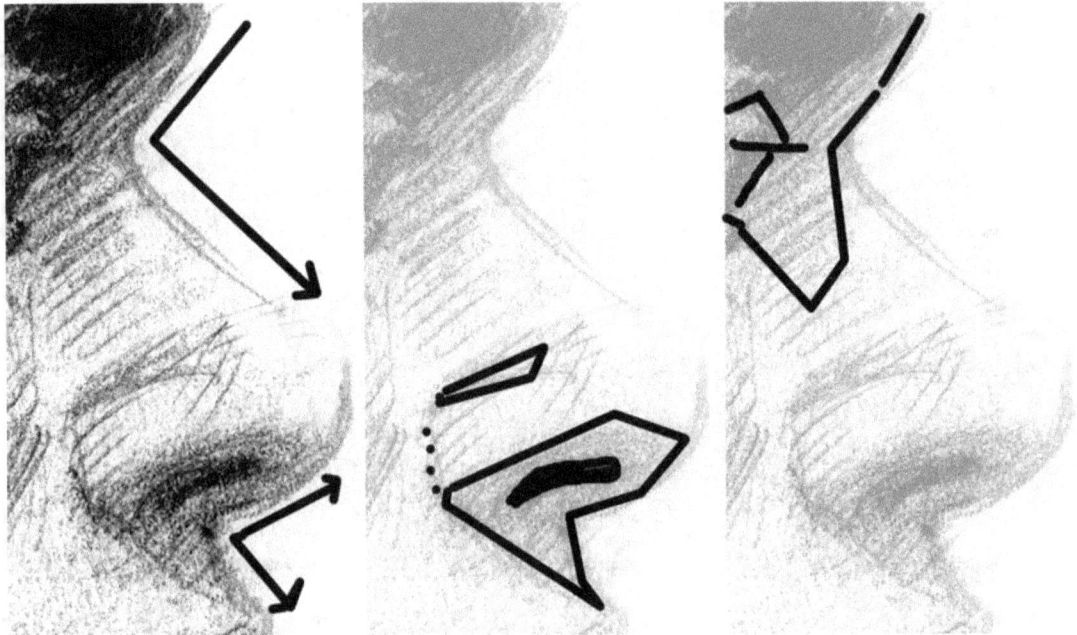

Many beginner artists find the nose particularly tricky, but it needn't be so! One thing to remember is that the bridge of the nose "blends" into the side of the brow and the eye socket. Typically, there will no be any hard lines defining the edge of the nose—gradual shading looks more natural.

Don't overdo your rendering. Less is definitely more when it comes to the nose. If you begin to overwork the nose, it could start to resemble a snout.

In the illustration above, the picture on the left shows the sharp angle of Rogelio's nose in profile. In the center picture, I have simplified the shading around his nostrils. There is a shadow shape that indicates the underside of his nose and shows how the nose has cast a shadow above the lips. In the far right picture, you can see that the shadow from around the eye "migrates" down the bridge of the nose. The shading of the nose blends in with both the brow and eye, as well as the upper lip.

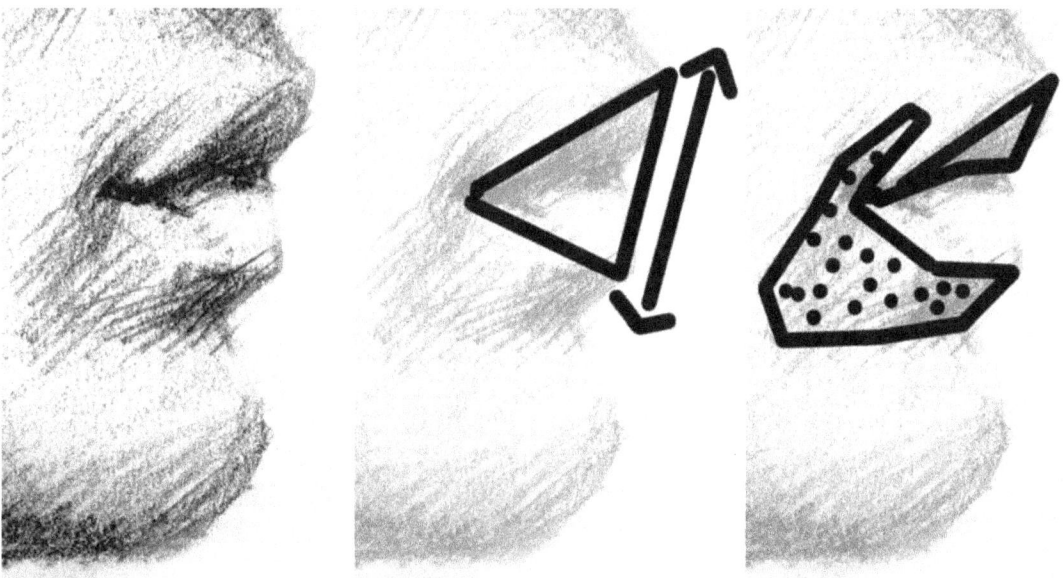

Just like with the eye when seen in profile, the mouth often takes on a tilted triangle shape. The lower lip tips in, and the upper lip often juts out (sometimes by only a subtle amount). The shading around the mouth (the dotted area in the picture on the right) is usually darker directly under the lower lip, as well as at the outer corners.

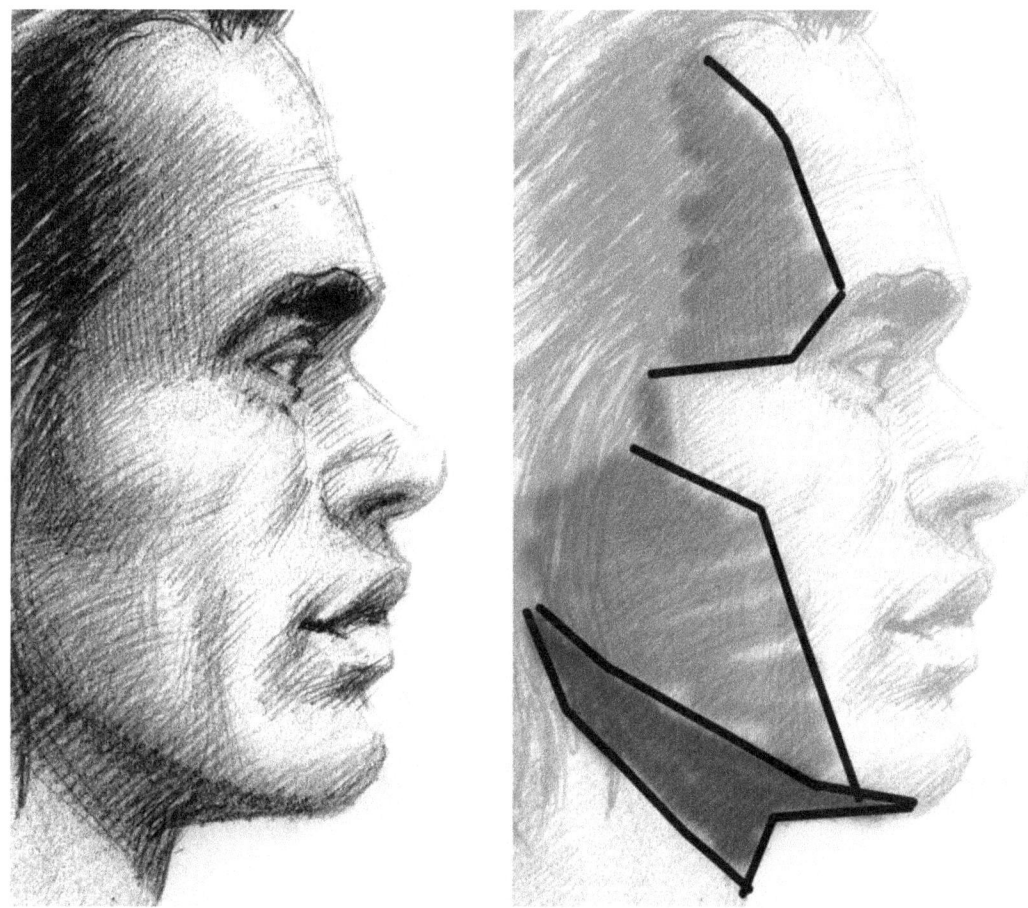

All of our heads have a front plane (the front of the head, where the features are), side planes (cheekbones, jawline), and a back plane. Here we see the side plane. The darkest shadow is underneath the jawline because it faces away from the light source. There is a large shadow on the side of Rogelio's head, which is somewhat interrupted by the cheekbone; the cheekbone itself juts out a little and attracts more light.

You will add details and nuances to the shading of the head, but first, you should familiarize yourself with these basic, simplified shadow shapes.

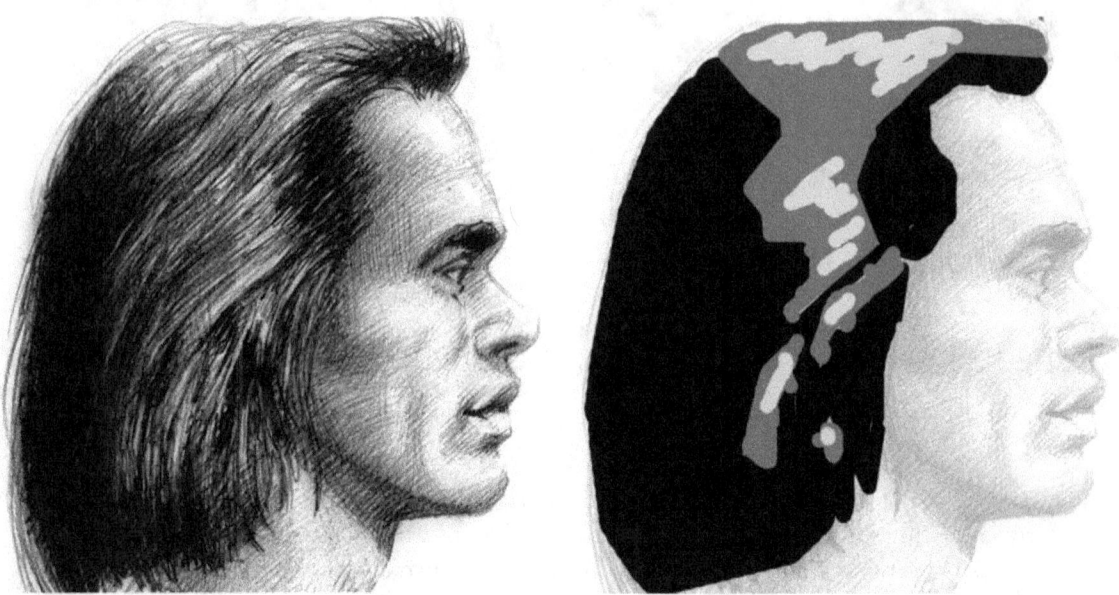

It's easiest to "block out" large shadow shapes in the hair first, then add a few individual strands and highlights last. You can use an eraser to pull out some extra highlights if necessary. Remember, DO NOT try to draw in every single strand of hair. If the shadowed areas are shaded in first, you will be surprised at how little intricate detail the hair needs, in order to look very "hair-like"! Again, less is more!

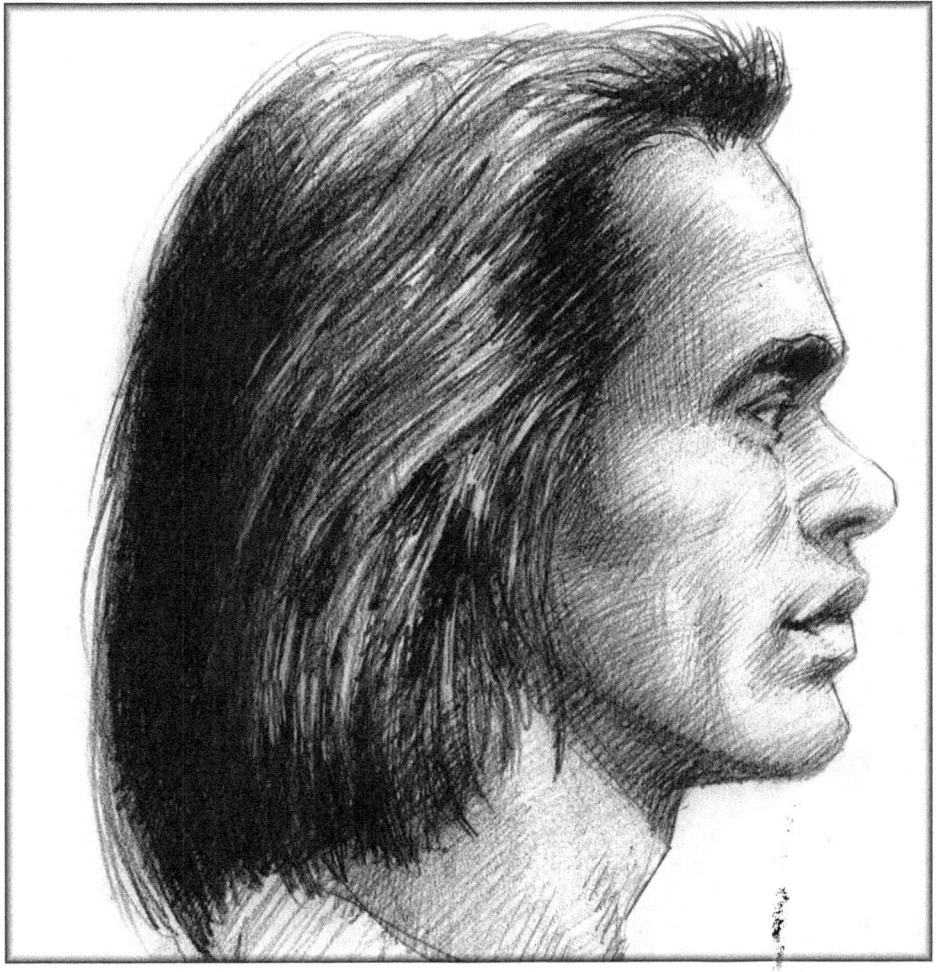

Is there anything different you notice about this picture? I've added some new lines to his face. There is now a pronounced outline all down the edge of his profile, from the top of his forehead, down the edge of his nose, and around his lips, chin, and neck.

But does it really look better? Compare the outlined Rogelio picture to the original Rogelio:

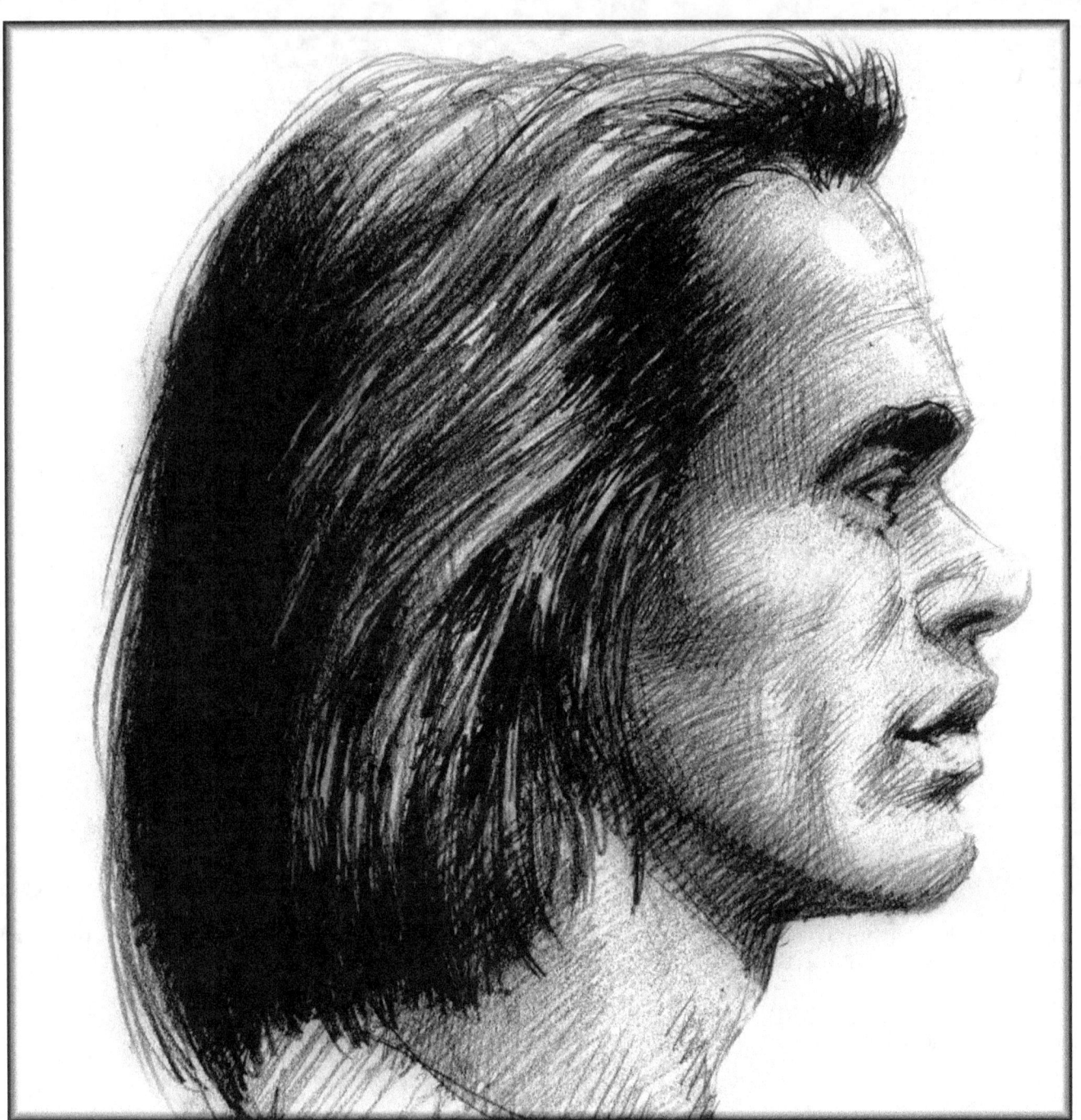

The non-outlined Rogelio leaves the highlighted parts of his face (the forehead, edge of nose, bottom lip, and upper chin) as a lighter value. The edges are lost, because the background of the drawing is white, and these areas of the face are also lighter. So, we have a highlighted area of the face up against a white background.

It becomes obvious that we don't need to see those outlines after all. In fact, his face looks more three-dimensional without them, because it keeps the values true and intact. Would we see a heavy outline over the edge of his profile in real life? Of course not. So why draw it in his portrait?

Here's another example of lost edges:

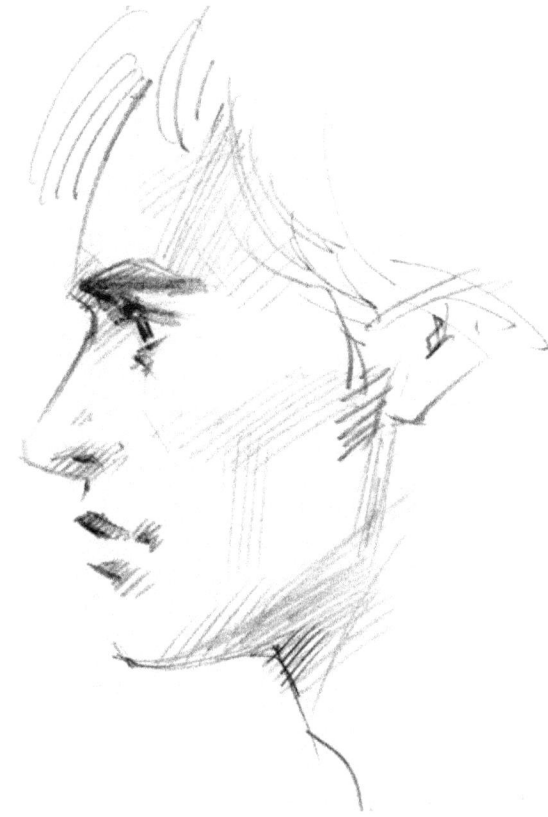

This is a simple little doodle I found in one of my sketchbooks. It probably took two or three minutes to draw this, so it's not very detailed. Do you see the lost edges? Let's look carefully:

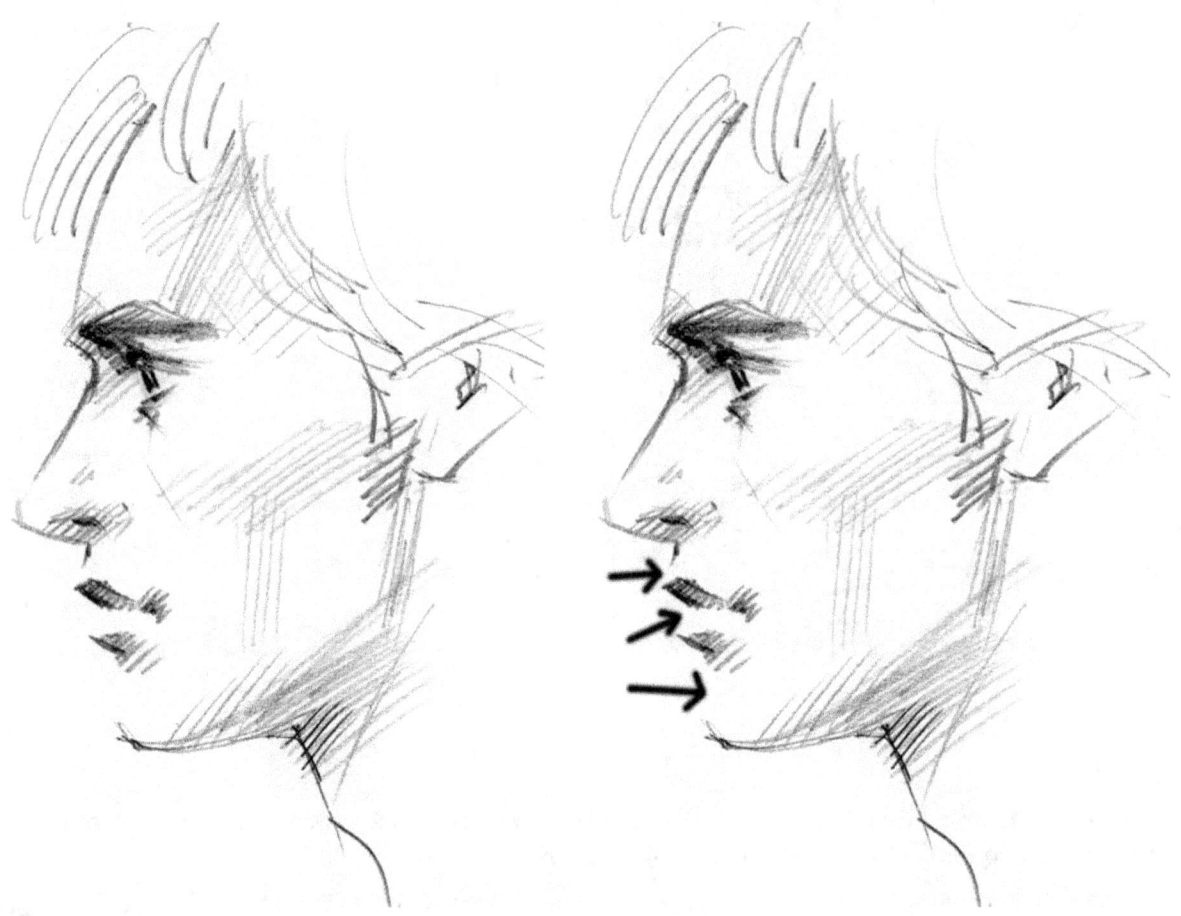

Our eyes fill in all the necessary information about his face. We don't need to see the entire border of his upper lip, lower lip, or upper chin, to know what's there.

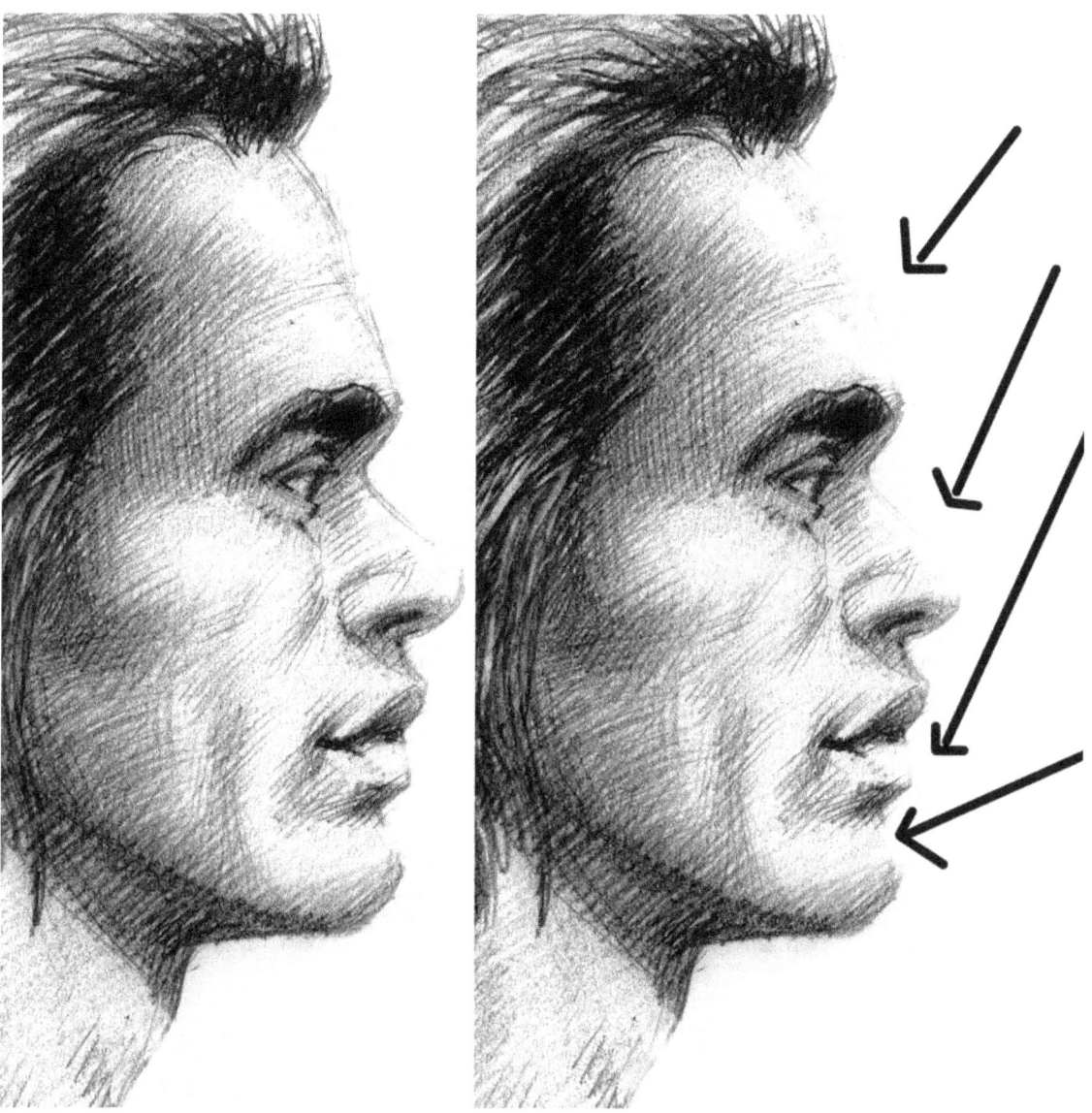

Now I've gone even farther and removed more outlines from select spots on Rogelio's profile. Where there is light hitting his face and creating highlights (see where arrows point on the illustration on the right), hardly any outline is needed.

I'd argue that it looks more elegant to omit these types of outlines. As I often tell you, less is more!

EXTRA WORK

And now for some extra practice. I present you with Gustavo!

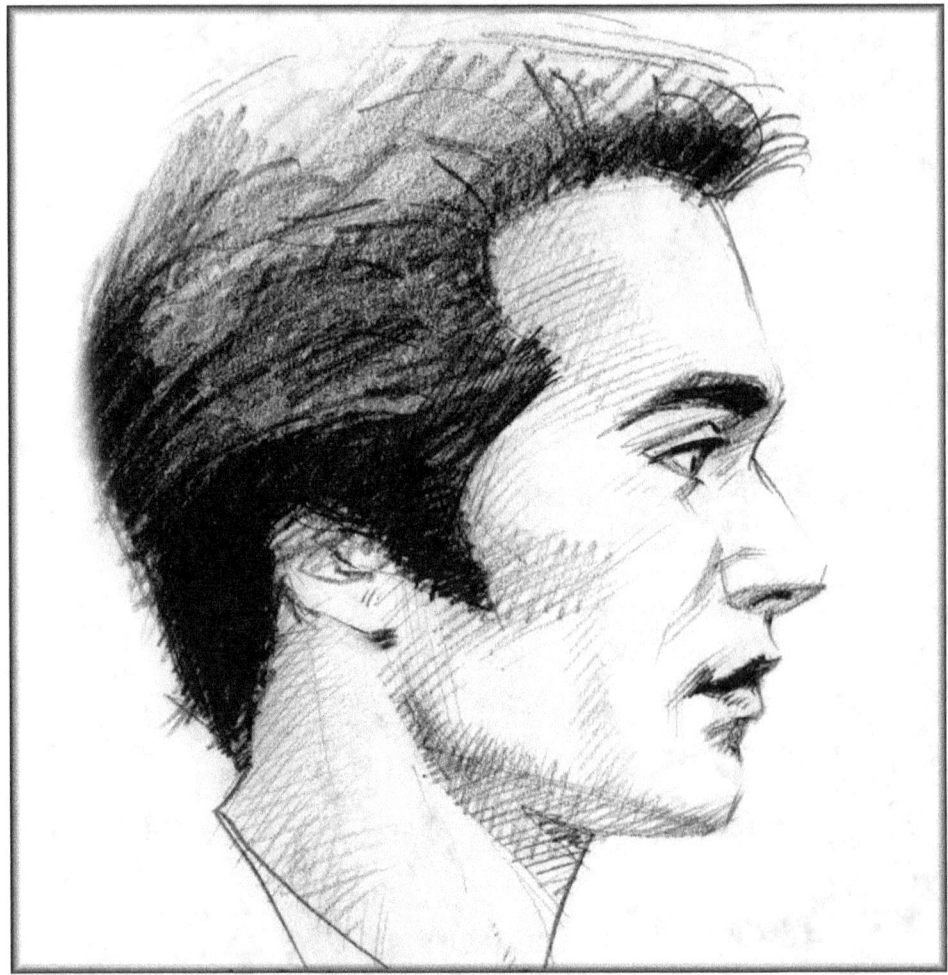

Gustavo started out as a smaller sketch so he will do fine being copied as a smaller drawing. You can draw him on a 5 inch or 6-inch square.

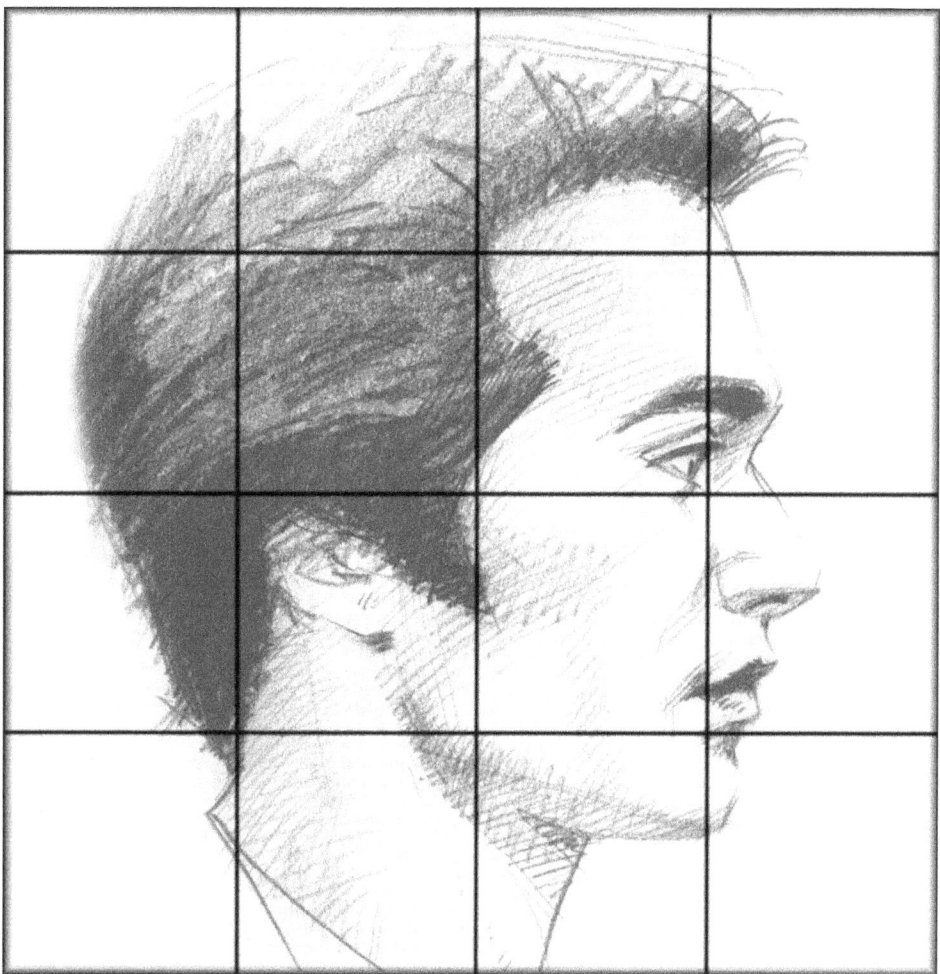

There are only 4 squares vertically and horizontally with this one. Make 1-1/2 inch squares (1-1/4 inches if your drawing will be a total of 5 inches) to complete the grid.

With larger squares, this means you have fewer grid squares overall. You will have to do more analysis and more looking at shapes, angles, and negative space in order to get the drawing accurate within each square. This is a good thing! It will be a challenge, but I know you can do it.

Gustavo has a very angular face. Notice the angles of his brow, chin, and jaw. These are common in the male profile.

Do you see some lost edges (not outlined)? Remember: don't draw in an outline if you don't see it in the original picture.

SKILL BUILDING LESSONS FROM CHAPTER FOUR:

You continued to learn more about values, lights and darks and middle tones. You have completed a new portrait with the aid of the grid and discovered some new details about the features of the face, as well as about the structure of the head. The idea of "lost edges" and soft edges was introduced to you in this chapter, and you will be repeating, "Less is more!" when you are tempted to overdo outlining parts of your drawing.

CHAPTER FIVE: A THREE-QUARTERS VIEW PORTRAIT

You did notice that I was making you work with only profiles before, didn't you? That's because I believe profiles are a little easier to comprehend at first. But, now you've graduated to the three-quarters view.

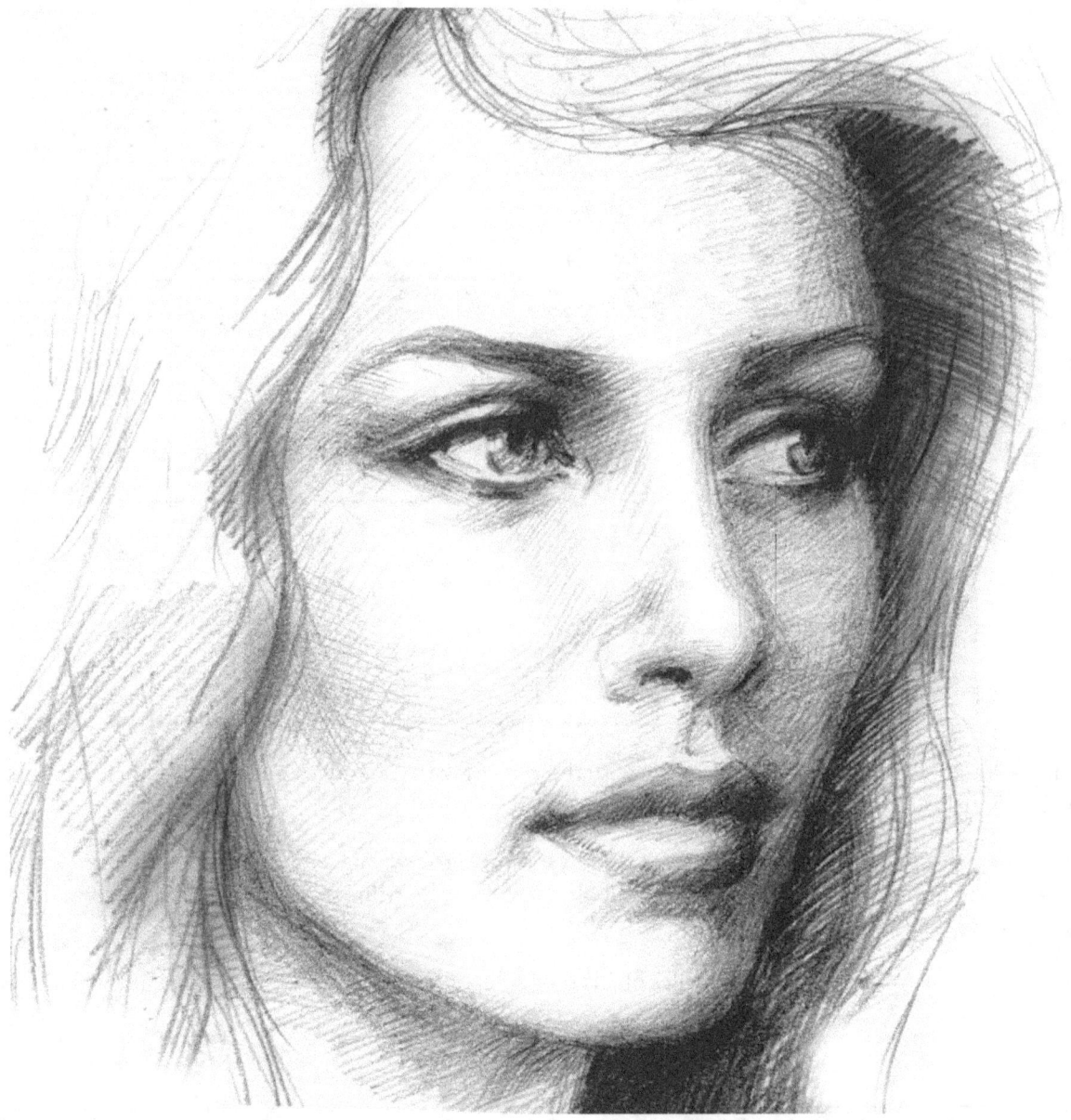

I call her "Cynthia." She looks like she comes straight out of some '80s sitcom!

You've probably noticed that I always frame these portraits into a square shape. That's because it's so much easier for you to make your own grids (using either inches or centimeters) when you're always dealing with a simple square for everything.

This time, I was unorthodox and made seven squares. Let's live on the wild side with our seven-squared grid!

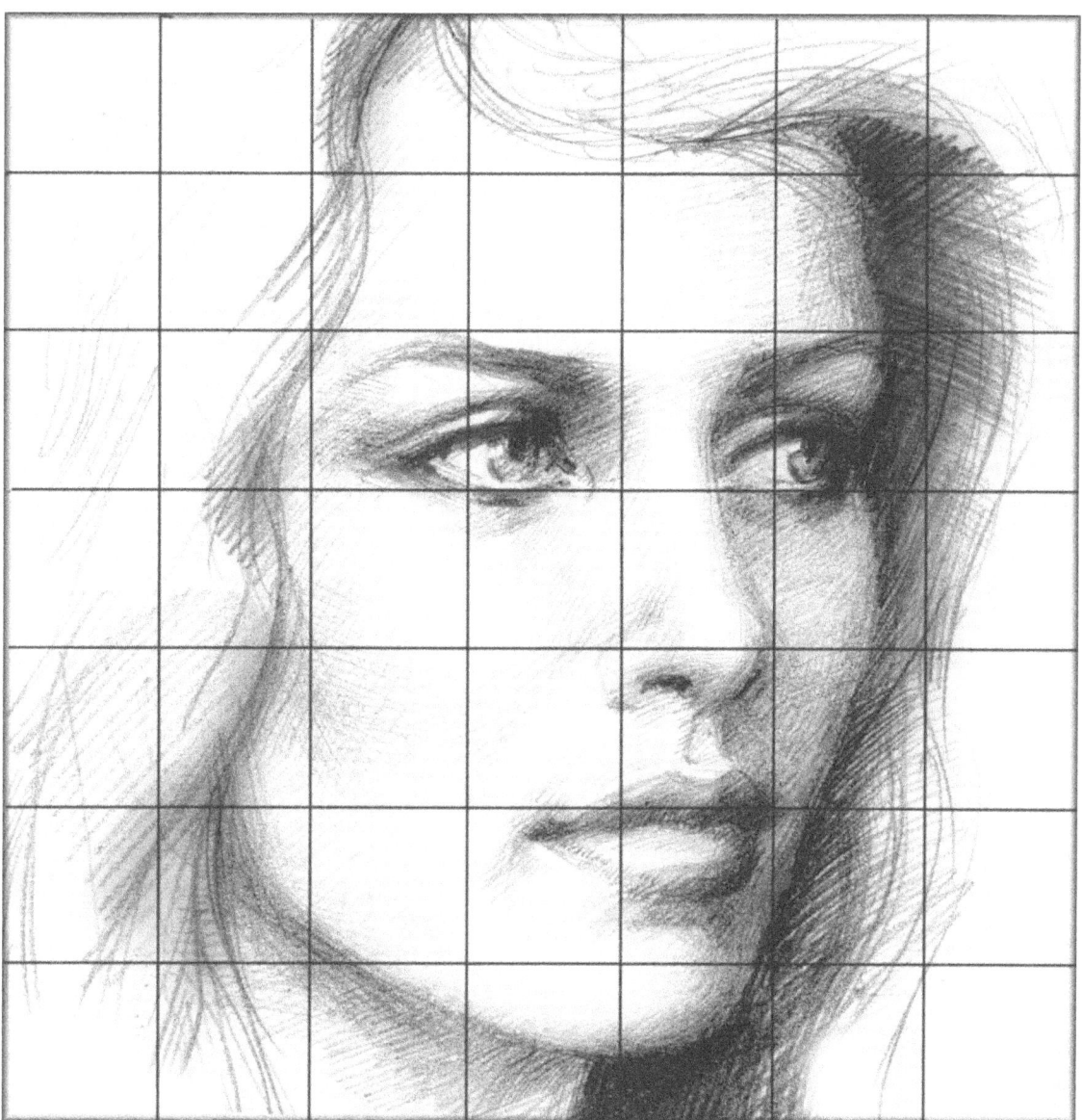

(I lightened the values on her portrait a little, so the black grid lines would show better. When you've got your outlines and angles drawn in, please consult the previous un-gridded picture in order to finish your exercise.)

Mark off 1-inch (or 3-cm) intervals and then create all your little squares. You should have 7 squares both vertically and horizontally. Or, you can go larger if you like, as long as the squares are all consistently spaced and sized.

You're returning to the smaller grid squares with this drawing, because the 3/4 view is unfamiliar to you, and therefore will be a little trickier. The smaller squares will help you get everything correct!

You'll notice in this drawing that my crosshatching sketching is slightly "tighter" (more detailed). There's no trick to doing this; just use smaller, more careful crosshatching. I used a 0.5 mm mechanical pencil for this drawing, but 0.7 mm would probably work well, too.

Here are some things to look for:

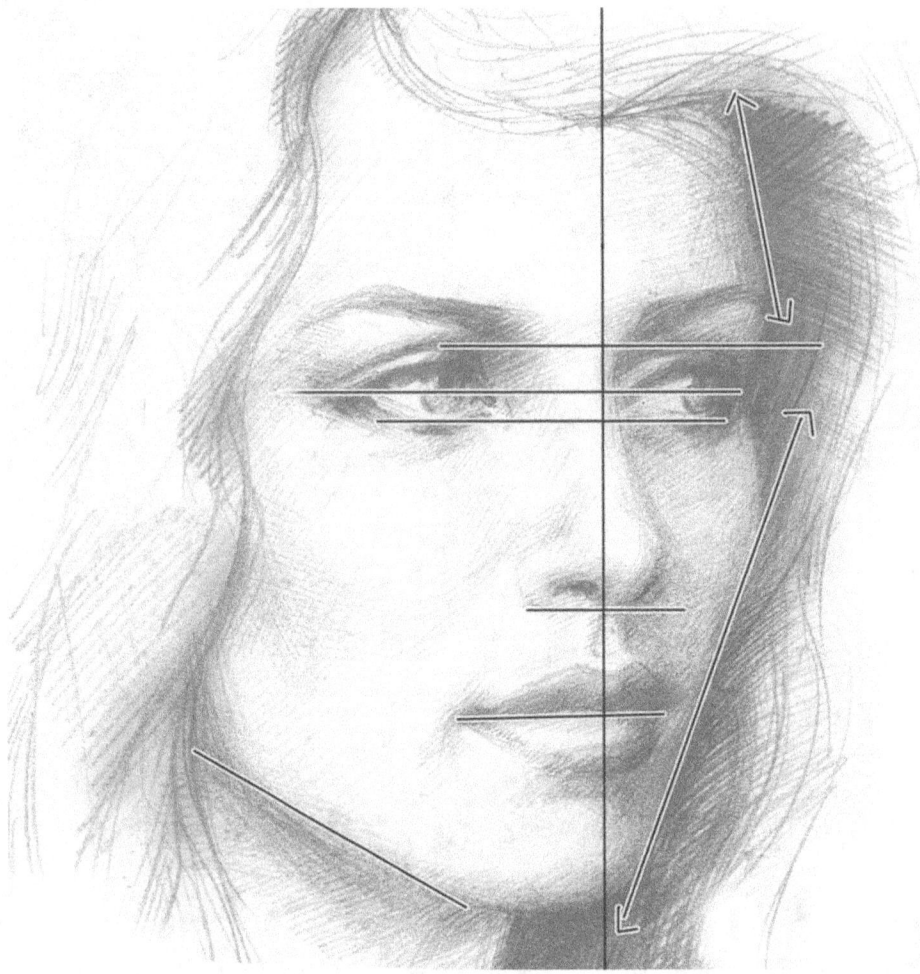

Notice how the nose angles out from the center of the face (the center is marked with the black vertical line).

To make sure the eyes aren't crooked, you can lightly draw straight lines through the center (and upper and lower lids) to confirm that they line up. (You will, of course, erase these alignment lines later.)

The edge of her cheek on the shadowed area angles down (as seen in this illustration) and the angle of the brow slopes in a little bit. Pay attention to the angle of the jaw on the left side. You don't want this angle to be too shallow or too deep.

On the subject of lost edges (which we first learned about in Chapter Four, with Rogelio), take note of her mouth:

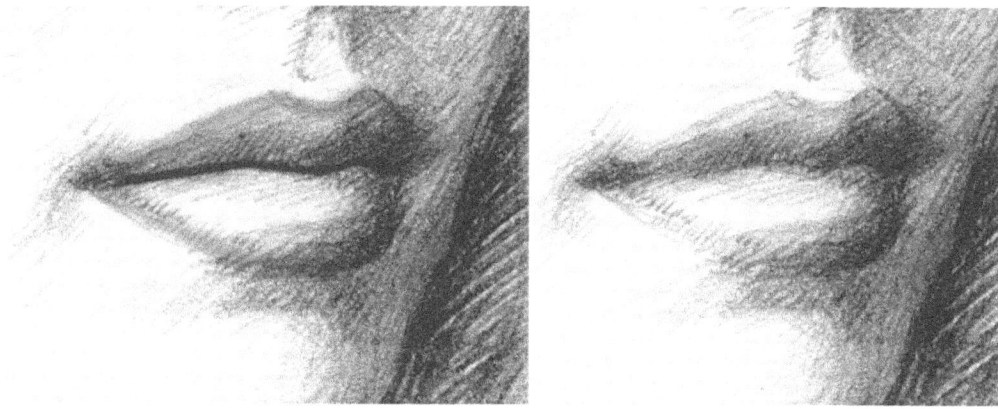

On the left image, I've added a heavier line between her upper and lower lips. I've also given the outer contour of her lips a darker outline. But are these heavier lines necessary? I don't think so. Without those darker lines, her lips look softer and more delicate.

Here is another example:

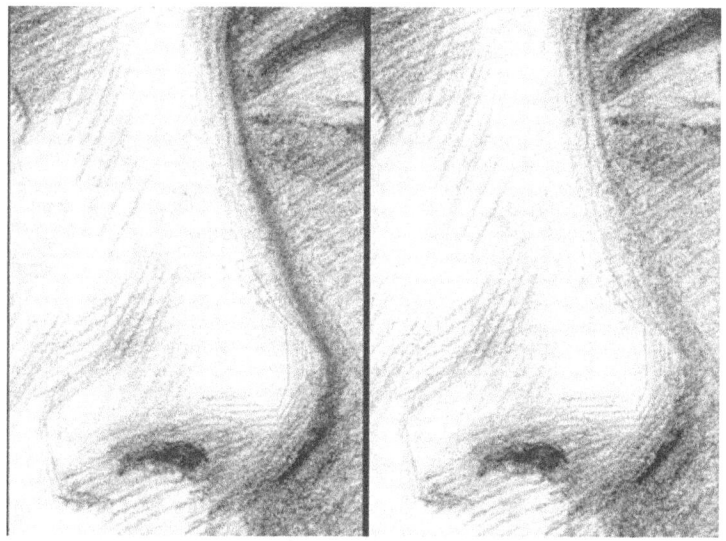

I've added a heavier outline along the right edge of Cynthia's nose in the picture on the left. But does the drawing need that? Did it look wrong before? I don't think it did.

The nose, in particular, can have a lot of edges that DO NOT need to be distinctly defined with heavy outlines or exaggerated shading. In fact, there is no line defining the left side of the bridge of her nose. (I added a few shading strokes, but no defining lines going down the length of the nose.) On the right, it is slightly darker along the side, and that's enough for you to identify the edge.

Try to identify the softer edges in a person's features. Don't be too quick to outline everything. Remember, less is more!

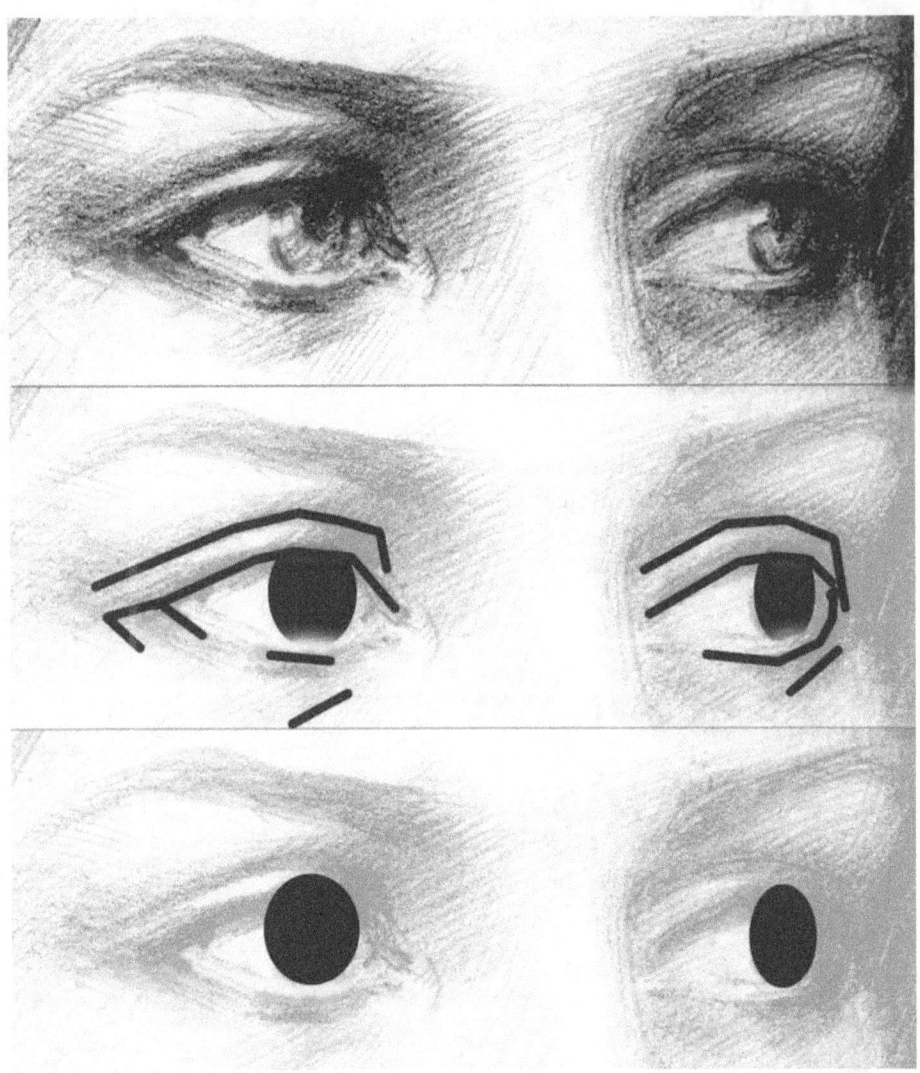

Because Cynthia is seen from a 3/4 view and is looking off to the side, the irises in her eyes will not be perfectly round. Instead, they will be oval. In the illustration above, the bottom panel shows the oval shape more clearly. The middle panel shows how the tops and bottoms of these ovals of the iris are obscured by the top and bottom eyelids. Additionally, we see that the shape of the eyelids is unique, due to her being seen in 3/4 view.

Also, make sure that you draw the pupils of her eyes as oval, and have them be concentric (perfectly in the middle) with the iris.

To accurately capture Cynthia's lips, it's easiest to simplify everything down into a few values and more abstracted shapes:

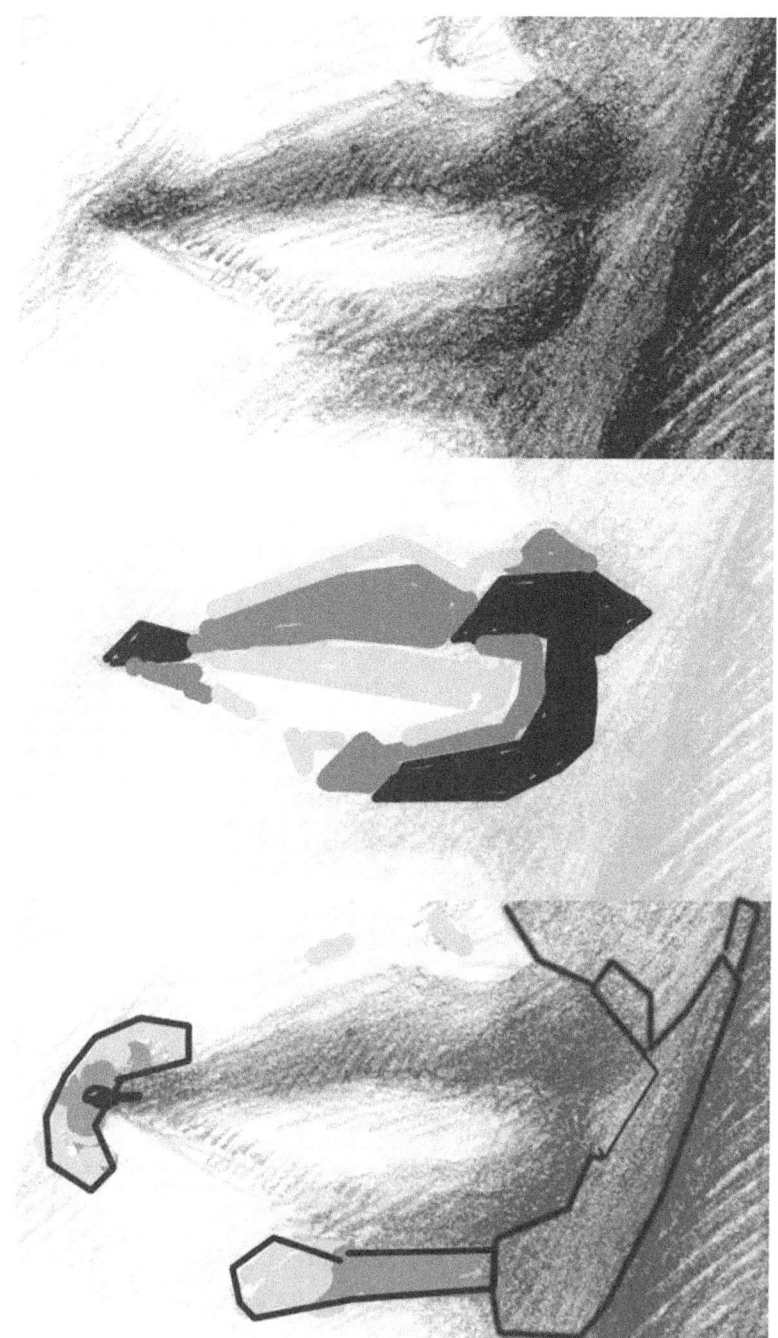

The middle illustration above shows where the shadows are the darkest, on and around her mouth. Then there are the medium dark areas, the medium light areas; the areas untouched would be the white.

The outer left corner of her mouth is quite dark—this is very common. Most of us have a darker "accent" at each corner of our mouths.

As we saw in Chapter Four with Rogelio, there is shading around the mouth, most noticeably under the bottom lip and radiating from each corner of the mouth. Don't overlook these details!

The structure of the nose seems to give many artists a lot of trouble. A good way to think of the nose when drawing it from 3/4 or front view is as a wedge…

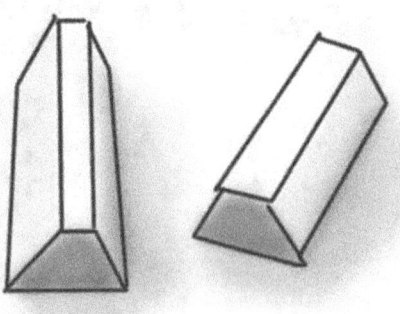

There's a top plane, and two side planes sloping down, and a bottom "underside." The underside is where the nostrils are, and usually has more of a shadow. The wedge-nose will cast a shadow on one side of the face or the other (depending on which side the light source is coming from).

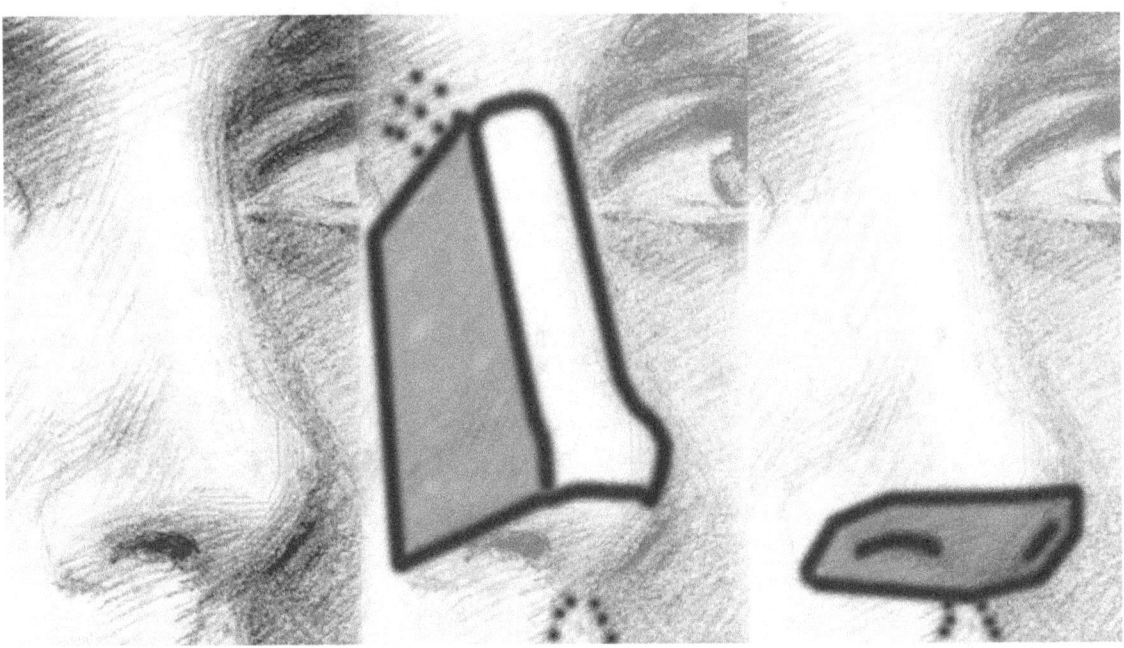

Here we can see that Cynthia's nose has that same wedge shape. I shaded the side plane (to our left) so it is easier to identify. However, in the actual drawing, that side of her nose is facing the light source, so it has very little shadow. The underside of her nose has more shadow (as I have highlighted in the illustration on the far right) but, as you can see, I've made the nostrils very dark and pronounced. This proves the point I made earlier—if you overdo the nose with heavy detail and strong outlines, it will soon look like a snout. Avoid the snout look! Shade the nose gently and with soft edges.

EXTRA WORK:

Here is Ana Paula:

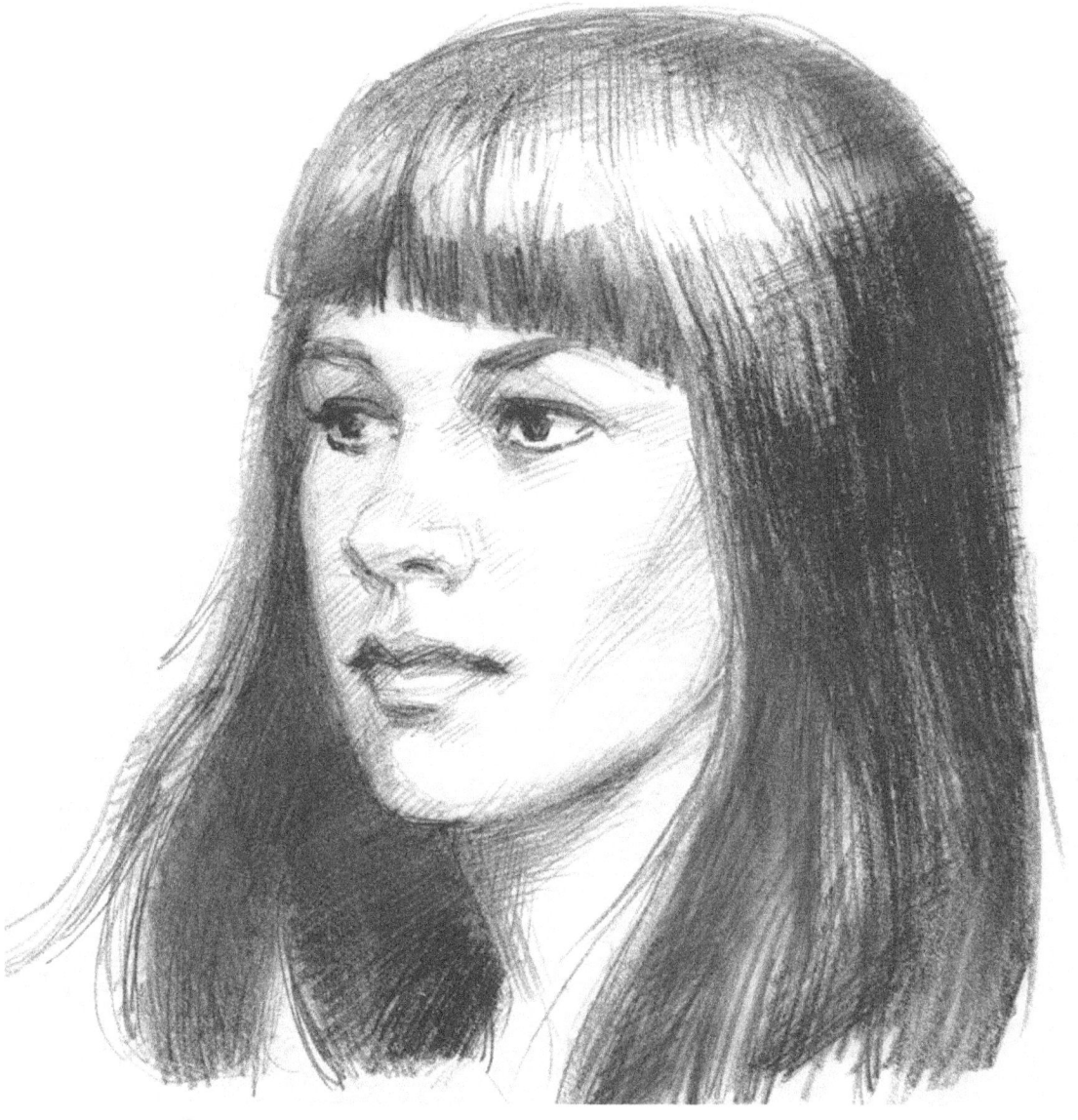

There's a lot of work to do on the hair in this drawing!

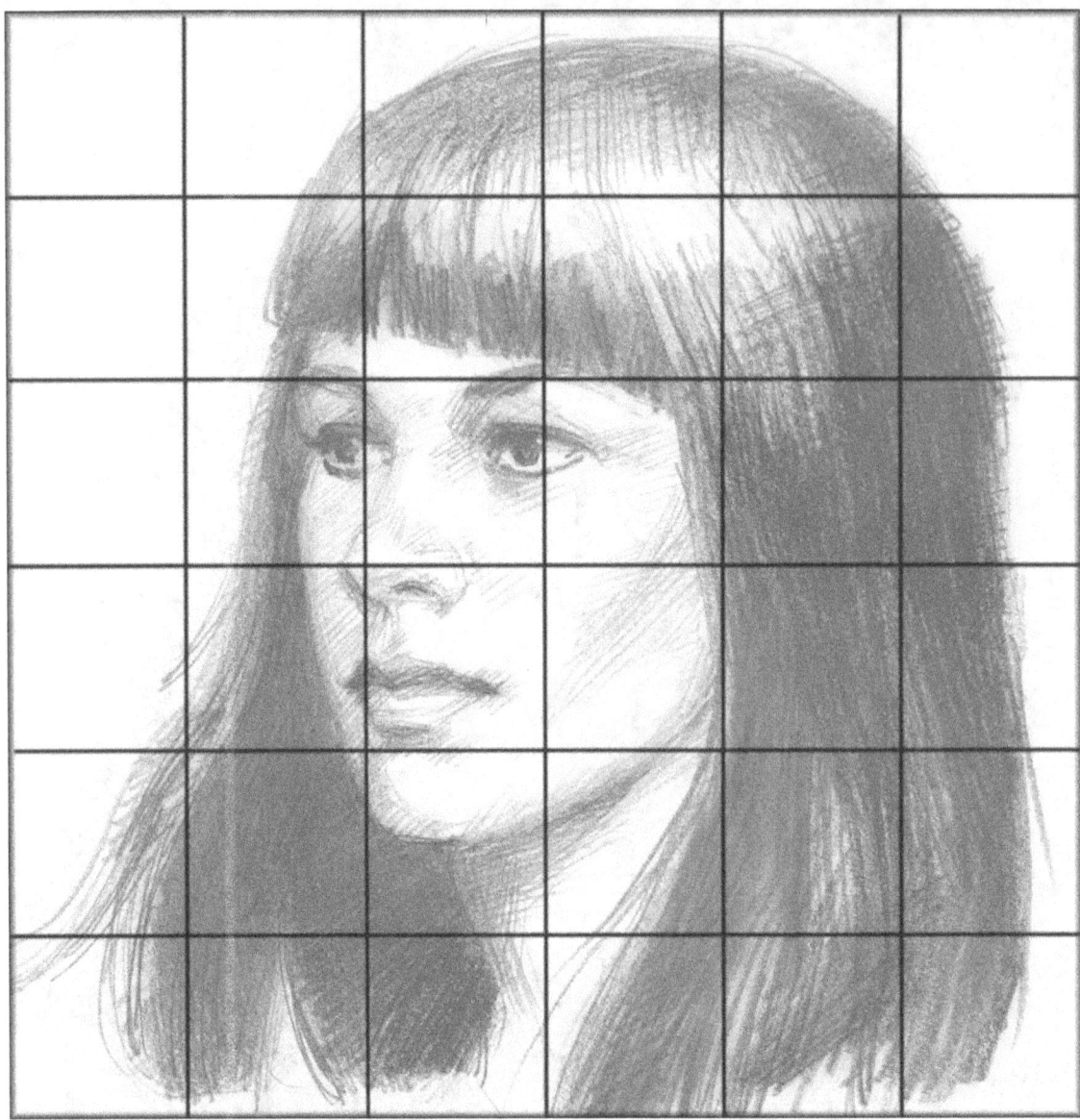

Yes, it's another standard 6-square grid.

As you can see in my sketch, I wasn't aiming for a very detailed, smooth rendering of the face or hair. So, your primary focus should be in studying the angles of the 3/4 view face. In addition, you can have some extra practice with hair. Remember, don't draw the hair as individual strands. You should first think of it as masses of value (dark and light).

SKILL BUILDING LESSONS FROM CHAPTER FIVE:

You have now successfully completed a 3/4 view portrait. You've learned to look for angles and alignments in the head when seen in the 3/4 view. You now understand that the iris of the eye is an oval shape when seen at this angle and that the pupil is always concentric with the iris. More information and details were given to you about losing edges and not heavily outlining some of the features of the face. You learned more about the structure of the nose, and how it resembles a wedge. You now know how to take more care when drawing the shading and structure around the mouth, especially its edges.

CHAPTER SIX: TACKLING THE FRONT VIEW PORTRAIT

To mix things up a little, this time we'll be copying a painting which has been digitally converted to black and white.

This is one of my old, abandoned oil paintings. Finally, it can be put to good use. It needed lots of time in Photoshop to be brought up to snuff. So many things were out of whack! The funny thing is, I had no idea it needed so much correction when I originally painted it. I guess that means I've been improving.

That's something to remember. You never should stop improving. No matter how long you've been drawing and painting, you ought to always be seeking to better yourself. Expect that there will continually be something in need of improvement.

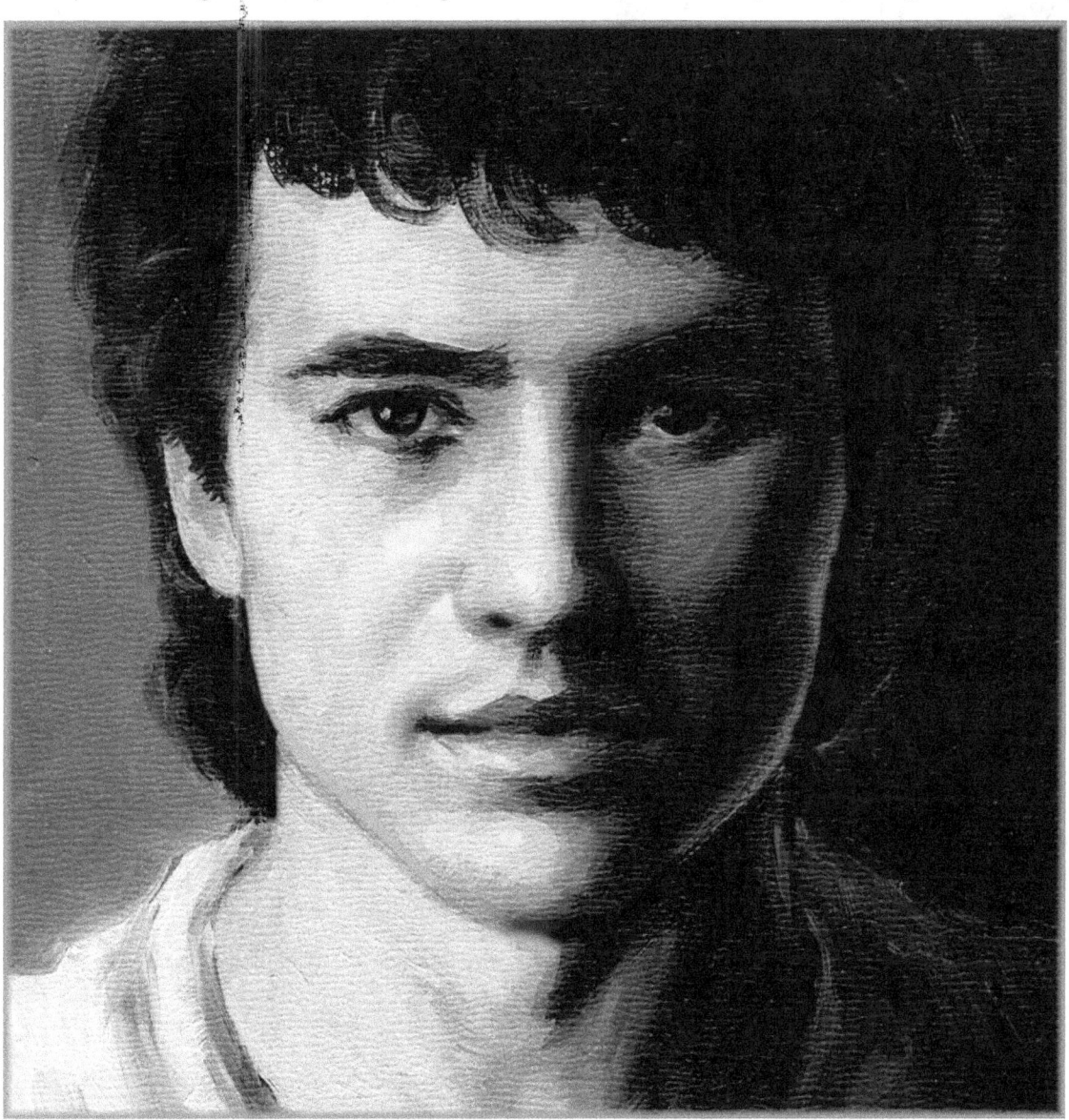

I'm calling him Bruno. You can see some of the canvas-like texture, as well as some brushstrokes in this picture. You'll ignore that texture when you start your pencil drawing!

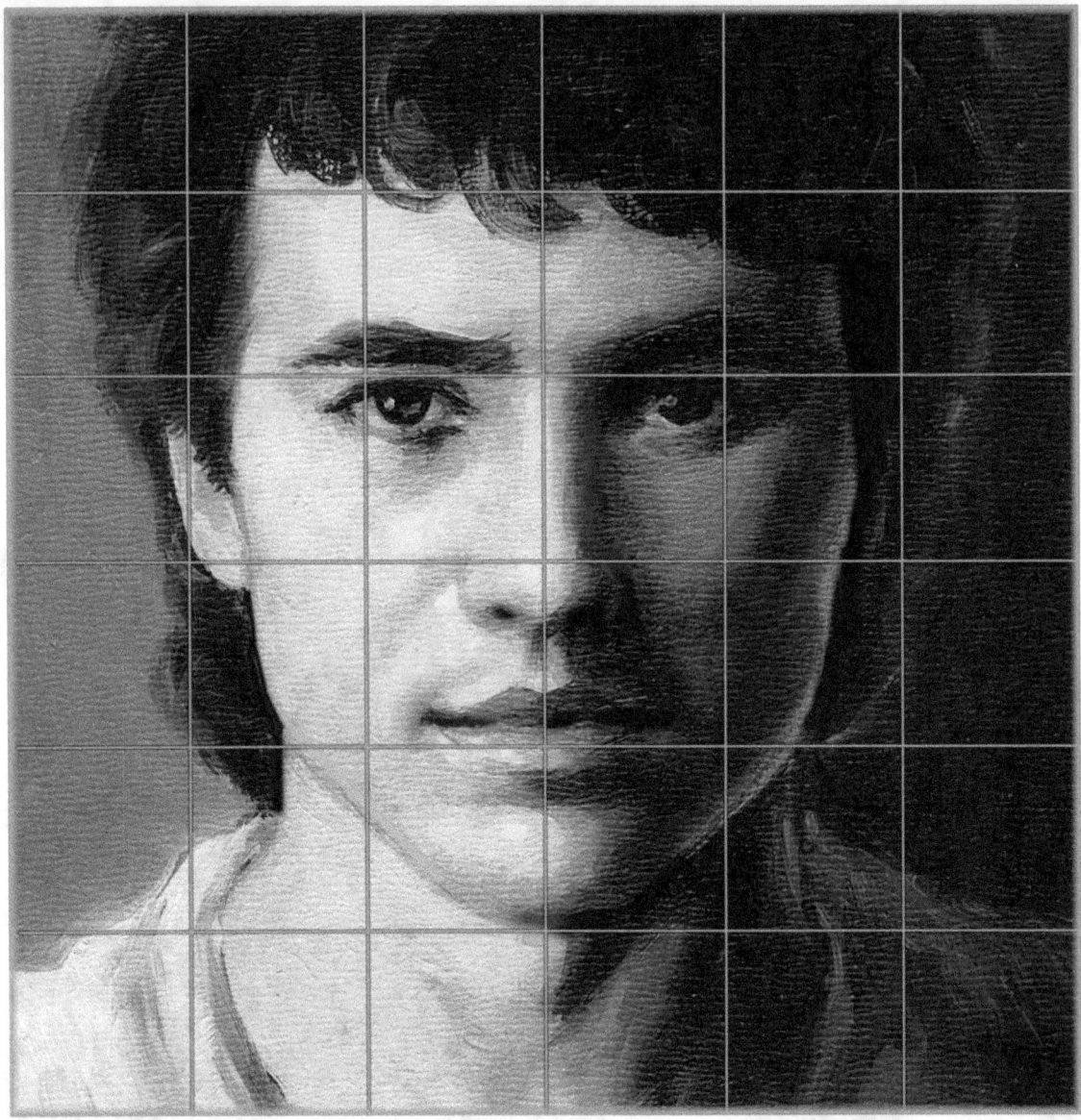

Again we will work with another 6-square grid. (The original painting is also 6 x 6 inches.) If you want to make your square bigger than 6 inches, that's fine, just as long as it has the same number of grid squares.

When you start drawing, be extra-careful to keep everything lined up correctly. This is particularly noticeable with full-face portraits. It's common to get the eyes a little lopsided and the mouth slightly crooked.

Watch for the jawline! Don't feel bad if you draw something out of whack; it happens to all of us. We just have to keep tweaking and correcting it until it's better.

ALIGNMENTS AND OTHER DETAILS

When you start to draw any portrait, even when using the grid as your aid, these techniques will come in very handy!

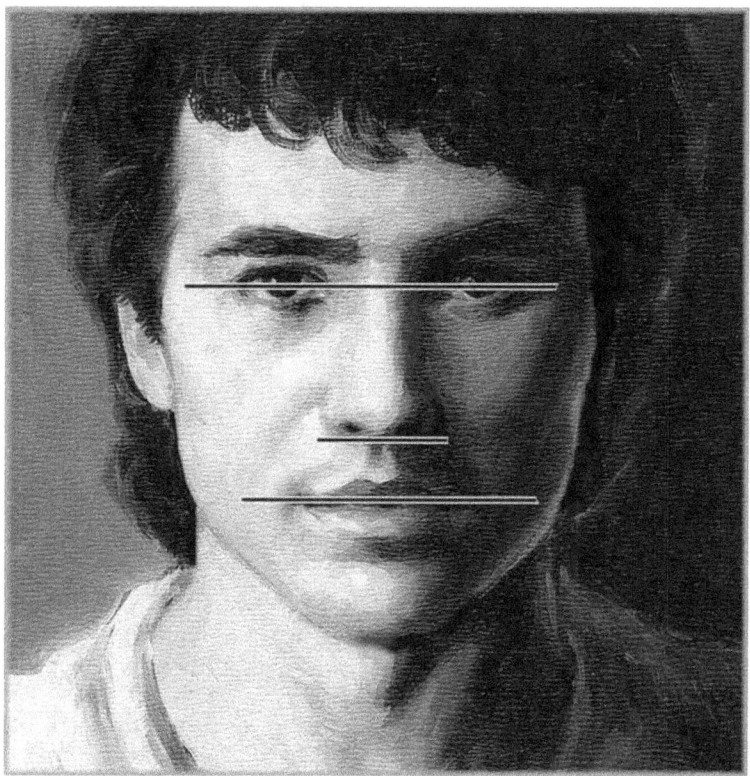

I've added an overlay of some lines to confirm that the eyes, nose, and mouth are parallel to each other and not crooked. Don't assume that you're getting it right just by eyeballing it. Always verify! Your eyes can fool you, especially when you've been working for a while and have become engrossed in the progress. The longer you work without a break, the more likely you will lose objectivity. You may believe your art looks great at the time. Later on, when your head clears, you will suddenly notice all these terrible, terrible mistakes! (Every artist has been there!)

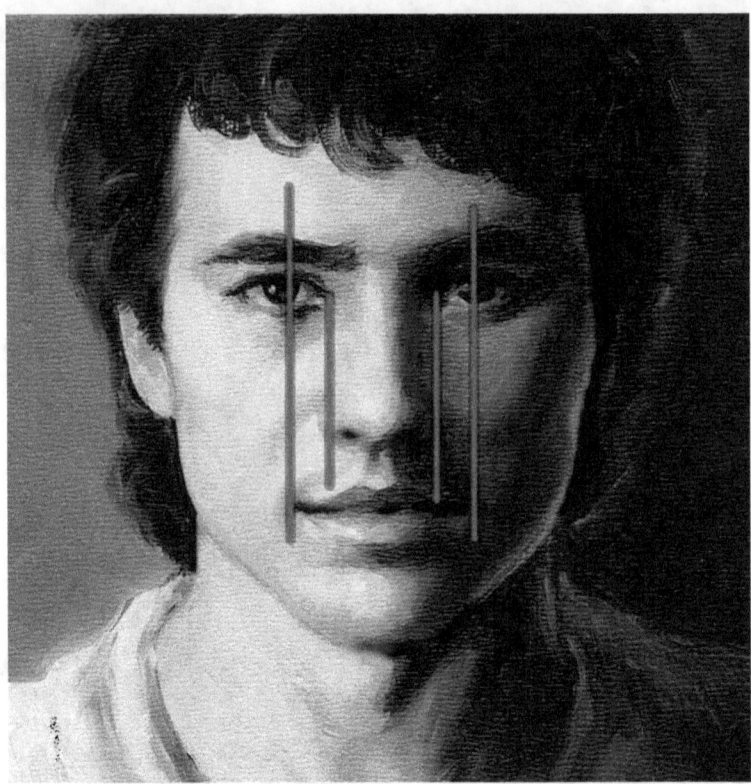

If a person is looking straight ahead, as we see in this painting, the pupils of the eyes often line up with the edges of the mouth. In Bruno, they almost do. The inner corner of the eyes typically line up with the outer edge of the nostrils. Each person is a little different. This particular face, being male, had a nose that is a little wider. This is not uncommon.

Look for where these landmarks line up on your model, and confirm that they're lining up at the same place on your drawing.

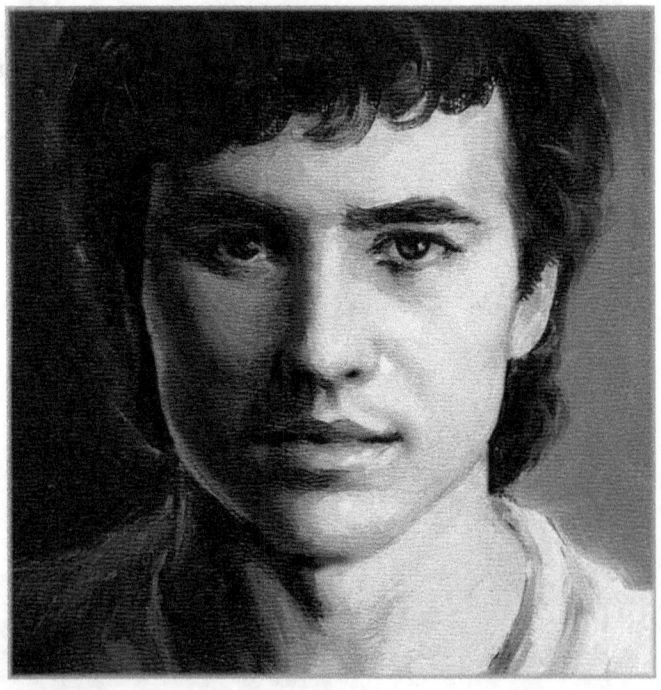

Another way to see if everything's lining up okay (is not all crooked and out of whack) is to look at your picture in the mirror. (Or, flop it in Photoshop, as I have done here.) I always do this with all my portrait art, whether it be a profile, 3/4 view, or full view.

This "mirror test" can be brutal. Rarely does a picture look perfectly normal when it's flopped! But that's true in real life as well. If you've ever seen a photo of someone (like a celebrity) inadvertently flopped, you'll notice that they often look slightly odd. Few of us have perfectly symmetrical features.

The mirror test will help you see where things are truly (and in my own experience, sometimes horrifically) crooked. When you find these errors, take a deep breath, note what's incorrect, work on the drawing some more, and check again…fix some more…check again. Finally, it'll start to look much better, and then you'll know that you've got it as good as it's going to get!

Now that we've covered some valuable techniques that will help us with proportions, alignments, and keeping symmetry in our drawings, let's look at how such a portrait would be crafted.

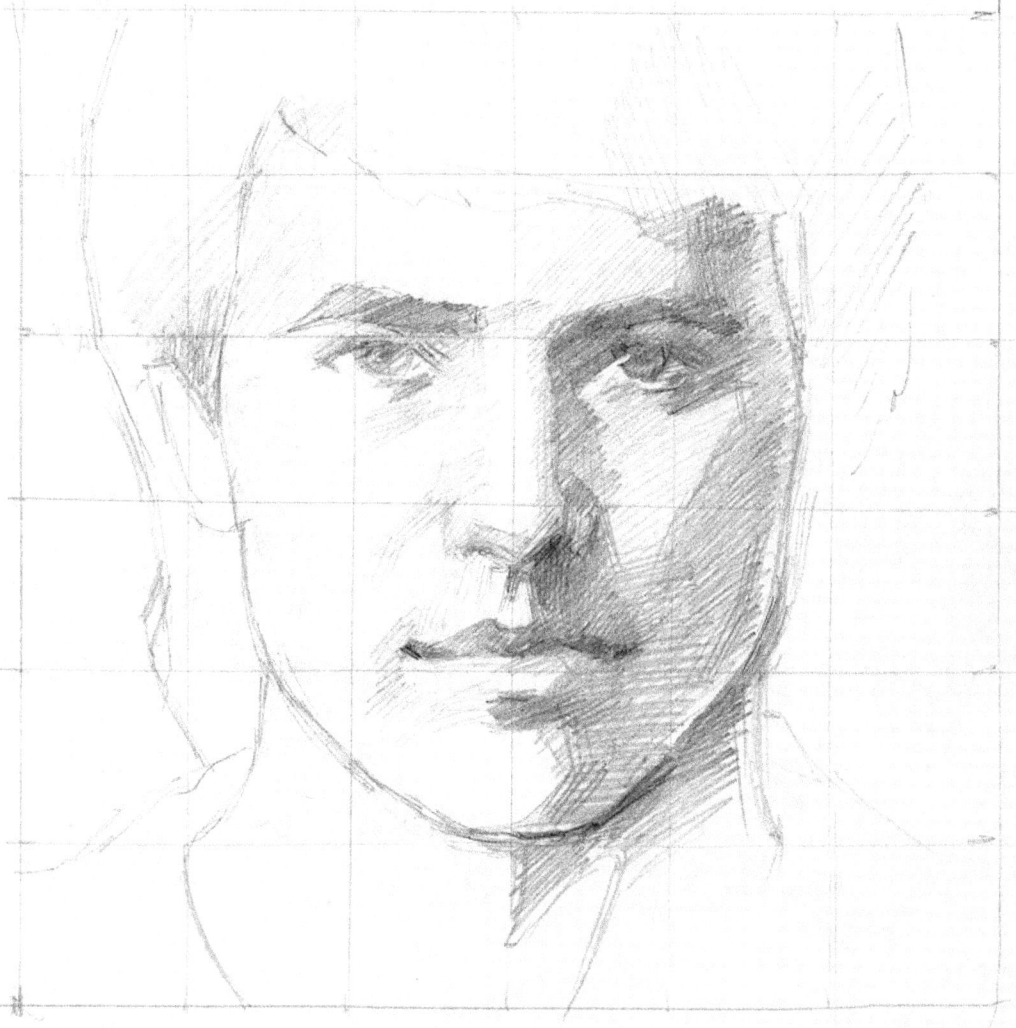

I did my own example grid drawing, to show you how I approach working on a more finished, thorough drawing. The previous projects in this book were more simplified sketches, but this time, we are copying a picture with a full range of values.

First, I work on the outline and make sure everything is in its place. Then I start lightly blocking in my values. At the earlier stages, I don't go much darker than a medium grey. I see how things are looking. If there's an error, it's easier to remove a medium grey area than it is to erase something that almost black!

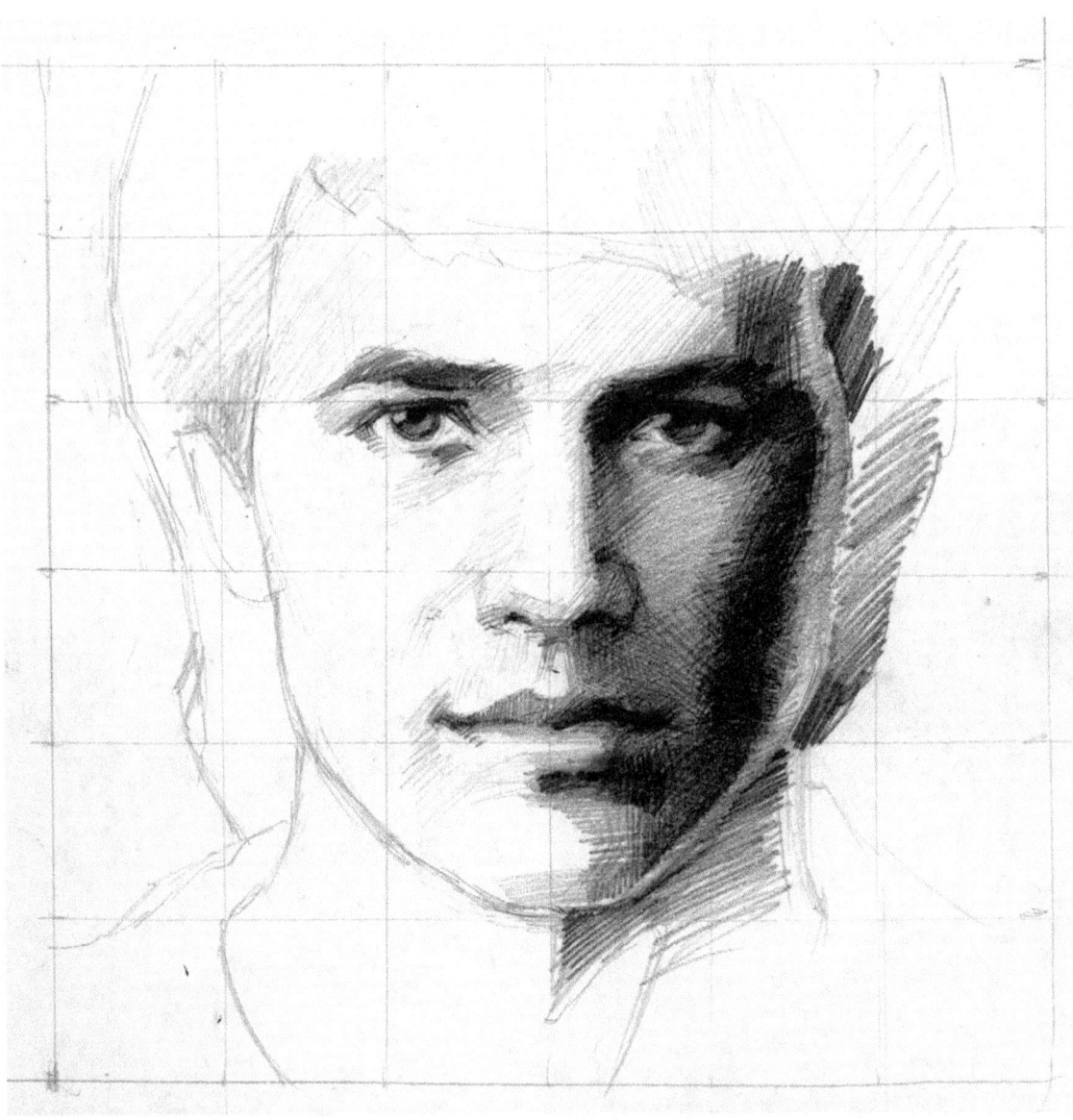

As I continue to work and am establishing my values, I am feeling confident enough to start putting in the darker values. This is a gradual process. I don't focus only on one feature or a single spot on the face. I move all over, trying to bring in more detail to the face as a whole. It is easier for me to see if my overall values are correct if I'm working on the complete image all at the same time.

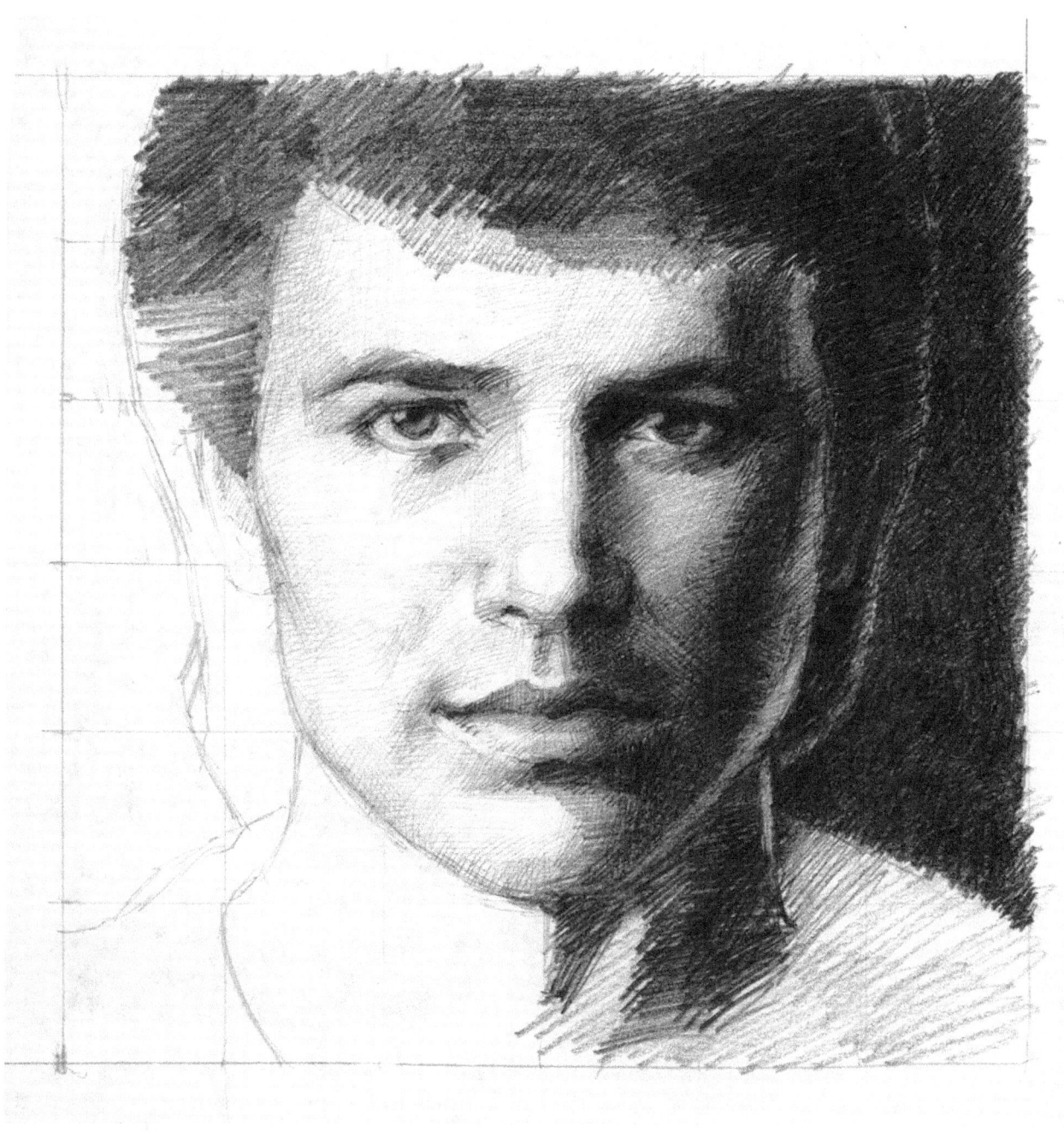

I work on adding more detail to the face, while also working over the background and hair, and other spots that will be the darkest values. This would be a good time to use a B or 2B softness pencil (4B or 6B is even better) because they have darker, softer pencil leads. They will help you with those large, dark areas in this drawing. But be careful, because dark, soft pencil lead smears like crazy!

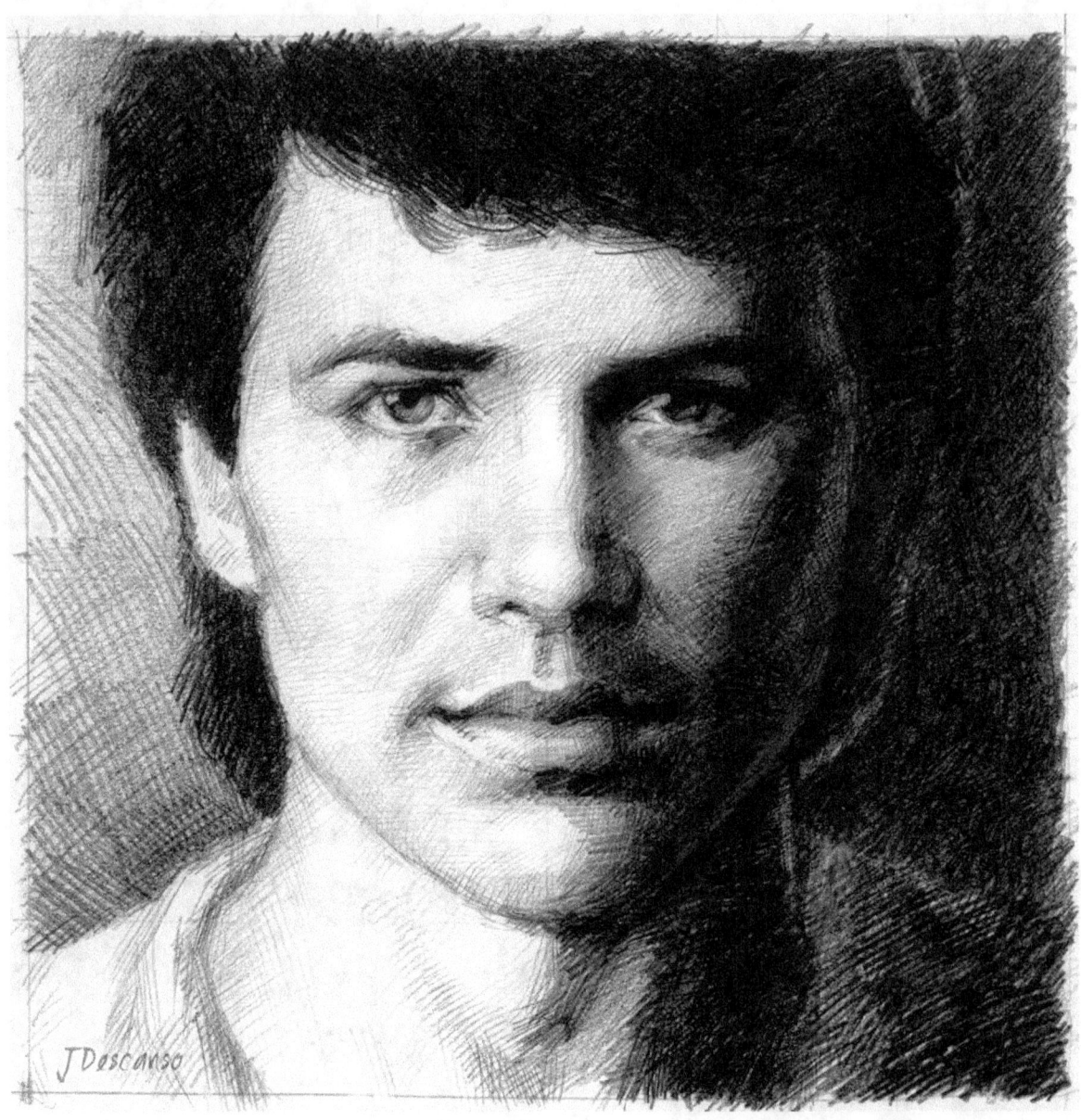

Finally, done! I get the values where I like them, in the foreground as well as background. You'll notice that the details in the face are "tighter" (more evenly rendered and with smaller, finer pencil strokes). In contrast, the background and some parts of his collar, shoulders, and even neck are drawn with coarser, "looser", and broader sketch marks. There's a reason for this.

The focal point is the features of the face. As we stray farther from this focal point to the background and the edges of the drawing, the focus gets looser or "blurrier," kind of like the way we view things in real life. The center of attention is seen with sharp clarity, but anything off to the side—in our peripheral vision—is less noticed and kind of vague. Many artists apply this same concept with their artwork, and will purposely lose some of the detail in the areas of artwork that are away from the center of focus.

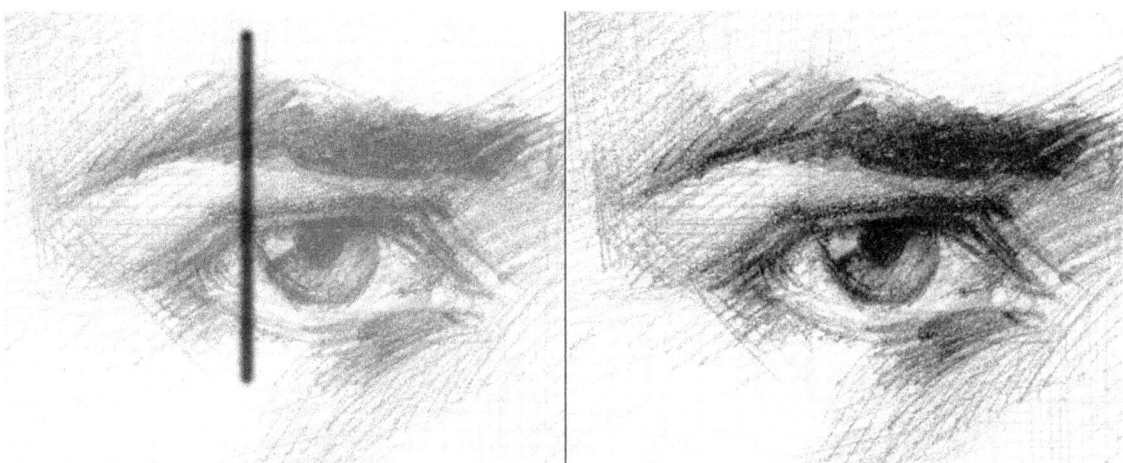

If you look closely at the square on the right, you can see a not-quite-erased grid line going through his eye. This is one of the drawbacks of using the grid—you must always be vigilant to erase (or at least conceal) the lines in your finished drawing. I think I did a fair job doing this overall, but a few spots have a faint remnant of the grid if you know where to look. Yet another reminder—keep your grid lines faint, so they're easier to erase later!

You'll also notice in this detail that the whites of the eye are not that white. In fact, I've lightly shaded the whole white of the eye, with slightly darker shading at the top (where the thickness of the top lid casts a slight shadow). Look carefully at the whites of the eyes and capture their value accurately! They are commonly a grey, not a stark white.

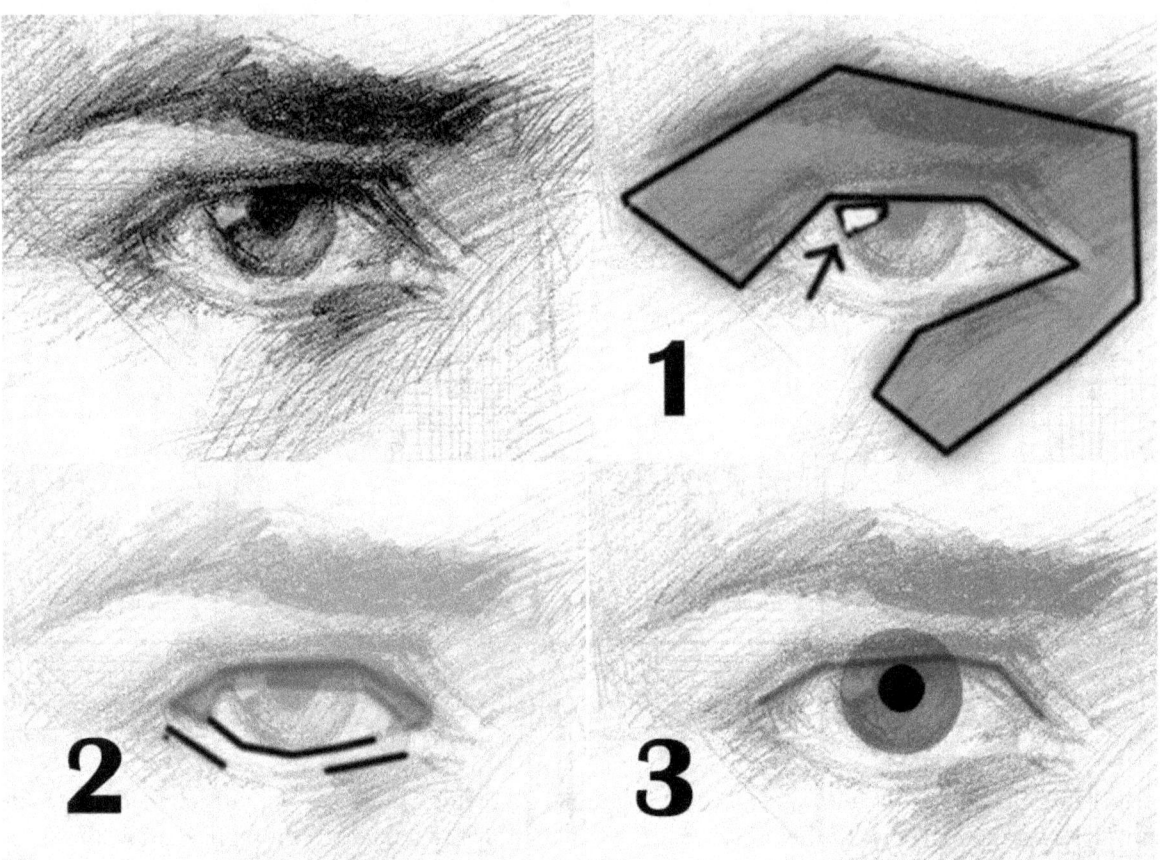

1. The eye sockets recede in slightly, and the brow usually juts out, thus casting a shadow upon the eyes. I have emphasized the shadowed area in #1. The arrow points to the catchlight, or highlight, in the eye.

2. Another reminder that the thickness of the upper eyelid casts a shadow over the top part of the white of the eye. Don't forget to draw the thickness of the lower eyelid, but again remember—less is more! Don't outline the lower lid thickness heavily. Use subtlety.

3. The iris of the eye is always perfectly round, as is the pupil, when seen from the front view. The pupil is completely concentric within the iris. Avoid making an oval or lopsided-shaped iris. This is a major art crime in my opinion! As you learned in Chapter Five with Cynthia, the eye at 3/4 view will have an iris and pupil which are oval. From the front view, the iris and pupil are round. Also, the pupil is centered perfectly within the iris. In addition, notice how the upper lid obscures the top part of the iris. If the entire roundness of the iris were to show, the person would have a wild, wide-eyed, crazy look!

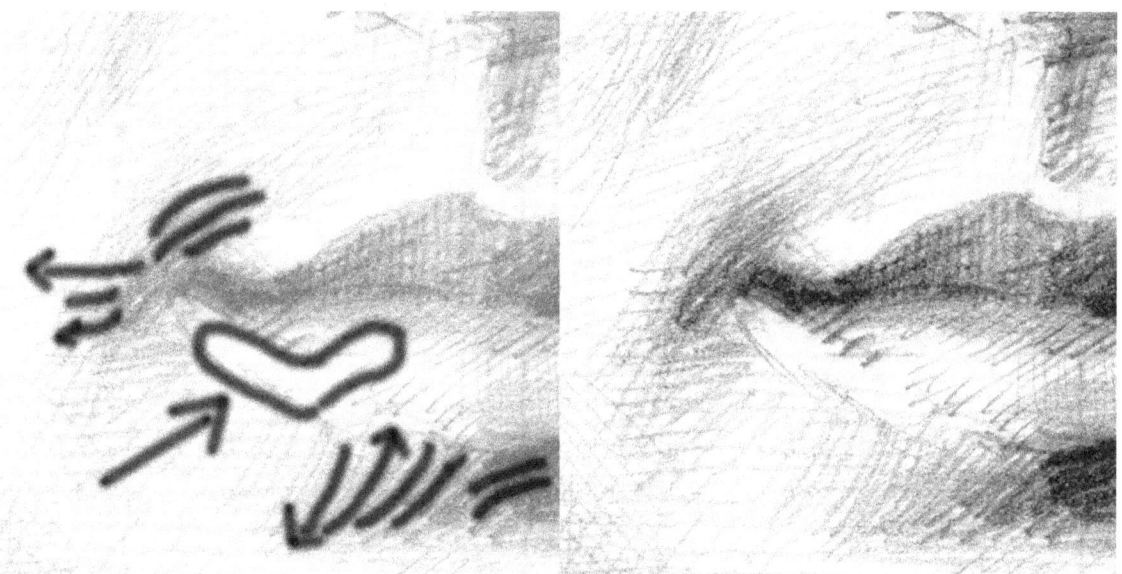

Here are some reminders of techniques that you learned in earlier chapters. The thick black lines in the illustration on the left highlight how some of the crosshatching lines around the mouth are "contour" lines, following the shape of the flesh around his lips. The crosshatching goes in many different directions—some of the lines are merely to indicate the value (a light grey) while other lines are helping "describe" the contours of the features.

There is an arrow that points to a sideways "L" shape, which is where the highlight hits the side of the mouth. Notice how the lips are not fully outlined here. This is another example of a soft or lost edge, something you've learned in previous chapters.

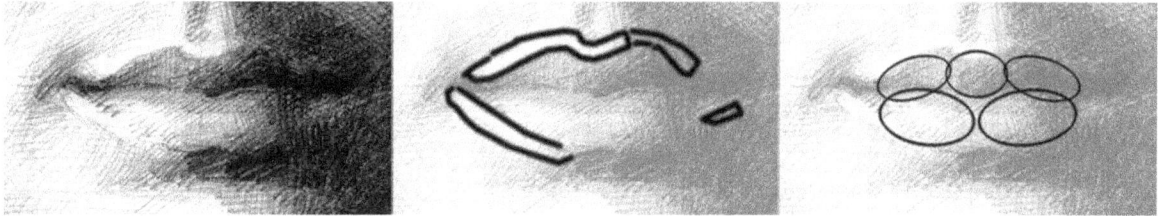

Here's something else interesting about Bruno's mouth, and in fact, everyone's mouth. Did you notice the light ridge that outlines the lips? No whiskers grow here on men, but women and children will have a lighter area here as well. I've outlined where you can see this ridge in the center picture above. Shadow obscures some of the ridge, but it's very visible on the left side of the mouth.

The picture on the right shows how the lips have five distinct sections to them—the bottom lip seems to be divided into two sections, and the top lip has a rounded area right in the center (underneath the nose) and two rounded sections on each side.

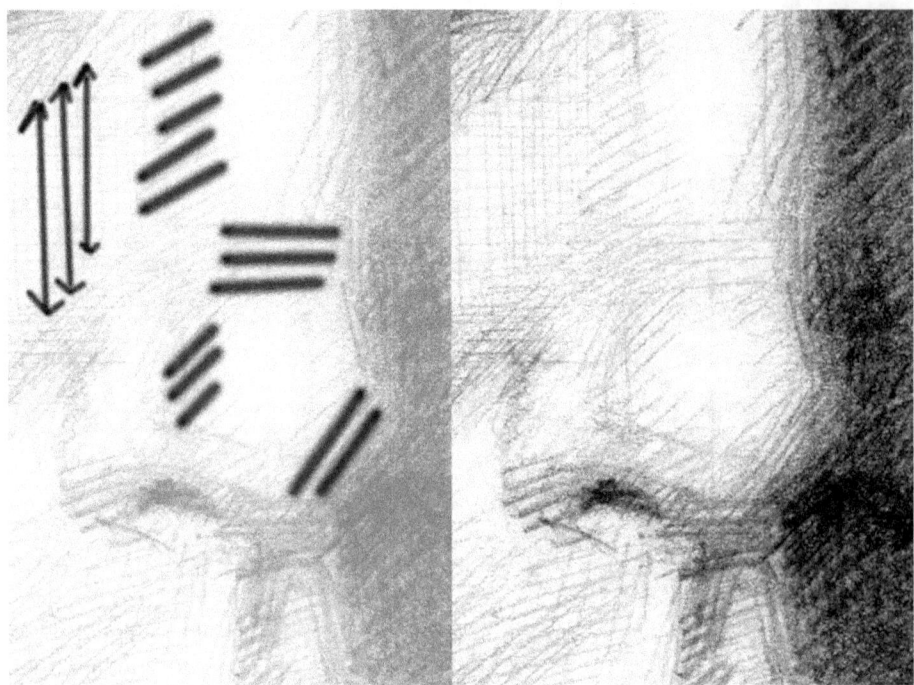

Bruno's nose doesn't have a lot of hard, defining lines. The lighter side of his nose is suggested with various crosshatching strokes. I put a few arrows to the left of his nose—I call these "value strokes", meaning that the crosshatching was only meant to create the necessary value (light or dark)—it isn't a contour line that is any way trying to follow the structure of the nose. However, the other lines I highlighted are more contour in nature. Notice how I have a few hatches going across the top and sides of the bulb of the nose. There are also some lines going down from the bridge of the nose. These contour lines are all helping "describe" the shape of the nose.

SKILL BUILDING LESSONS FROM CHAPTER SIX:

Now you have completed a front view portrait, which can be the most difficult. You learned how to check for lopsided features and misalignments by flopping your work-in-progress in Photoshop or looking at it in the mirror. Some important details about where the features line up were discussed. More information about crosshatching techniques was given. You learned some exciting new tidbits about the details and nuances of the mouth.

CHAPTER SEVEN: A SHORT OVERVIEW OF FACIAL STRUC-TURE, RACIAL AND AGE DIFFERENCES

You've completed several portraits and built a lot of skills along the way. But now it's time to take a little break and review some bits of information about the head, as well as learn some interesting new facts.

THE STRUCTURE OF THE HEAD:

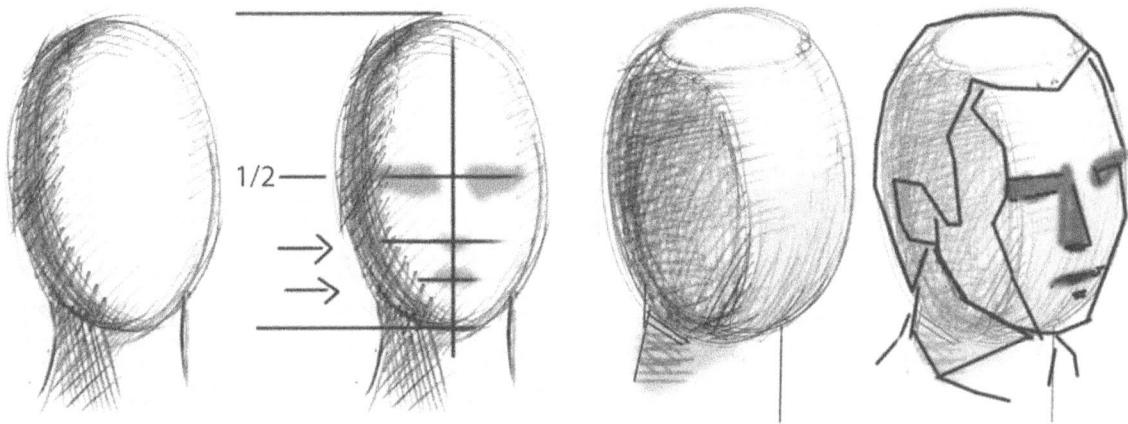

Because you've been drawing with the help of the grid, you have not needed to worry about understanding the placement of the features as much—the grid has been your guide. But it's important to understand the structure of the head and know how things line up.

The eyes are located about halfway down the head. A lot of beginner artists cannot believe that the eyes are placed that far down, but do some measuring for yourself and you will see! The nose is placed approximately halfway between the eye-line and the bottom of the chin, and the mouth is a little less than halfway from the nose line to the bottom of the chin.

Think of the shape of the head as being an egg shape, except the sides and top of this egg shape are gently flattened. Then imagine that there is a wedge sticking out for the nose, as well as a wedge shape slightly jutting out for the brow.

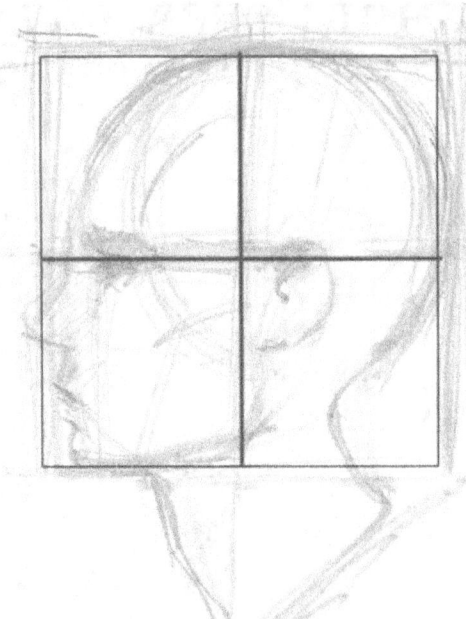

A very common artist's mistake is to make the back of the head too shallow. As you can see from this diagram, the jawline and the front of the ear are located halfway back on the head.

THE EYES:

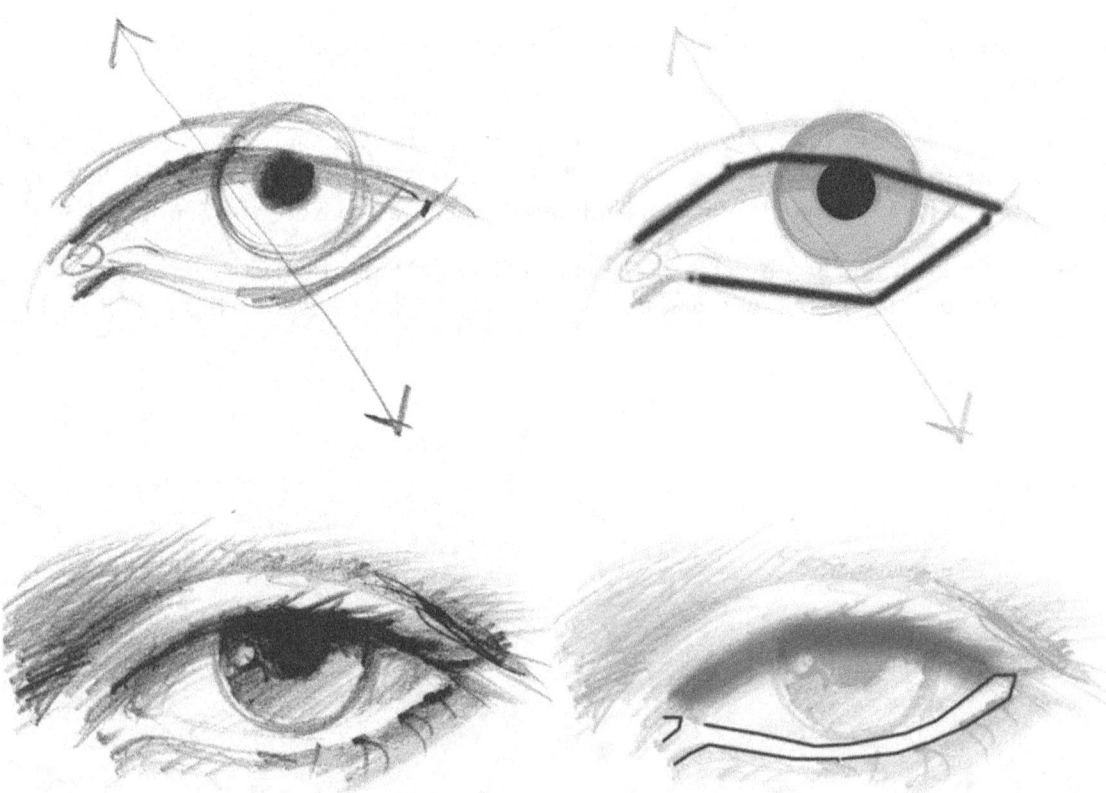

The bottom lid often has its widest part about a third way in from the outer edge, while the top eyelid may have its widest part approximately a third way from the inner corner. (There will be many exceptions to this, as everyone's eyes are unique.)

It cannot be repeated enough: The pupil is completely round when seen at front view, and is perfectly concentric with the iris, which should also be perfectly round. Do not overlook this important detail! The iris should never look lopsided or off-center!

The upper lid has thickness and because of this, casts a shadow over the white of the eye. It also has thickness, which can often be seen (see bottom right picture, where we can see the shadow from the upper lid and the thickness of the lower lid).

The eyelashes are not heavily defined here. I made a few suggestions of clumps of eyelashes, mostly only on the outer half of the eye. It's overkill to draw in every single eyelash and can quickly start to look unnatural.

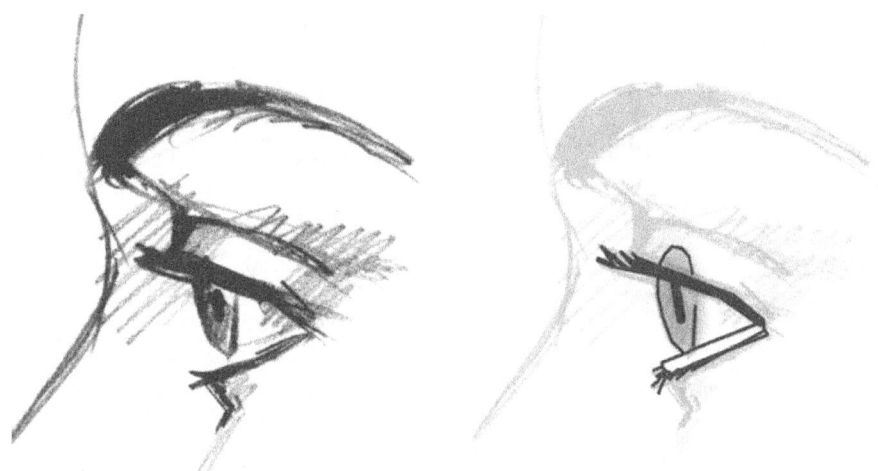

Here you can see the thickness of the eyelids from the side view. Also, remember that often the upper lid (and sometimes the lower lid) covers up part of the iris.

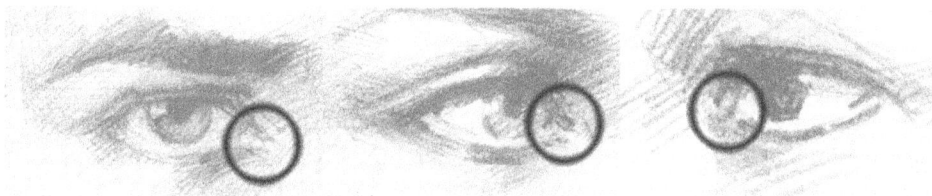

"Less is more" definitely applies to tear ducts. You don't want to leave them out (that always looks strange), but you don't want to overdo or heavily define them either.

THE NOSE:

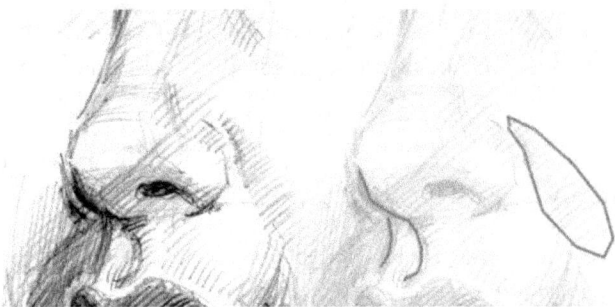

The "smile lines" that start on each side of the nose and travel down the edge of the mouth shouldn't be overdone. You know what I'm going to tell you—less is more! Unless you are doing a portrait of an older person with heavy, defined smile lines, it looks better to avoid outlining the area at all. In this illustration, I've hatched a soft shadowed area which gradually fades away. Few vertical lines are following the "smile line."

The contour of the tip of the nose seems to continue on down to become the philtrum (the gentle groove above the center of the lips). Always center the philtrum right below the center of the nose.

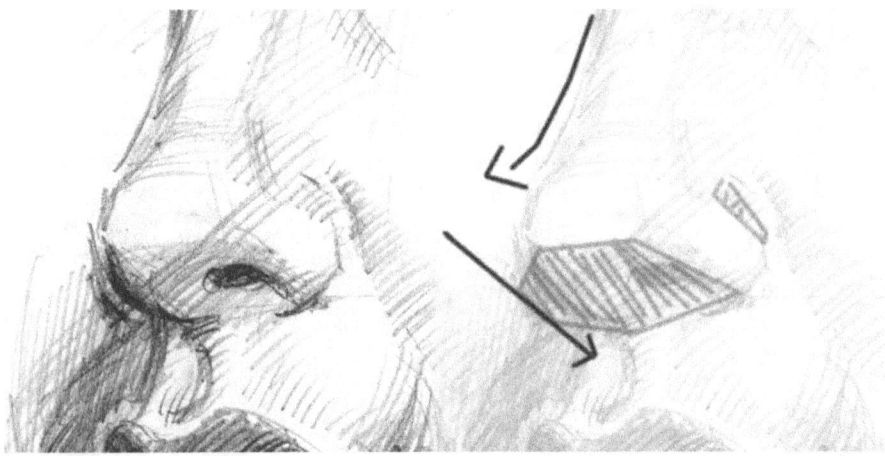

The underside of the nose usually faces away from the light source, and therefore will often be in shadow. Try to avoid heavy outlining of the edges of the nostrils. Some more gentle hatching lines can be used to suggest a lot of the nose—less is more! Heavier outlining and fussy details painstakingly rendered around the nose area can make it look more like a snout, as I said.

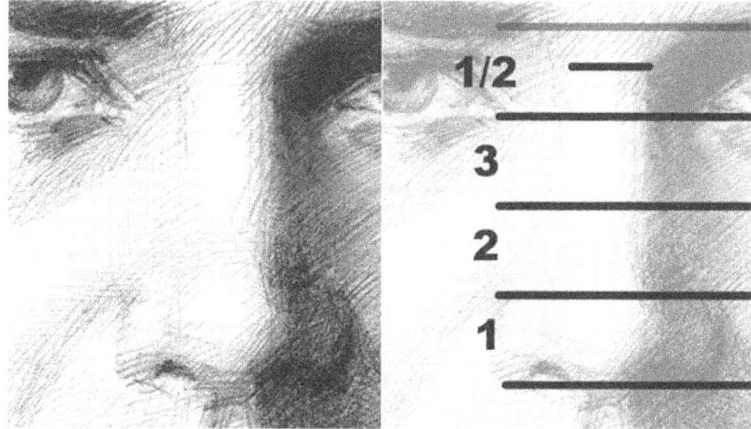

The "wings" of the nostrils (the part of the nose right above and on either side of the philtrum) should not be too short. The length of the nose (from the bridge down to the bottom of the nose) should be approximately three or three-and-a-half "wing"-heights.

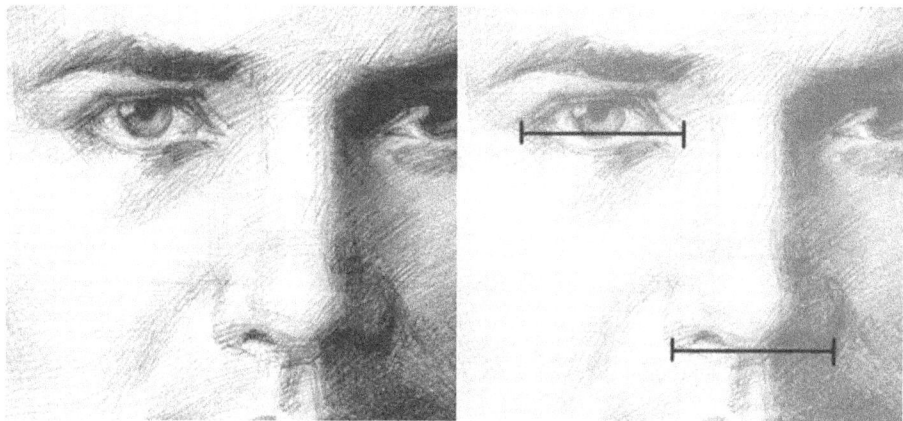

While this will vary depending on the person, in this face you'll see that the width of the edges of the nose (at the base) is equal to the width of the eye. Another common mistake made by new artists is to make the width of the nostrils too narrow. Measure to make sure you get it correct!

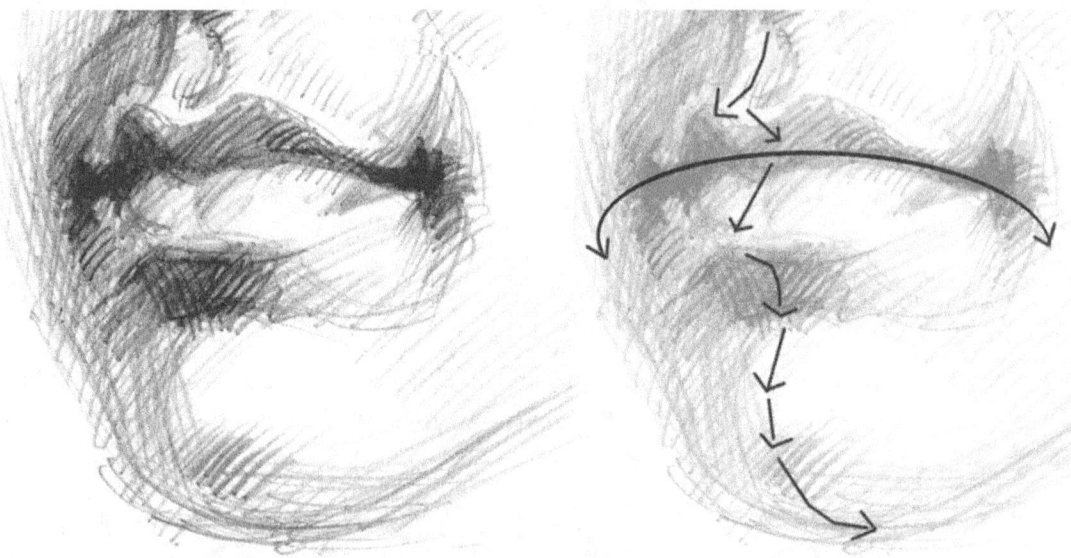

The mouth is not positioned on a flat surface. Remember that the lips are wrapping around the teeth. They will have shading to suggest this roundness.

Also, see that the upper lip usually juts out farther than the lower lip. It dips in to meet the center of the mouth, and then the lower lip juts out (just not as far as the upper lip). Underneath the lower lip the face tips in again, and then we follow the roundness of the chin.

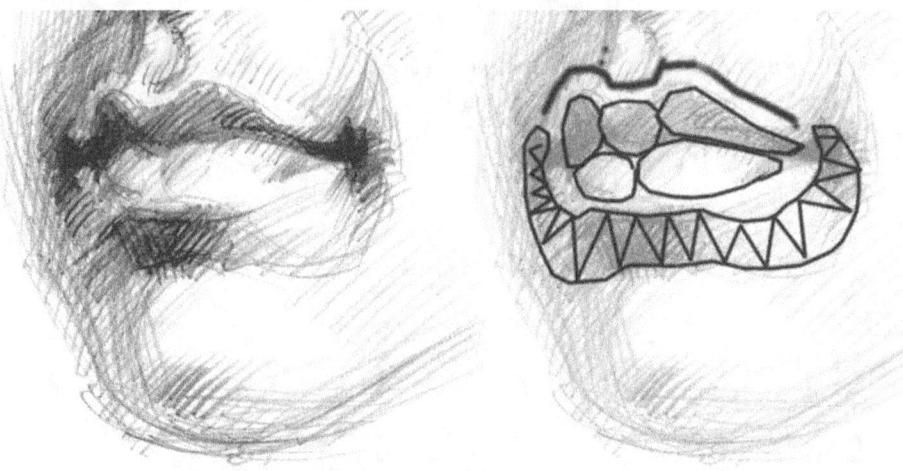

In this drawing, we can see the oval sections that gently divide up the mouth. Three oval-shaped segments make up the top lip, and two sections make up the bottom. The shading that often goes around the bottom lip is more visible here, and again we see that ridge around the lip where no whiskers grow. (In this illustration I drew a line following the ridge on the top lip, but remember that this ridge is also present around the bottom lip.)

AGE DIFFERENCES

So far this book has dealt with drawing younger adults. But, most of us will want to draw portraits of people of all ages!

CHILDREN:

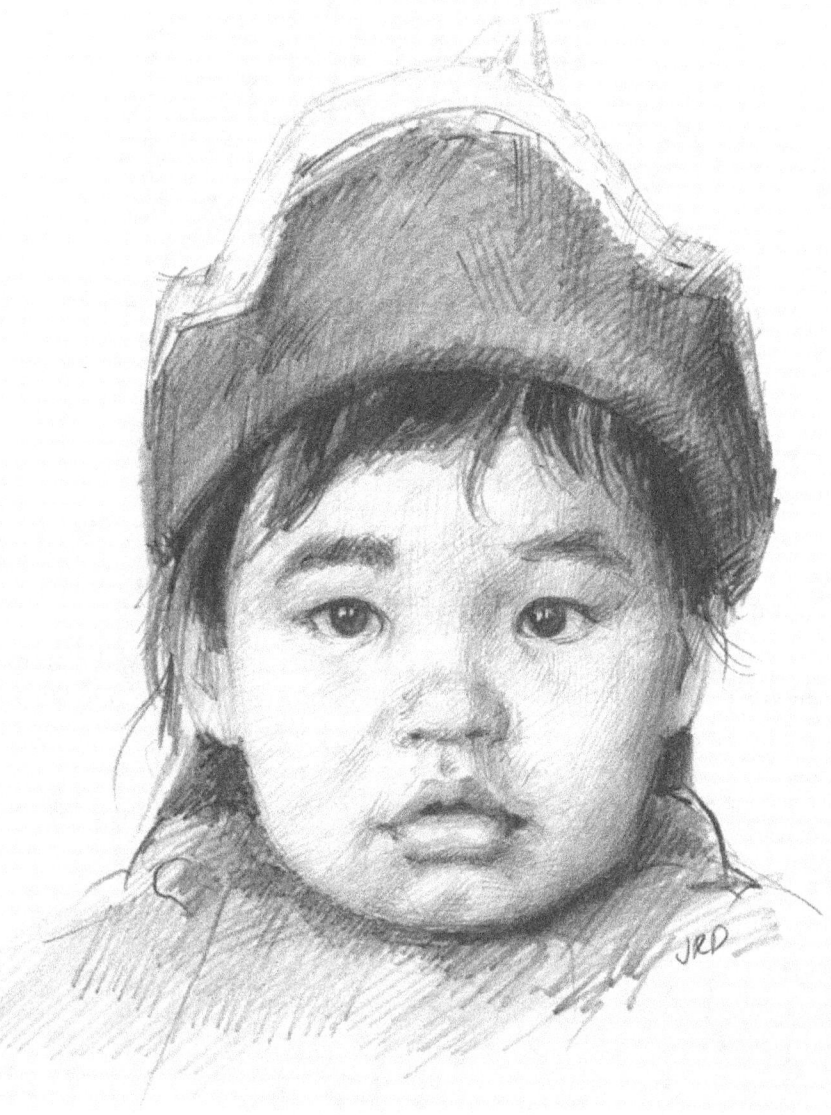

Notice the proportions and spacing in this child's face. The length of the chin is very shallow. The eyes are spaced farther apart. (There is more than one "eye-width" between the eyes.) The angles and contours of the face are soft and rounded.

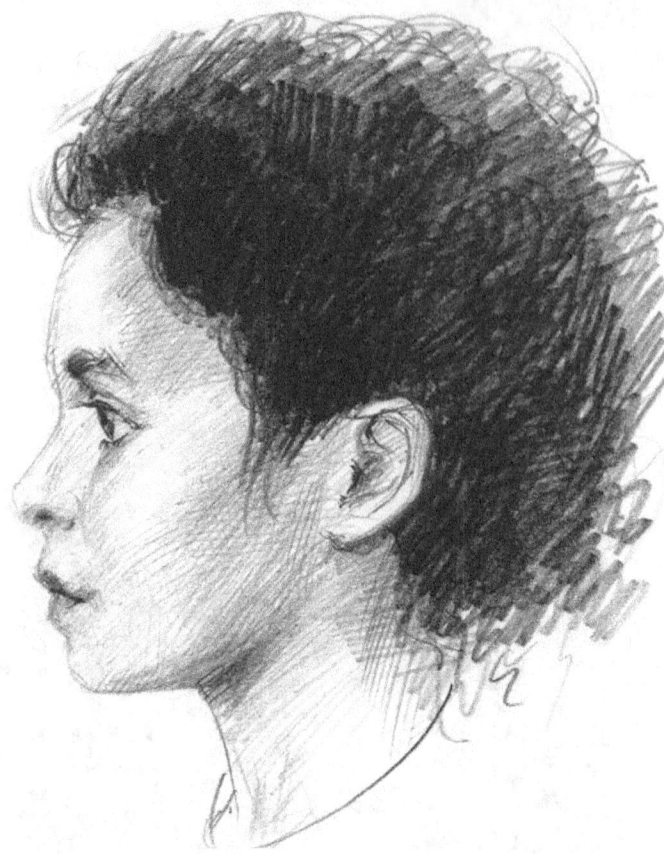

The eyes are larger on a child. In fact, the eyes are one of the things that doesn't grow all that much as we age. A child's eyes are about as large as an adult's eyes. As the years pass, the rest of the child "grows into" the size of the eyes.

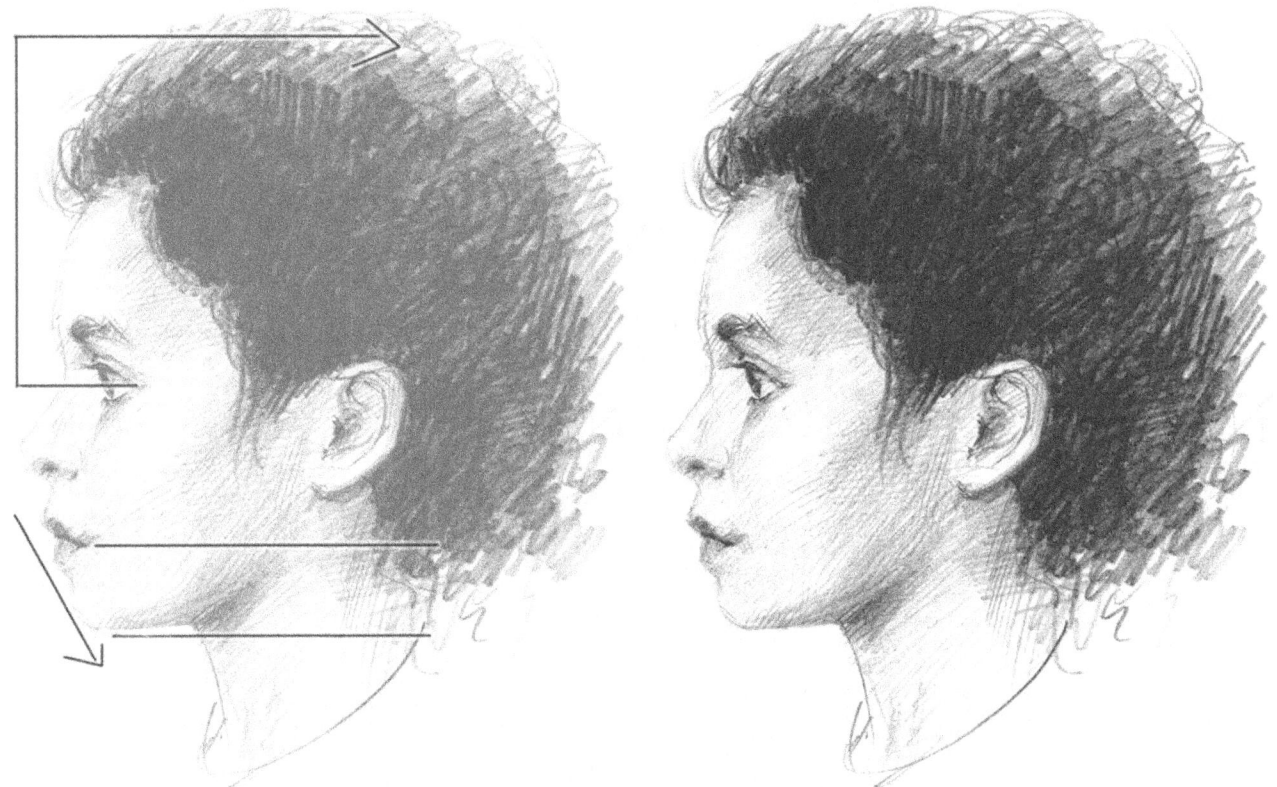

Characteristics of a child's face:
eyes located lower on head
larger eyes in proportion to head
sloping chin
shallower chin

A baby's eyes are placed lower on the head. (They have the appearance of much higher forehead.) As the child grows, the position of the eyes gradually moves closer and closer to the half-way mark. The eyes then remain at the half-way mark on the adult.

The angle of the neck is more erect (up-and-down) in children, and the chin is shorter and more sloped. A child's ears often seem larger in proportion to the rest of the head.

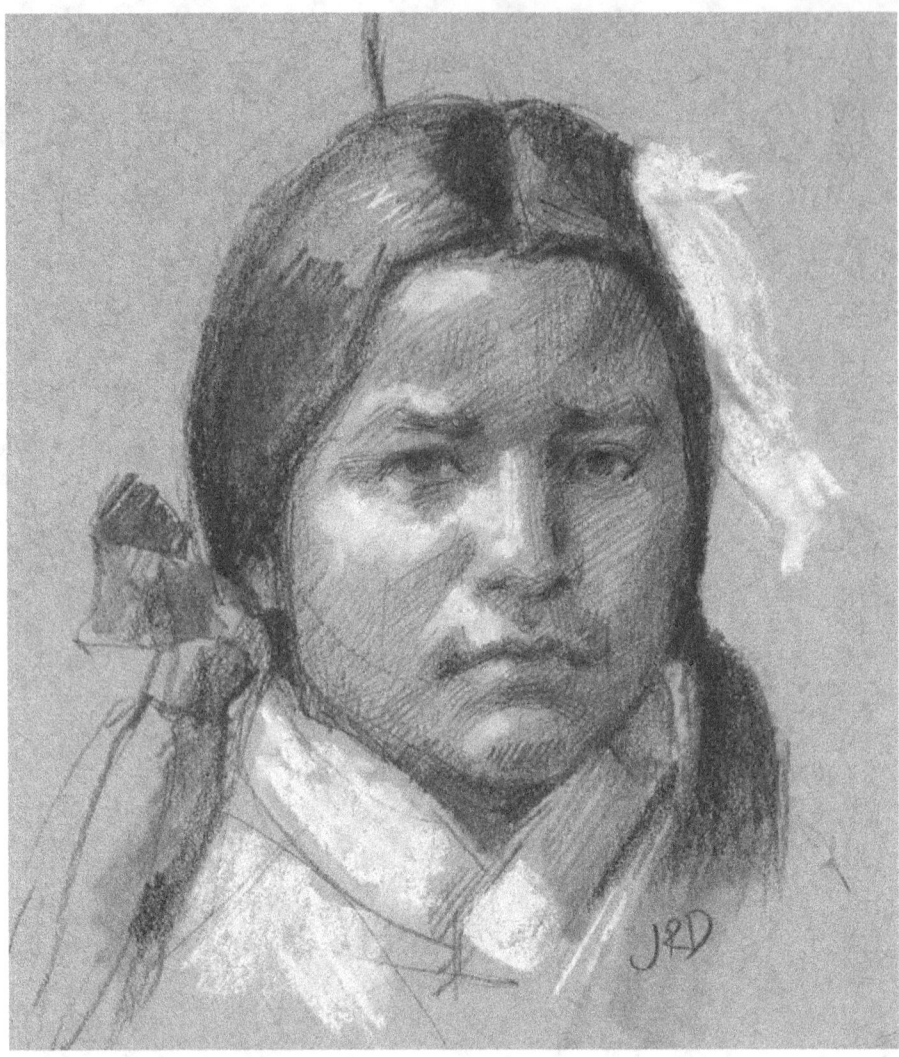

I used an old public domain photo as reference for this sketch of a Native American child (drawn on toned paper with graphite and chalk). I fear I may have "matured" the face a little bit, by not correctly capturing the roundness of the jaw and cheeks, drawing the eyes a little too small, and by making the features slightly too angular. Be careful when drawing a child's portrait—it is extremely easy to add years to their appearance by making these small errors in proportion.

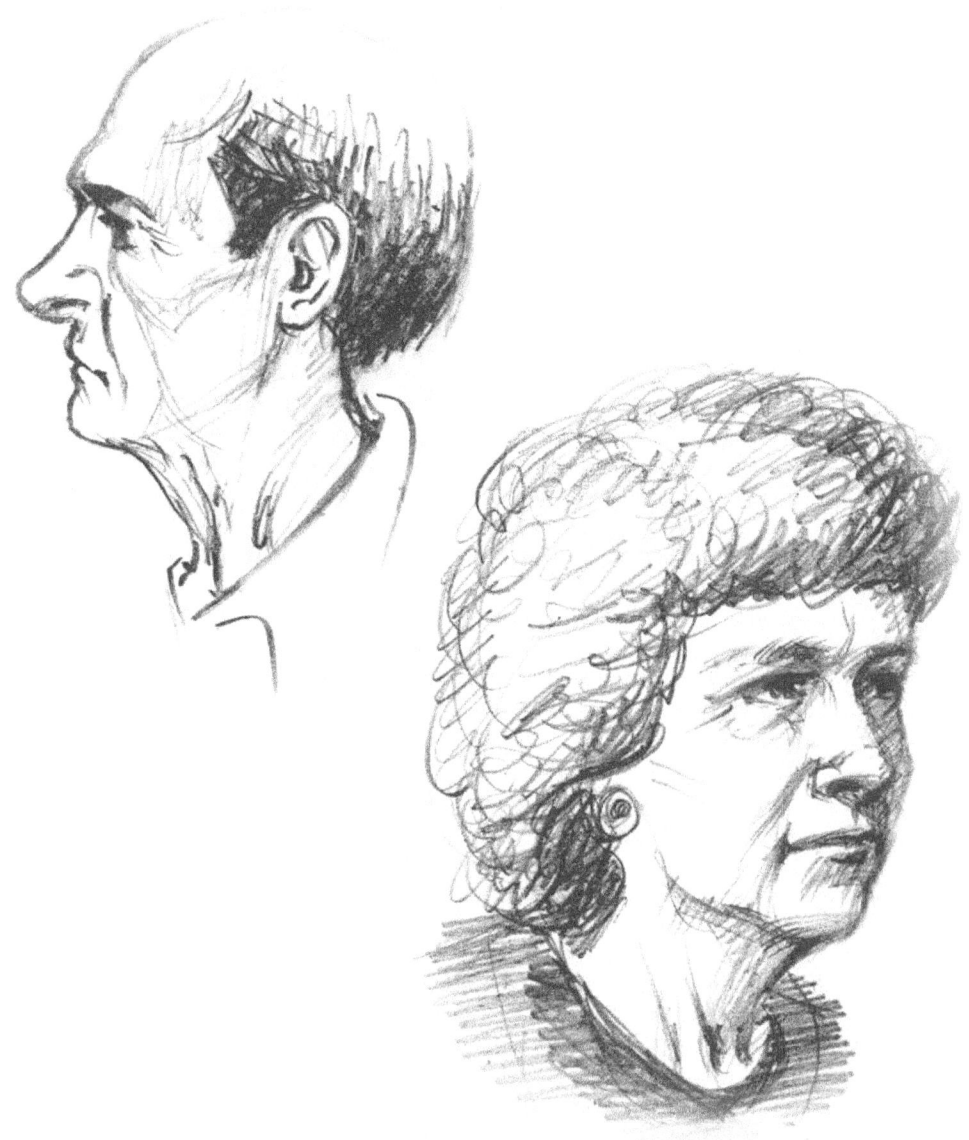

The changes to our faces are gradual as we age. The bulb (tip) of nose may become larger and droop down. Lips will thin. The chin will recede and the jawline and neck sags and becomes less refined. Creases and wrinkles appear around the nose, mouth, and eyes.

RACIAL DIFFERENCES

The world has increasingly become a huge melting pot, which means that many of us are a mixture of many ethnicities. The best way to capture each person's uniqueness is to look for overall proportions and angles. Don't *assume* that because a person belongs to a particular racial group, that they must possess all the characteristics common with that ethnicity. Observe, measure, verify!

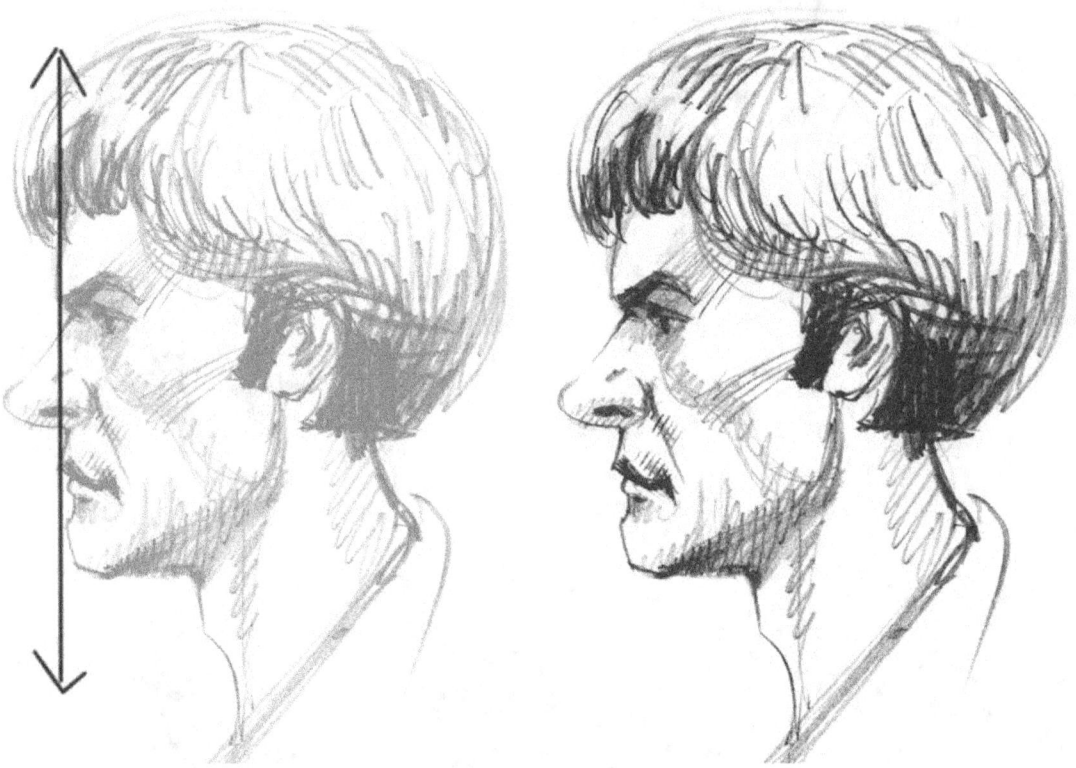

Only the rather large nose extends past the line of this man's profile, and both his forehead and chin barely slope back from straight up-and-down line of his profile.

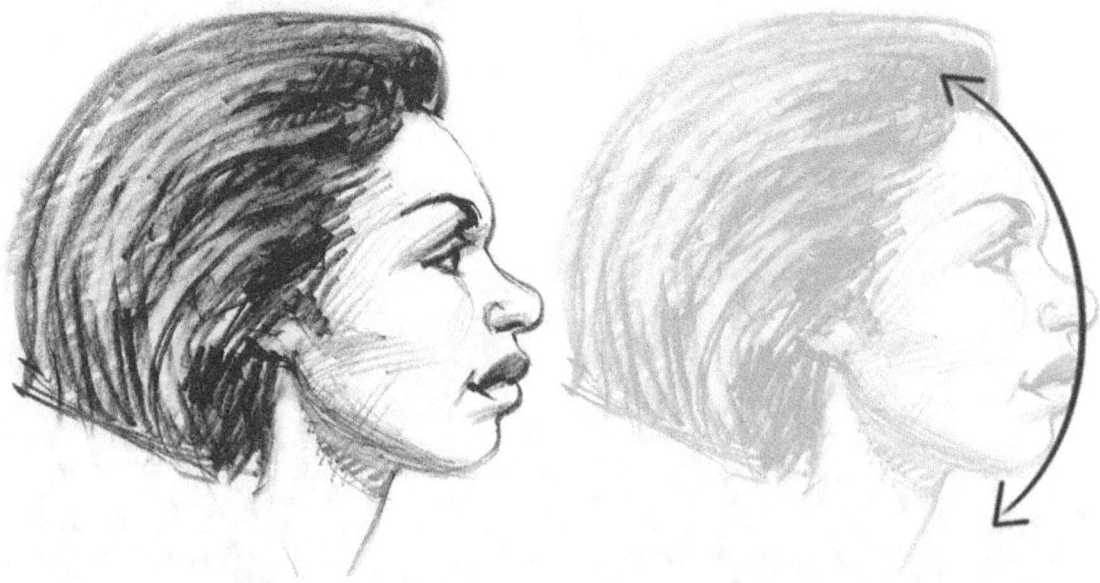

In contrast, this woman's profile is very curved! Her forehead slopes back dramatically, as does her chin.

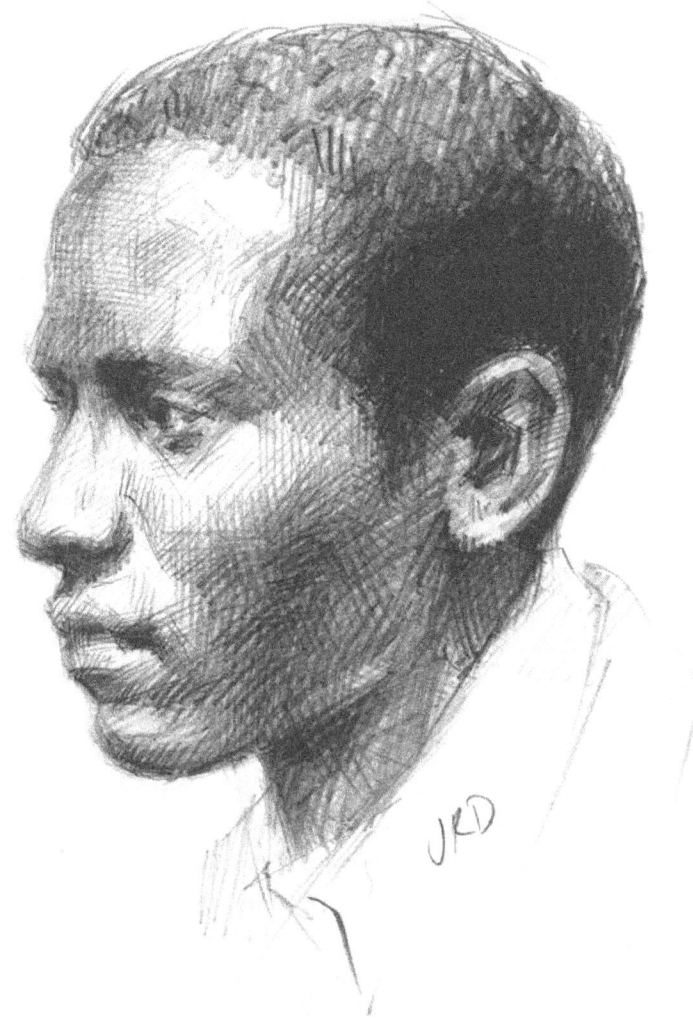

There's no special "trick" to shading someone with a darker skin color. Look for the values and capture them as accurately as you can. In this young man's face, there are still a few highlights where I left the paper blank, but the middle and dark values are more pronounced than they would be on a lighter-skinned person.

SKILL BUILDING LESSONS FROM CHAPTER SEVEN:

You have learned more about the intricacies and nuances present in the head. You have been reminded of some of the important details that you should look for when drawing the eyes, nose, and mouth. You learned about how to draw portraits of people with varying ethnicities, as well as young and old.

CHAPTER EIGHT: COPYING PHOTOS VS. DRAWING FROM LIFE

GOING OFF THE GRID

In this book, you started out with the grid because it's such a helpful, encouraging, and effective way to begin to learn drawing. It does help you to "see" better, to look for angles and negative space. But, it hasn't been my intention to encourage you to use the grid forever.

"BUT THE GRID HELPS ME BE MORE ACCURATE!"

Many artists believe that they must continue to use the grid since they have difficulty getting accuracy without it. What they fail to realize is that their problems with accuracy are a symptom of a deeper problem, and that is their lack of training (and practice) in freehand drawing. Everyone's drawings are inaccurate when they start out. The only way to "cure" inaccuracy is with more practice and study!

Who believes that someone who is unsteady on a bicycle should keep on using training wheels forever? Training wheels are a temporary solution. The goal is for the bicycle rider to gradually strengthen his or her skills enough to no longer need the training wheels. That's how beginner artists should view the grid.

How do you wean yourself off the grid? Here are some tips:

- Start to gradually make your grid squares larger and larger, which means fewer squares in total. This will force you to do more freehand drawing within the much-larger squares.

- Then, you can start to use only an outside image border as your guide. As an example, crop a photo reference so it's a perfect square. Mark a perfect square on your paper. Then look for angles, negative space, and other landmarks and placements within the square of your reference photo and draw them on the same spot on your drawing. In other words, treat the outside border of your picture as one big grid square.

- If you're struggling with a difficult area on a photo reference, use some tracing paper and trace over the outline of the trouble spot. When you do this, analyze what it looks like—its shape, its angles. You may then be able to more easily replicate the same shape in your drawing. (I'm not suggesting you trace the outline directly to your drawing—but rather that you "see" the shapes better by outlining them with your pencil.)

It's okay to use a grid—larger squares or smaller—on an extremely complex image. I've seen artists whose drawing skills are beyond reproach use the grid when the composition is full of intricate elements that need to be positioned perfectly. Such circumstances don't come along that frequently for most of us, so when they do, there's no reason to not use the grid to help us out!

But, I will repeat: be wary of falling back on the grid every time something is taking a little longer to get correct or is slightly outside of your comfort zone. This will lead to over-dependence, and that is *not* what you want.

WORKING FROM LIFE

Now that you're being introduced to a world that is Beyond the Grid, it's time to talk about drawing from life.

Working from a live model continues to be wildly popular among many artists, even though many of us still sometimes use photo references. When working from life, we often get someone to formally pose for us, but other times we doodle and sketch "in the wild", without our models being aware. It's all tremendous fun!

Working from life is encouraged and touted by many artists, for other reasons besides its being fun. (Which it is, it is!)

These reasons include:

Photos distort and lie. Did you ever notice that some of your selfies look way off? Or those vacation pictures—the sky was more blue than that, surely?

The camera can lose something. The dark values flatten out (loses some of the subtle deep values and rich color), or maybe the lights wash out (like when that gorgeous blue sky you saw on vacation becomes a drab, pale grey). Photos can subtly distort perspective. That's why many artists work from life—they can record what they see and experience, with their own eyes!

I never completely understood all these benefits until I started doing a lot of portraits from life. I painted from the model for a few hours, then completed it later from a photo I had taken. Wow, what a difference between what I saw (and recorded on canvas) and what the photo was showing me! So much was changed. So much was lost with the photo! I'm a believer now.

Many art teachers expect students to work from life and/or draw freehand (without a grid). I sometimes hear students complain that these teachers are needlessly making them work the "hard" way for no tangible reason. But that's not what's going on. Most of these teachers are well aware of how photos can lie, which is why they insist that their students work from life.

Even though I still use photo references frequently, I've grown to love working from life. Pictured below are some of the sketches I've done of models, or drawn while roaming out and about. Wherever I may be, there's no reason to be bored, because usually there's an opportunity to draw someone. That's another benefit to working from life—the interesting people you meet, and the fun you can have as you draw them!

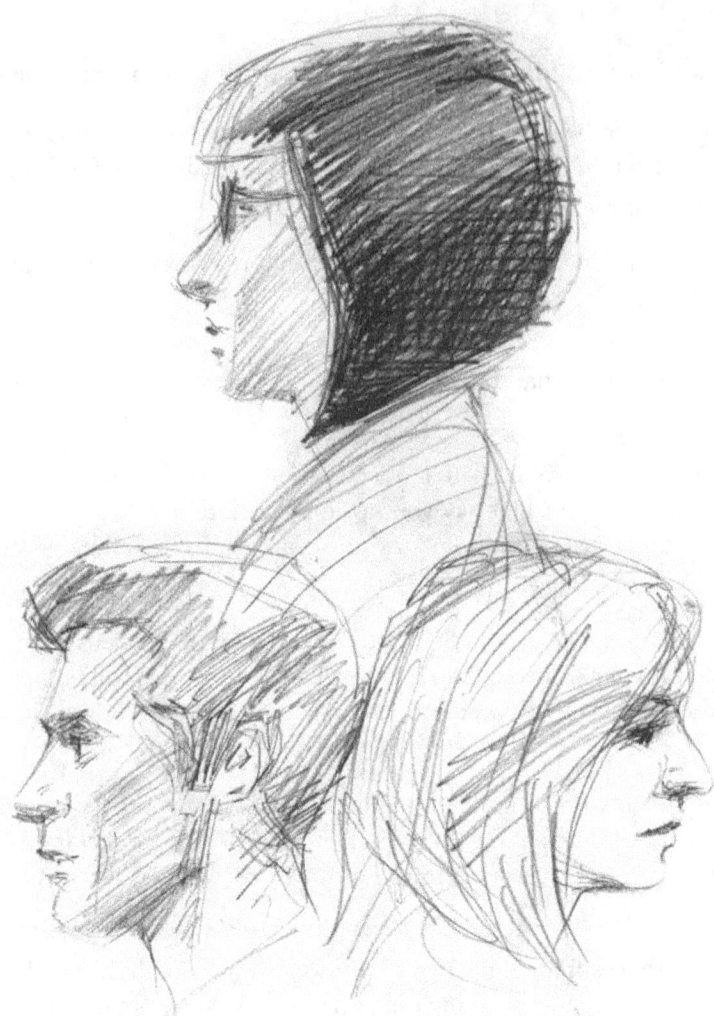

Above are some sketches done while I was roaming around with a fellow artist and drawing various people in the city. It's excellent drawing practice and always an adventure. Sometimes I only had a few minutes to complete each portrait, and the subjects were animatedly moving around as I sketched. (The speed with which I had to capture these sketches explains the spontaneity and unfinished look.)

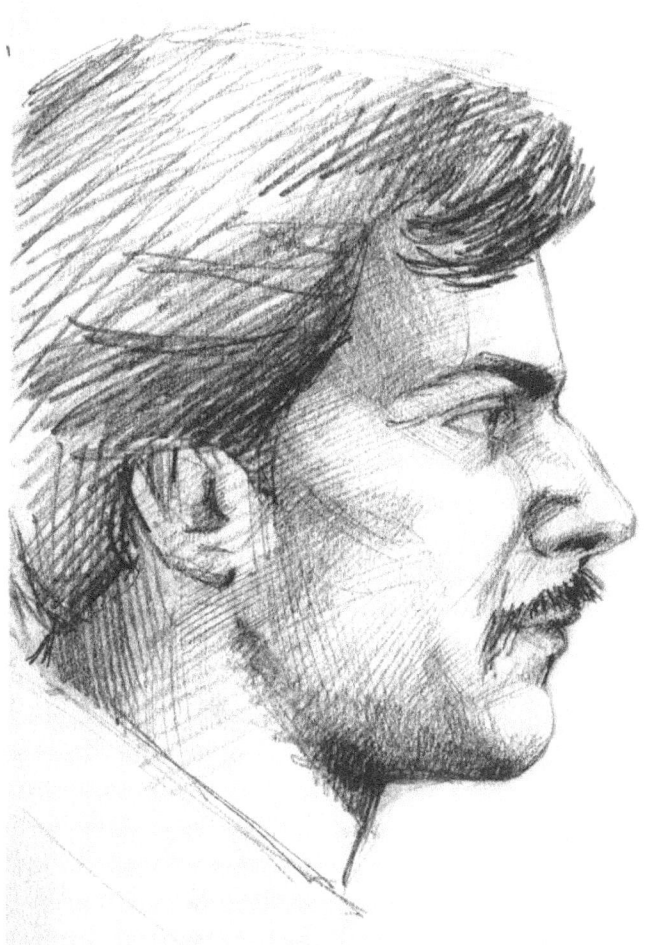

One of my friends posed for this portrait. Unfortunately, I didn't allow enough room for the back of his head on the paper. (But, it's better that I crop off the back of the head, rather than try to squeeze it in, making his head too narrow!) Sketching portraits of family and friends can bring back good memories later, and I encourage you to do it as much as possible!

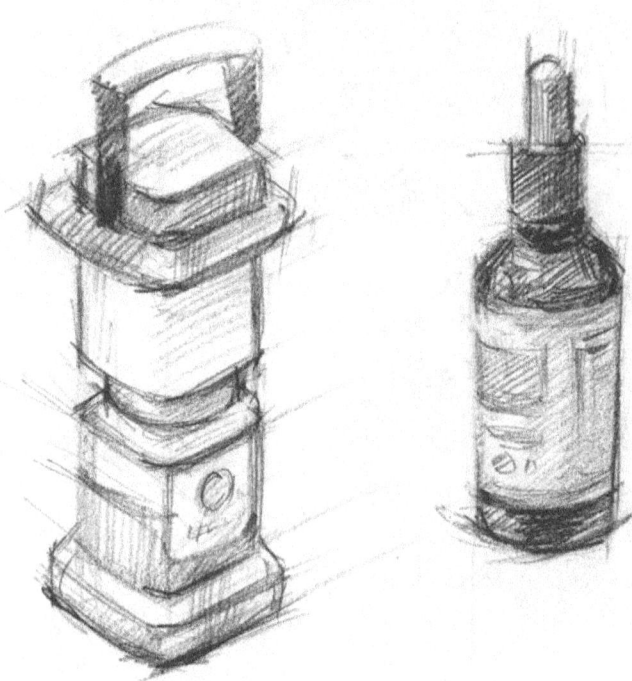

These were items I found around my studio. No object is too trivial to draw.

It is often said that portraits and figures are the hardest subjects to capture, and there is truth to that. Because we are much more familiar with how a fellow human being looks, we notice immediately when a person's features are rendered even slightly out of alignment.

I used to think that drawing anything non-human was a "waste of time", because many non-human and non-animal subjects aren't nearly as "hard" as drawing people and I wanted to put all my energy into drawing portraits. But now I'm understanding that any drawing, especially when done from life, whether it be of your shoe or a teapot, is helpful. Yes, it's true that you can draw the teapot slightly out of proportion, and no one may notice. But it still helps you improve your skills, especially if you are intently trying to draw that teapot as accurately as you can.

I urge you to start drawing anything you see around you. Even if your first efforts look terrible, that's okay. Keep on doing it! Most peoples' first attempts look pretty bad. (I know mine did!) The only way to move past that is to keep practicing.

Fortunately, your time spent working with a grid has already been helping you prepare for drawing without it. Here's a reminder of the various methods you can use to improve your drawing skills:

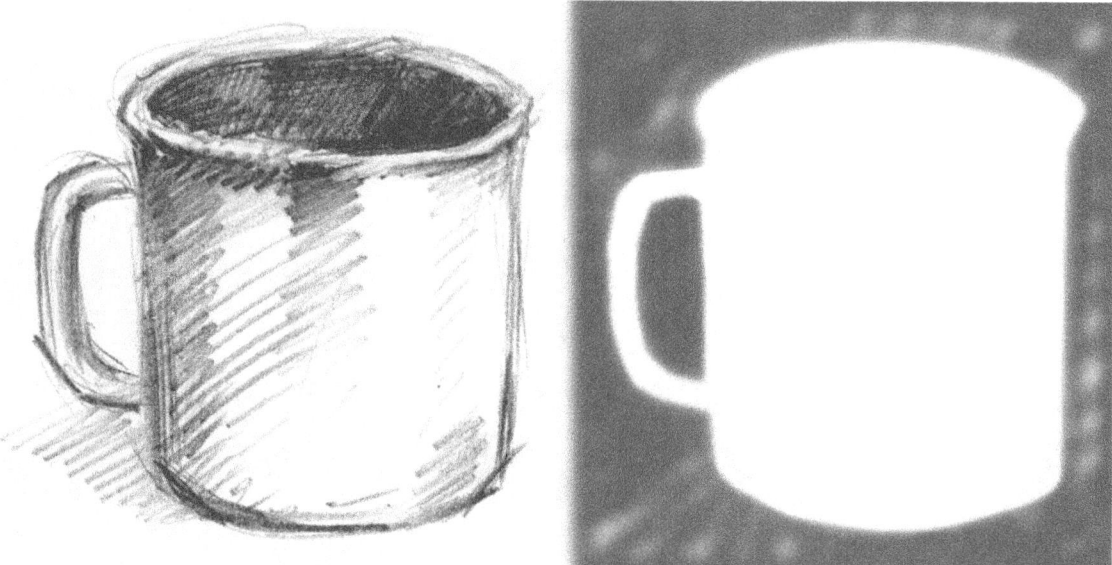

Negative Space: We've explored this in previous grid drawings. Instead of giving all your attention to the handle of the mug, look at the space inside the handle of the mug. Look at the shapes of the area around the bottom of the mug, the sides, and so forth. See if these shapes match up with the mug outline that you are in the process of drawing.

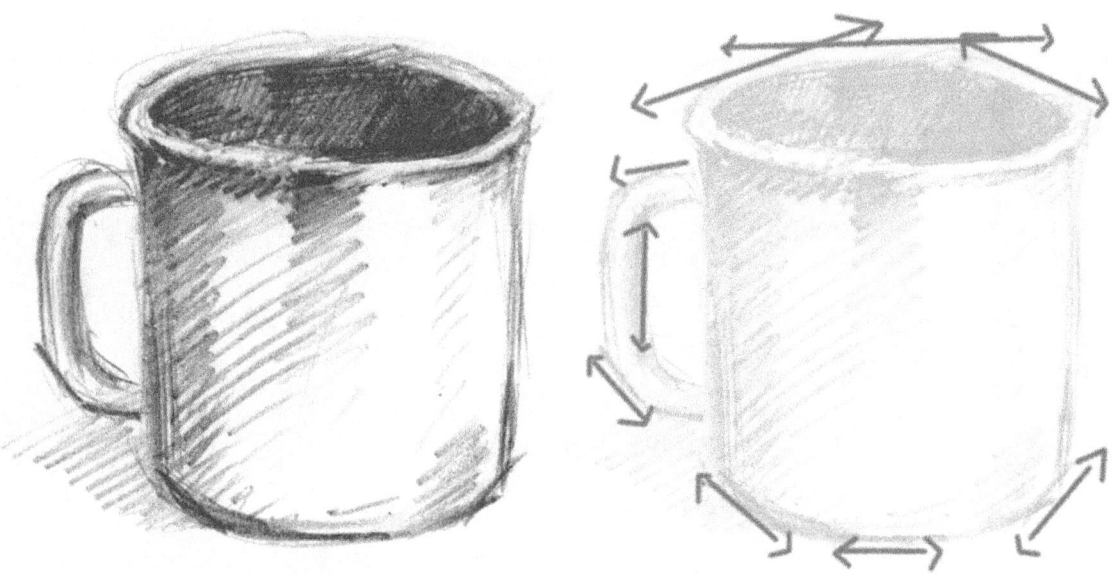

Angles: You should be very familiar with looking at the angles by now! Think of angles first. If you look at the finished mug drawing on the left, you can still see sketchy remnants of my "angles" (that I later refined to make more round or smooth). To identify the correct angles, think of the hour or minute hands of a clock and what angle they would be at any given hour of the day. What "time" is the lower curve of the mug handle? It looks like maybe 10:30 (or 52 minutes past the hour) to me. The bottom of the mug is 3:00 (or 15 minutes past the hour). Get the idea? This method is tremendously helpful and will work if you are copying photos freehand (no grid) or drawing real life.

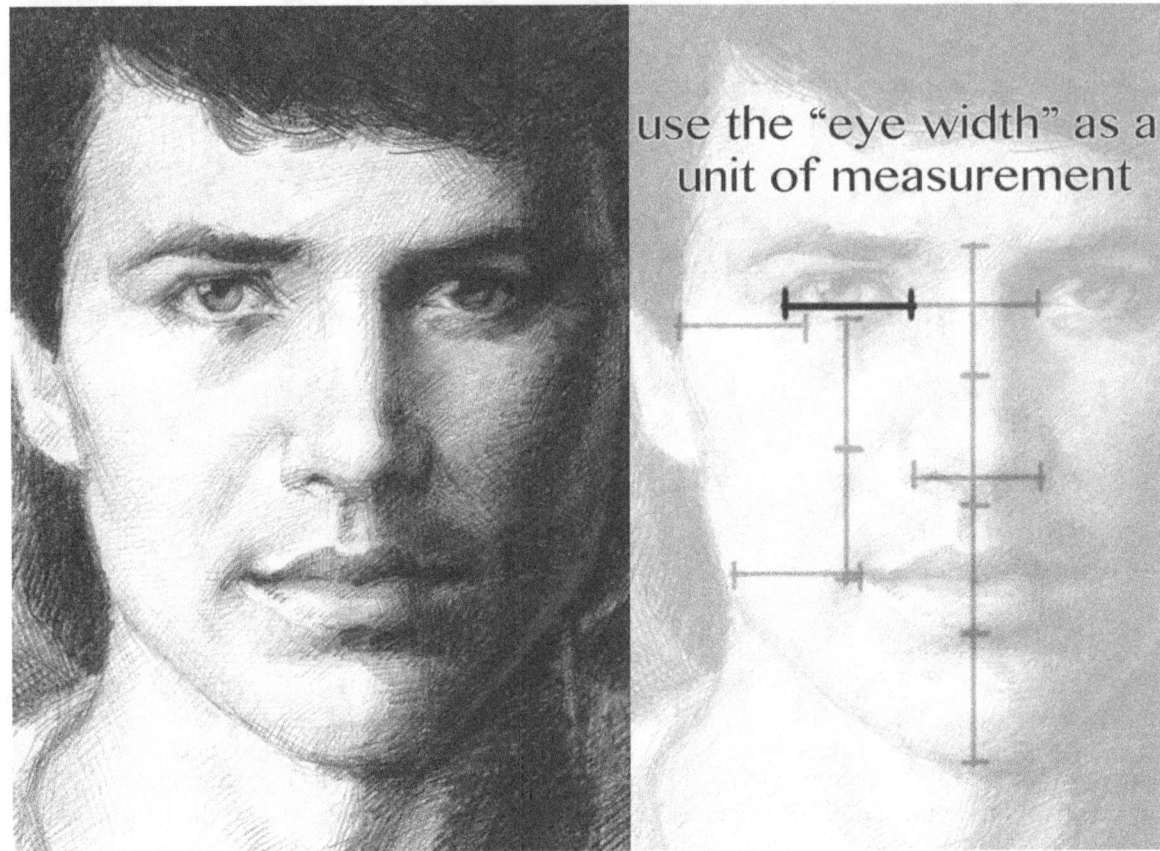

use the "eye width" as a unit of measurement

Measuring: Find something to use as a unit of measurement, and compare everything else in your drawing with that selected measurement. I have done this a lot when using photos as reference, and it can be used for drawing from life as well.

When copying a photo, get a strip of paper and measure off the selected "unit" (in this case, the width of the eye) in both your source picture and in your drawing. You'll make two eye width measurements: One for the photo, one for the drawing.

Check the various measurements in the reference photo by using the chosen unit of measurement. Then confirm the same measurements in your drawing. For example, the original reference picture says that there is one eye width between the two eyes. Is it the same on your drawing? The reference has the nose at two eye-widths long, from the top of the brow to the underside of the nose. Confirm that you've done the same in your drawing!

You don't have to use the eye width as the unit. It can be anything you wish, even the entire head height (especially useful if you are drawing a figure).

When drawing from life, artists have been using the "arm stretched straight out" method for centuries. You've probably seen it depicted in comics or in old movies.

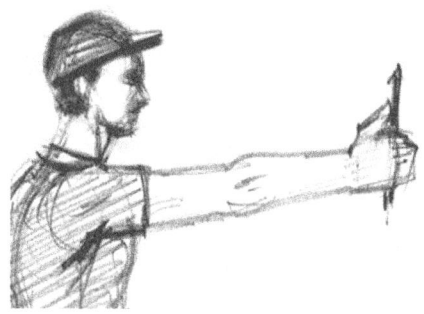

Look at your model or subject. Hold your pencil or pen in one hand, squint so you only see out of one eye and hold your arm straight out in front of you. (This won't work if your arm is bent by even a small amount.) Use the tip of your thumb or top edge of your fingernail to mark off the length or width of the thing you intend to use as your "unit of measurement." (It could be the eye width or the height of the head or anything else, remember!)

Being careful not to move the edge of your finger from its place on the pencil, check the lengths or widths of the subject you are drawing. Or, better yet—mark off the proper lengths or widths on your paper as you are first laying out the outlines of your portrait. That way you'll get it correct from the start.

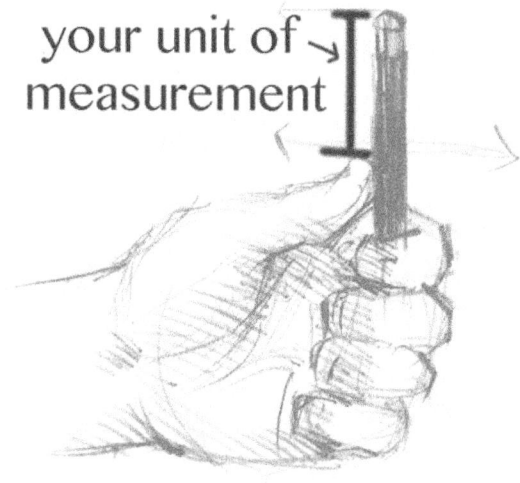

your unit of measurement

The top of your thumb to the top of the pencil will be the unit you'll use to measure anything you want to draw.

GETTING STARTED WITH LIFE DRAWING (OR FIGURE DRAWING)

When you decide that you want to draw models from life, I'd recommend attending a local figure drawing (also known as "life drawing") class. I call all of them "classes," but some have minimal or no instruction. Many will meet at a local college or perhaps someone's art studio, and a model (usually nude) is hired. Each artist pitches in for the model fee. (The cost varies, but a current standard is often something like $10-$20 per artist for a session.) Typically, the model will pose for a total of two to three hours. Most classes will have several poses in one session, usually starting out with a series of quick poses (a few minutes each) to warm up the artists.

You may find these figure drawing classes intimidating at first, especially if other artists are more experienced, but don't be scared off. Everyone is there to learn and nobody is going to look at you funny if you're a beginner.

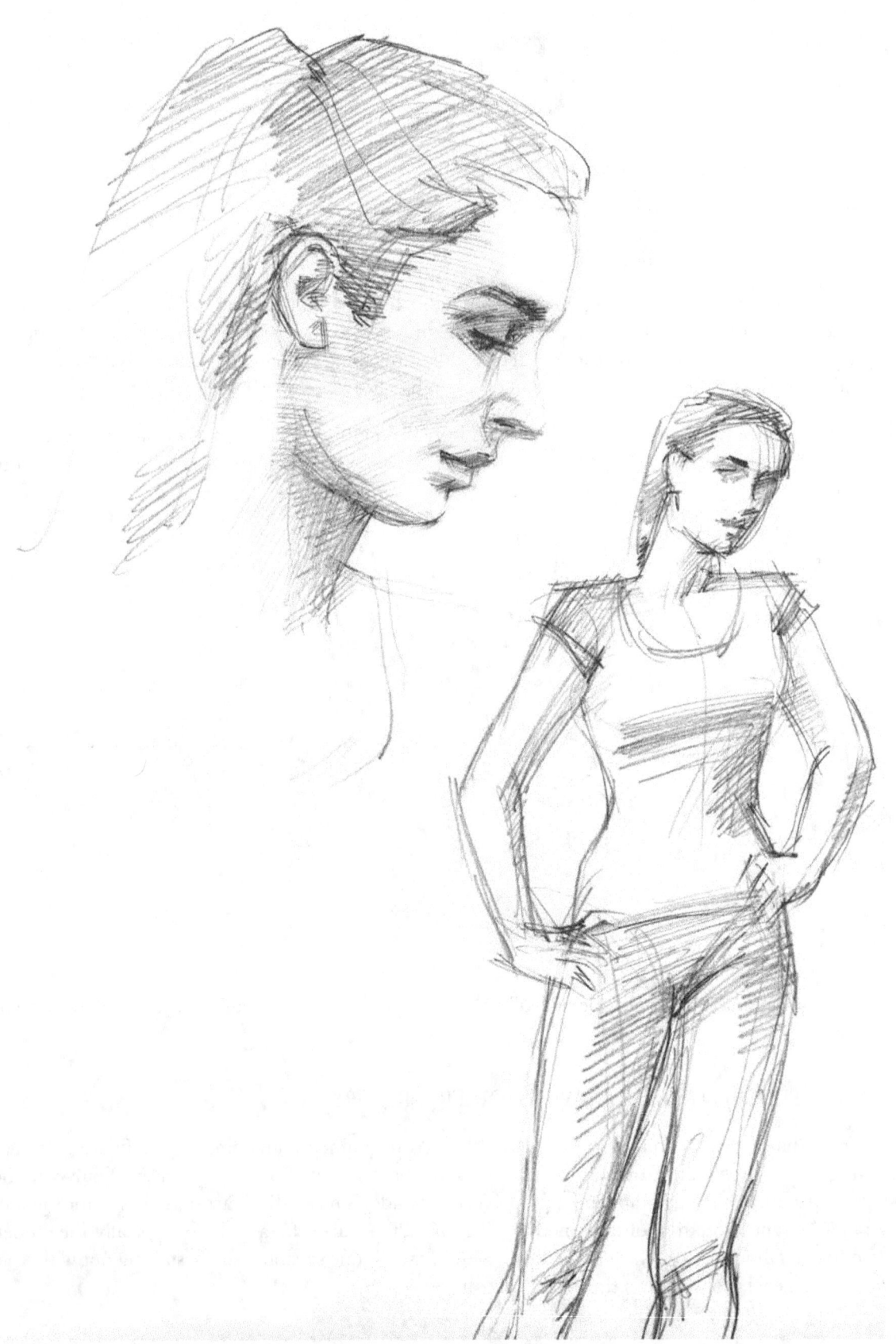

Skill-Building for the Beginner Artist: How to Draw the Portrait in Pencil

A very quick study found in one of my sketchbooks, drawn during a weekly figure drawing session. This lovely young lady posed for us fully clothed. It's just as common to find figure drawing sessions which feature a nude model, however.

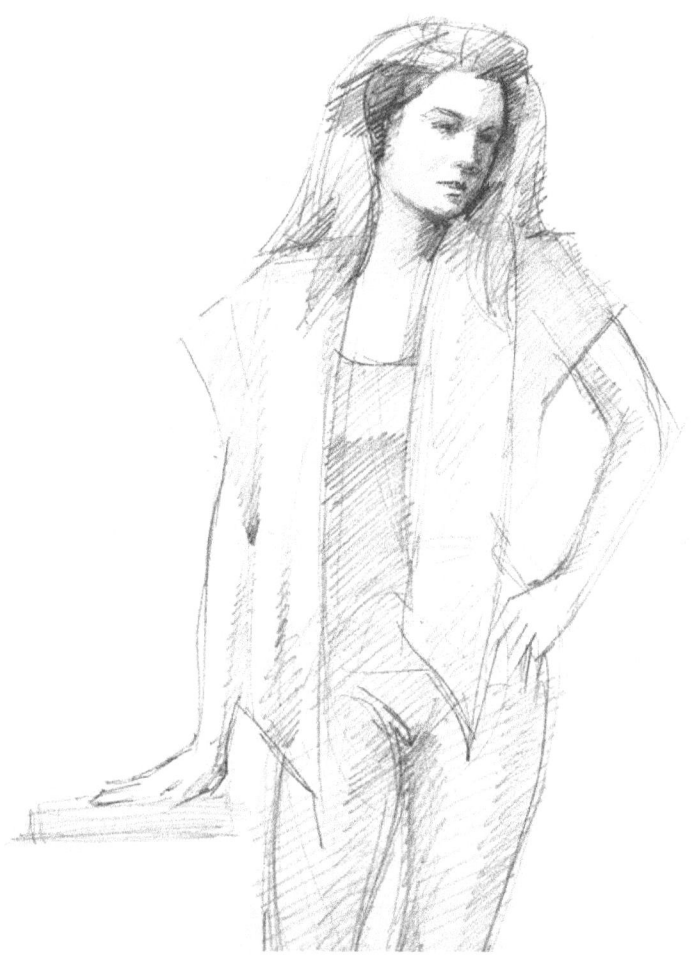

This sketch was done in about five or ten minutes. Drawing fast poses such as these helps sharpen your skills and will allow you to become more versatile and decisive in all your drawing.

I will not show any of my nude figure sketches here, simply because this is a portrait art book and many readers won't be expecting to see naked people. But you should understand that nude models will be common in these types of classes.

Many people are turned off by the idea of drawing nudes. But their fears are unfounded. Did you know that Norman Rockwell studied figure drawing? It's been considered a necessary part of an artist's education for many centuries. Even though Rockwell, the illustrator who is still much loved for his wholesome paintings, never painted a nude for his public work, he still saw the value in studying nudes in art school, because it helped him strengthen his skills.

Drawing the naked figure helps students to better understand human anatomy, and that in turn helps them depict people, either clothed or unclothed. Anyone who is interested in drawing, in particular in drawing people, is encouraged to start attending figure drawing classes. Don't worry about the nakedness of the models. When you see that everyone around you is more interested in getting their drawings right, and the nudity is treated like nothing out of the ordinary, then you begin to realize that it's going to be okay.

I attended my first figure drawing class (with naked models) right after I graduated high school. If you are under the age of 18 but want to attend a life drawing class with nude models, you may have to get special permission from your parents, or have a chaperone attend the sessions with you. Or, you can find classes where the models are clothed (or wear bathing-suit-type attire), until you reach the age of 18.

To find a local figure drawing class, check with a nearby college (a community college is often more affordable) or any community center that offers art classes. I'd also recommend looking at the site http://www.artmodelbook.com/ as it has a directory of available figure drawing classes. Classes are listed by state in the USA as well as in Canada. (At the time I write this book, there was a link on the left side of the main page to the directory.) Be aware that some listings may be out of date, but the guide is still very useful!

SKILL BUILDING LESSONS FROM CHAPTER EIGHT:

After completing several drawing projects with the aid of the grid, you now are being exposed to life beyond the grid. You have learned why drawing from life is important—and indeed, in some ways superior—to copying photographs. Some time-honored drawing secrets have been shown to you, to enable you to draw with accuracy without using the grid. You now understand that constant use of the grid may lead to an overdependence, which in turn can make it a crutch instead of a tool.

CHAPTER NINE: REFINING YOUR TECHNIQUE WITH A MORE "REALISTIC" PORTRAIT

Many beginner artists with an interest in portraiture have aspirations to make extra "realistic" drawings. This often will translate in their minds to "photorealistic."

This book won't be bringing a beginner artist quite to those heights; however, it can offer the necessary tools to help any artist vastly improve the realistic quality of their art.

If you look at this book's first drawing project, the portrait of Cynthia, you will notice that the shading is very simple. An adequate amount of detail is added to the face, but there are still large amounts of the paper that were never touched by the pencil.

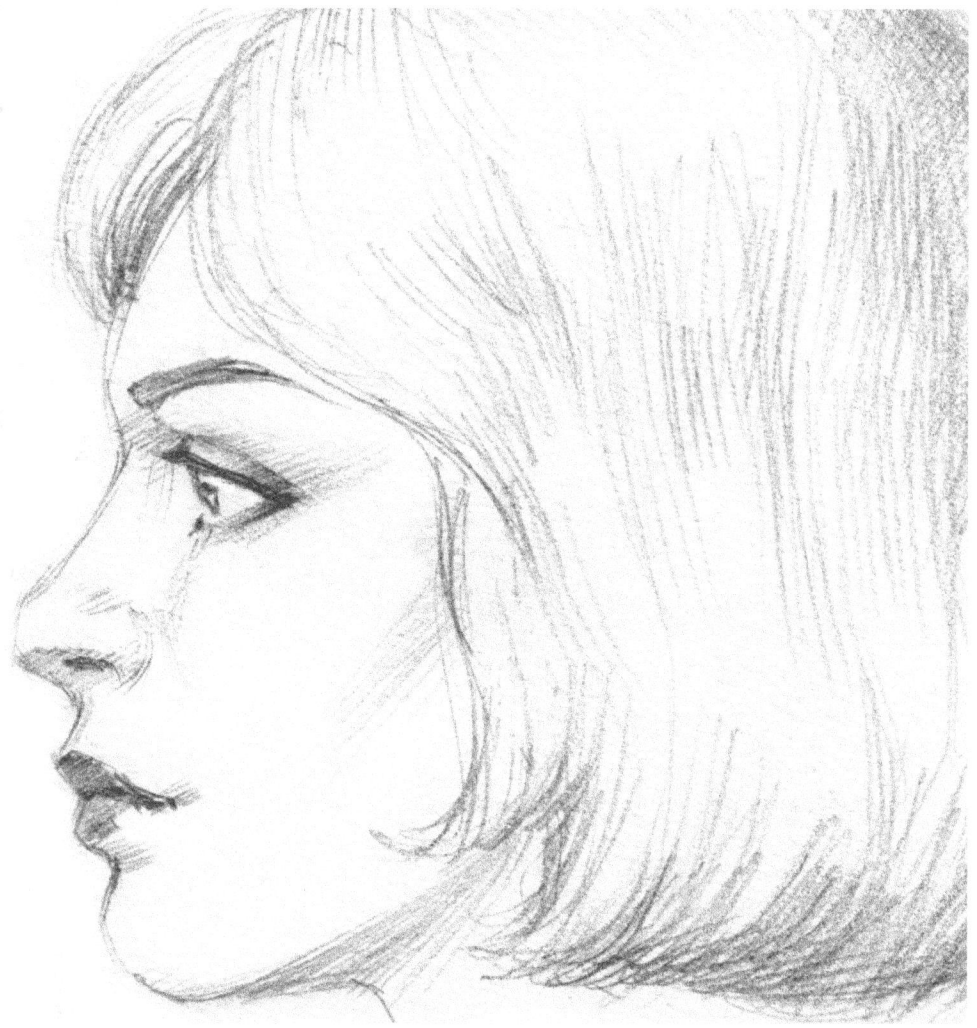

There's nothing wrong with this as a sketch, but it doesn't have an extra realism quality because the shading has been kept to a minimum. There's only a little shading under the jaw, the nose and mouth, the cheekbones; some additional definition around the eyes; and of course the shading of the hair.

Compare the portrait above, of "Cynthia", to the drawing on the next page:

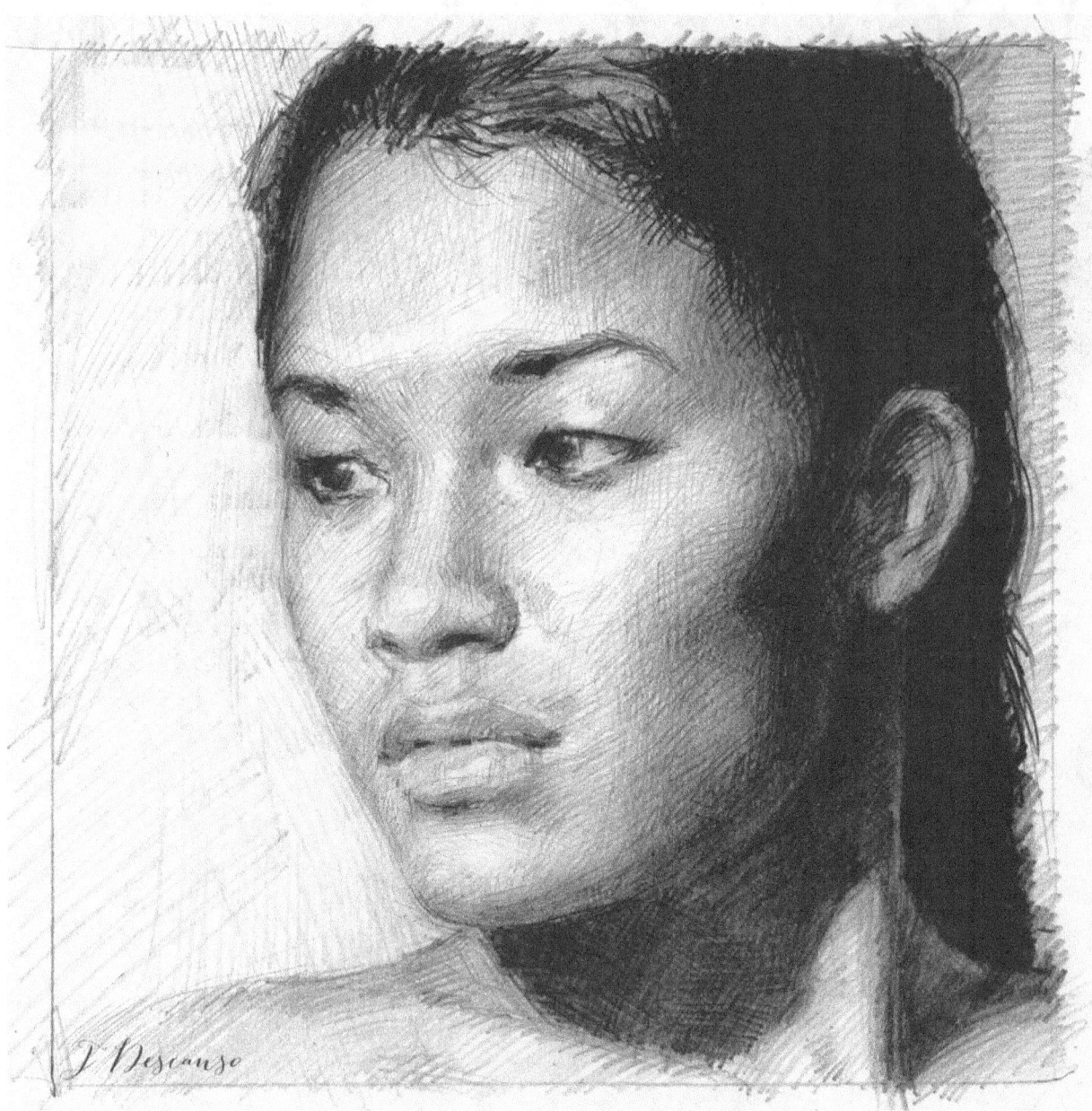

Almost every spot on this paper has some sort of pencil marks on it, including the background!

The main difference between these two drawings is not only the amount of detail (the second drawing has much more), but also the values. This second drawing has a much wider range of fully-defined values, from the blackest black, to the white of the paper, to all the shades in between.

CAPTURING THE TRUE VALUES

The key to capturing this realism in your own work is to first look at your reference picture or live model and identify the lightest areas. These areas and ONLY these areas will be white. Everything else on the drawing will have some pencil shading.

Let's identify some of the highlights on her face:

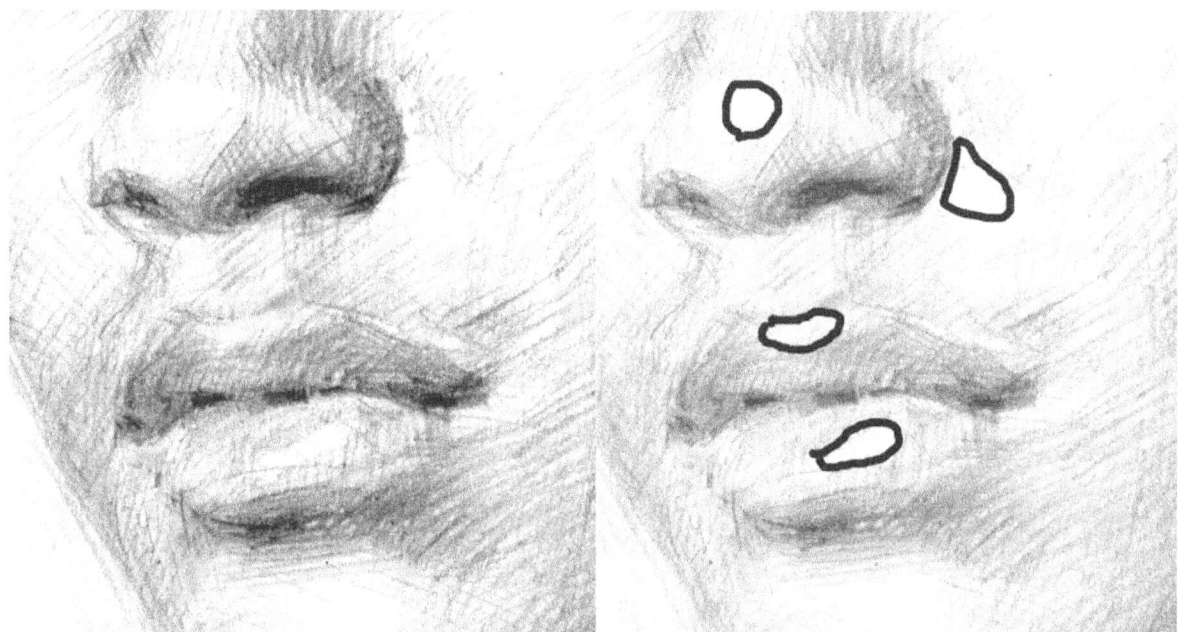

The lips have two main white highlights, and there's a highlight on the tip of the nose as well as at its corner. She also has a highlight on her upper eyelid, and in her eyes; highlights also appear in the inner corner of the eye on the right, and in a spot on the forehead. That's it! The rest of the drawing has to have some type of shading. Even if it's only the lightest of values, it still *has* to be there.

There's similar attention to values on two other more realistic-looking drawings from this book:

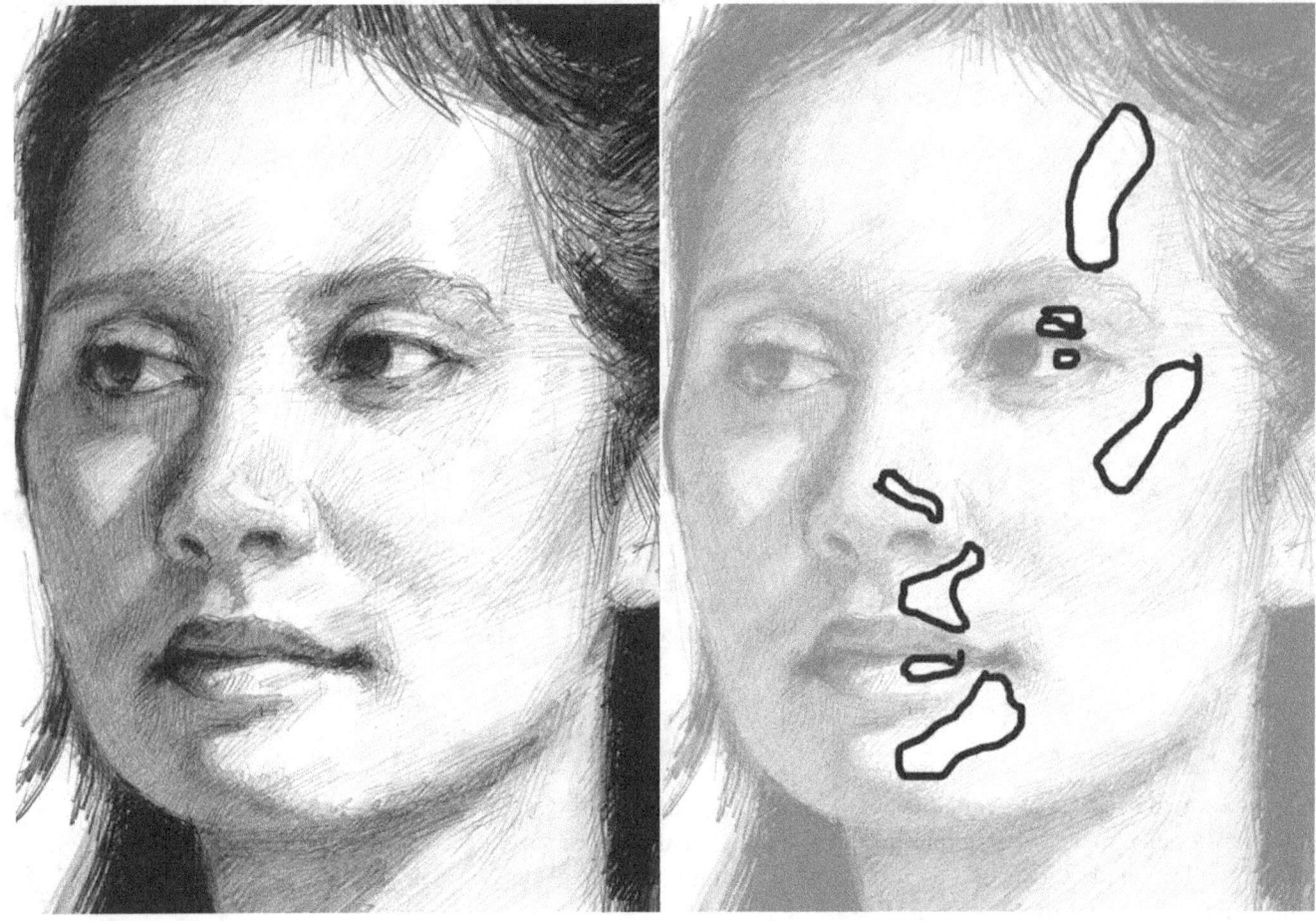

The highlighted areas are somewhat larger on this drawing, but even so, most of the face has some tone applied to it.

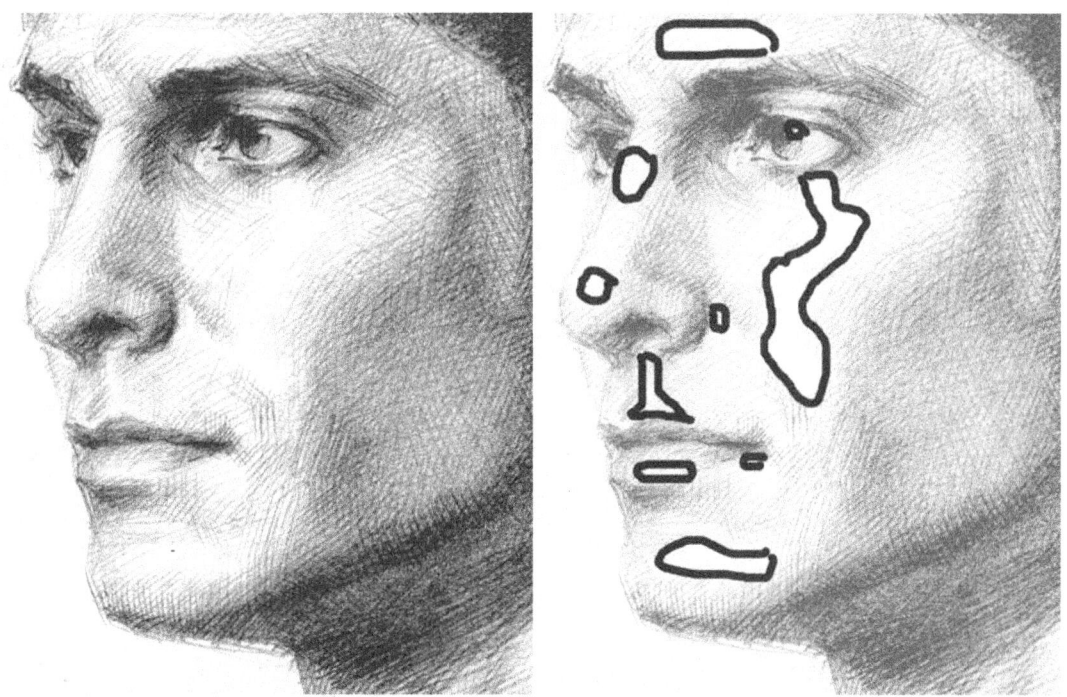

Some spots on this drawing are very light, but they are not quite white. The highlighted areas (untouched by a pencil) are still relatively small.

In order to identify the highlights, squint your eyes down halfway and look at your model or reference photo. When you squint, your vision should be slightly blurred. If you wear corrective lens, DO NOT take them off to get the blur. You must squint your eyes; that's what helps simplify the values for you.

As you squint, you will see that fine details are lost, but the basic shapes of light and dark will still remain. As you look at the blur, identify the lightest spots that pop out at you. Those are the highlights. Anything that is less than a pure white highlight will require at least some tiny amount of shading on it.

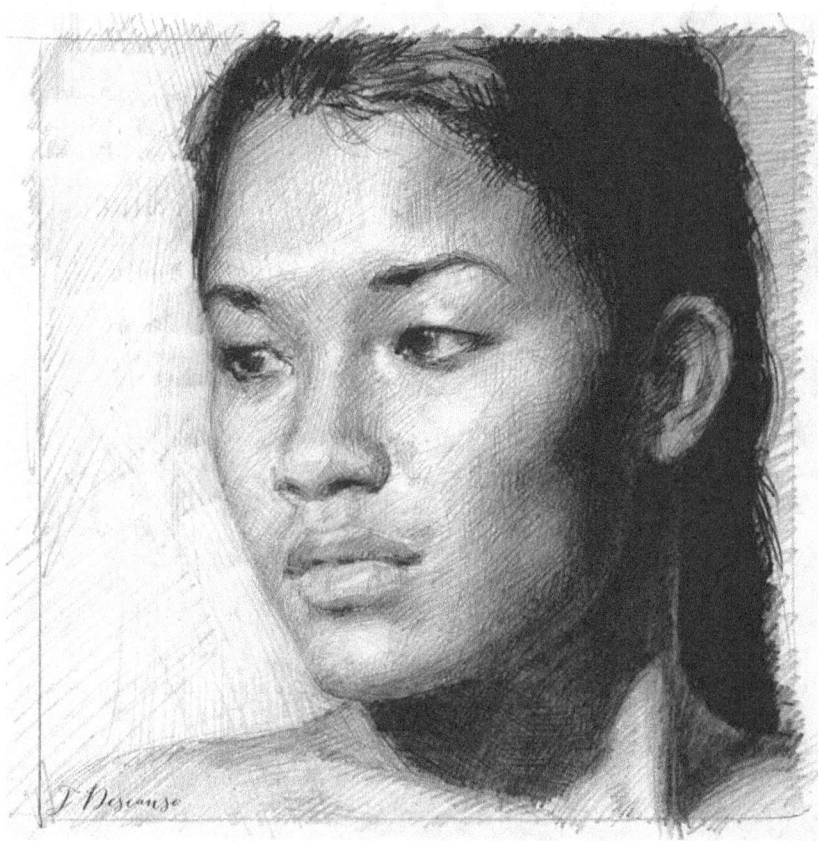

"Mercedes," 4x4 inches, graphite on paper

(I'm entitling this drawing "Mercedes", even though that's not the name of the model.)

Many of the following images shown of this drawing are bigger than its actual size. The original is a mere 4x4 inches. If you are reading the print version of this book, the picture above should be "real size." That's how small the original drawing truly is!

If you want to follow along and do your own version of this drawing, I recommend going up to 6x6 inches or even larger.

I don't own the rights to the reference photo, so unfortunately, I can't show it to you in this book. The photo comes from a .jpg file on the companion disk in the book, *Art Models 8: Practical Poses for the Working Artist* by Maureen and Douglas Johnson. I zoomed in on the model's face, cropped the photo and made it black and white in Photoshop. (These books contain photos of nude models in tastefully artistic poses, similar to what one might find in a figure drawing class.)

I highly recommend using photos from any of the books from the Art Models series, or else going to their site at posespace. com and downloading a set of reference pictures. You don't have to do a drawing using the same photo that I used. You can choose any photo that interests you.

You can do your drawing with or without a grid, but always remember that the grid's usefulness is limited, so sooner or later, you must move past it.

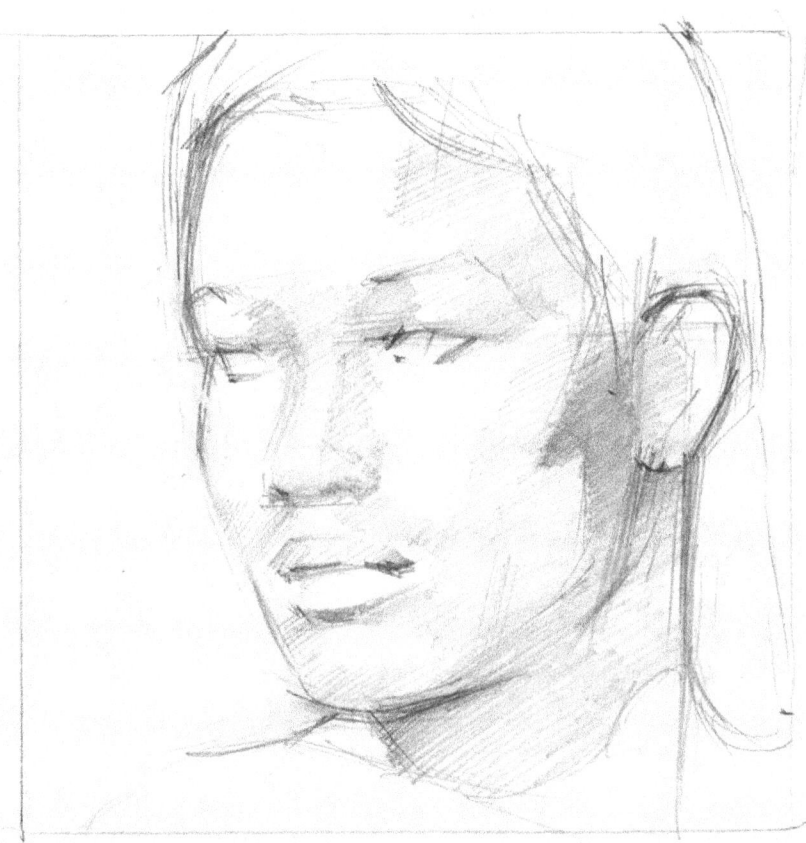

STEP ONE: I drew a perfect four-inch square and also cropped the reference photo so it was square as well. I then used the boundaries of this square frame as sort of single "grid" square. I looked for negative space, angles and borders in the source photo (with its perfectly square frame) and matched up the placement in my own square on the drawing paper.

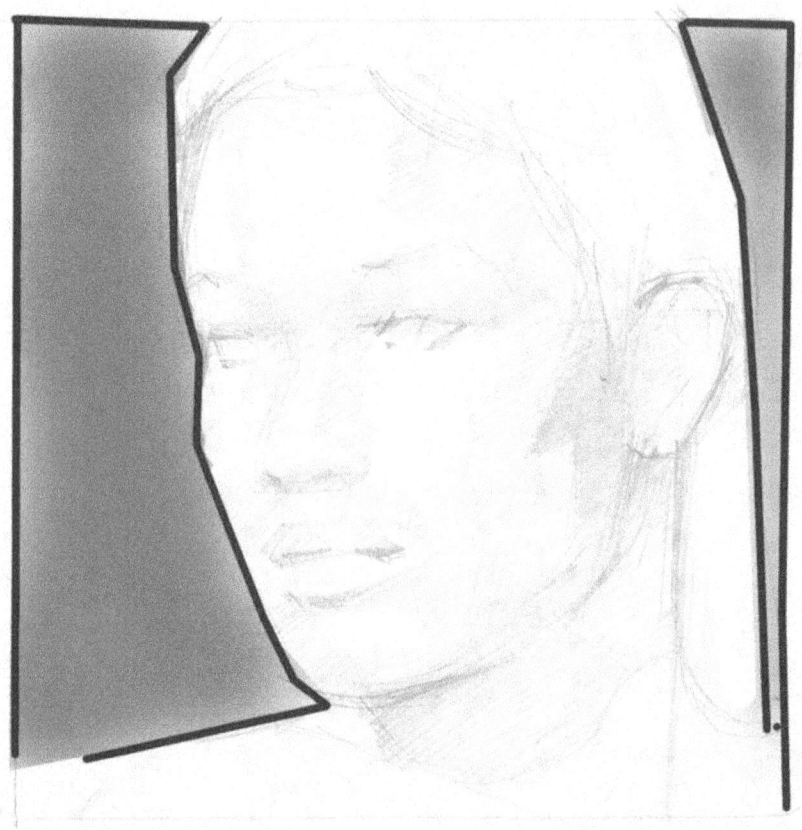

The first thing I did was focus on the negative space (seen here as the background, which I've shaded grey) in my reference photo. The right side of the picture has only a small sliver of negative space next to her head. There was more negative space on the left side. How far down on the square was the bottom of the chin? I looked at angles, like the side of her head, hair on the right side, and her shoulder, and the tilt of her cheek and forehead on the left side of the frame. I can also start doing measuring and comparing to make sure the proportions are correct in my drawing.

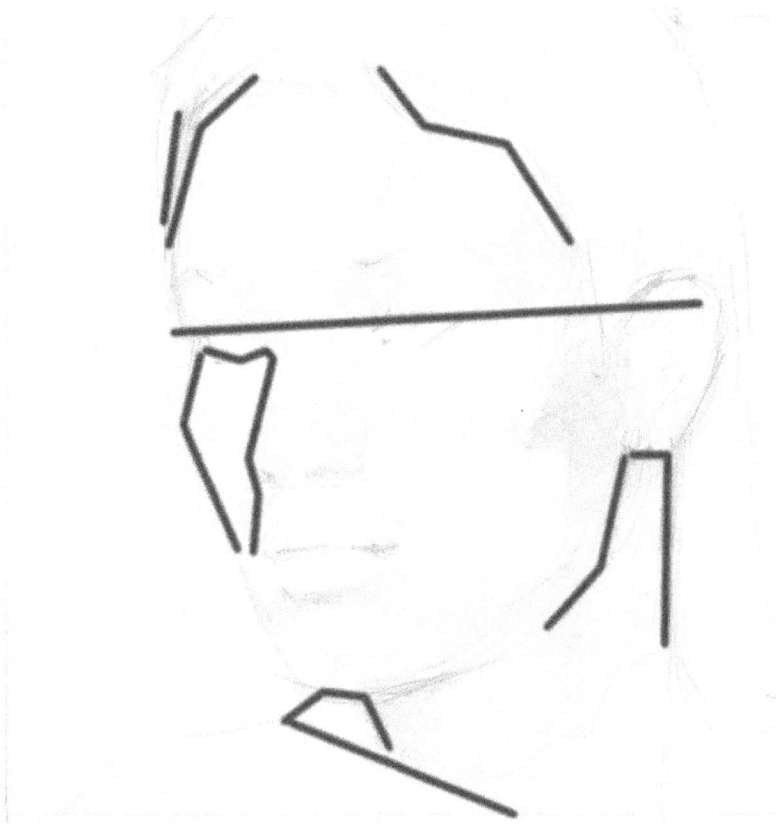

Here are some internal negative space areas that I worked to get correct. I looked at the shape that the shadow on her neck makes as well as the line of her collar bone. Then I identified the negative space made by the shadow of jawline (on the right side) that follows to below her ear, to the outer contour of her neck on the right side.

Getting the negative shape that was created by the side of her nose (on the left side) and the outer border of her cheek and extending to the lower edge of her eye also was crucial to getting her face in proportion.

I struggled with the outline of her hair and forehead. I had to force myself to look at the negative shapes to get the hairline more accurate.

You can see a very faint line on the sketch where I drew a line straight across her eyes. I often do this to make sure I don't get the eyes crooked. (Sometimes I still do, which means I keep on having to double-check!)

During this first phase of the drawing, I'm mostly concerned with getting the proportions correct. I also start to block out basic values and large shadow areas. I don't put in anything too dark at this stage, however. The accuracy of the drawing may still be wrong in some way, and there's no use in putting in darker values if all I end up doing is erasing them because I need to further correct the proportions.

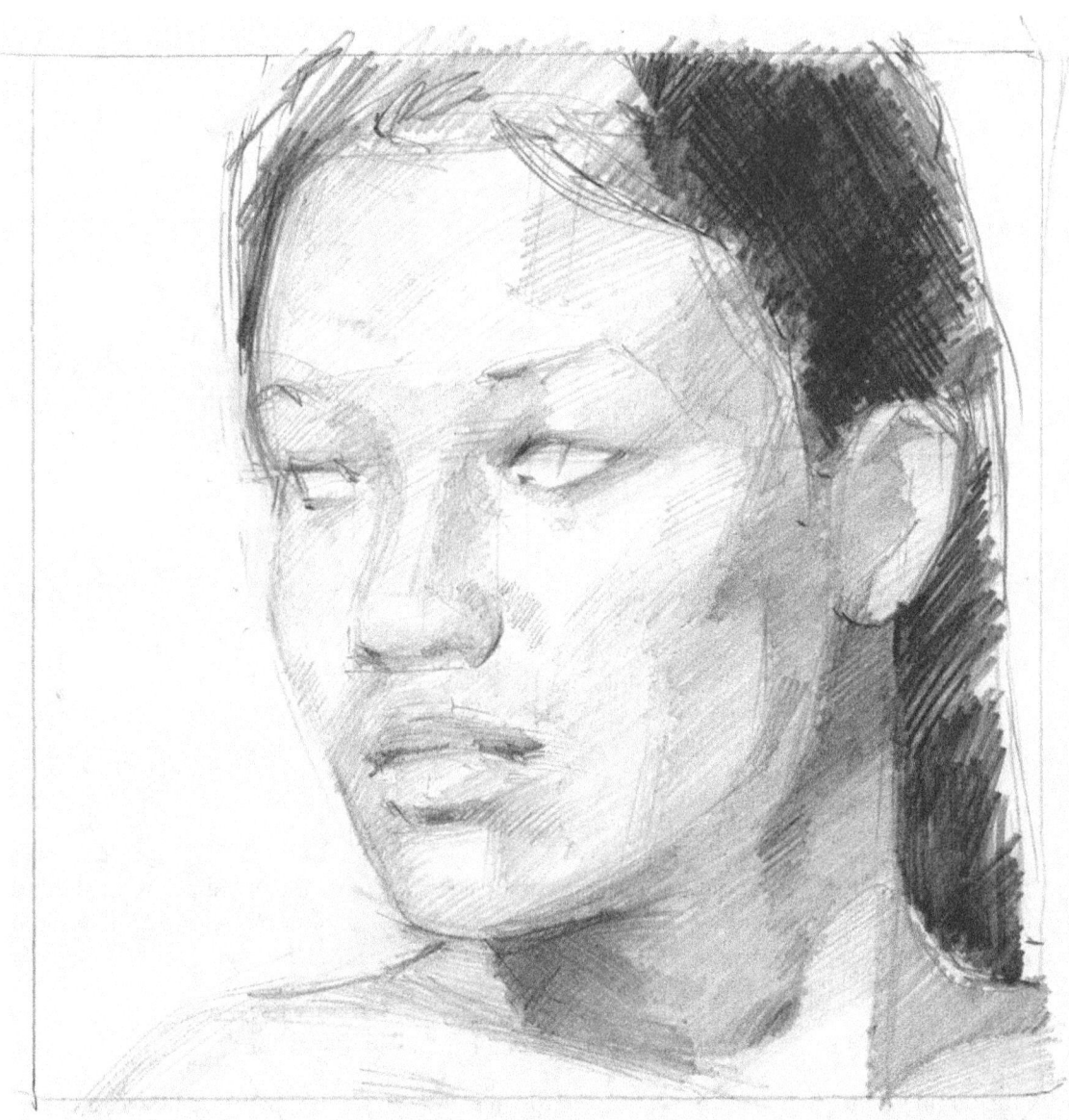

STEP TWO: As I become more confident of the placement of the features and the proportions, I start to block in the shadows more heavily. The hair is jet black with a few highlights, so I devote some time to darkening that area. Many other parts of the face are not yet rendered as dark as they will ultimately be; I'm working all around the face, continuing to model parts of the head and correct and adjust little details as I go along.

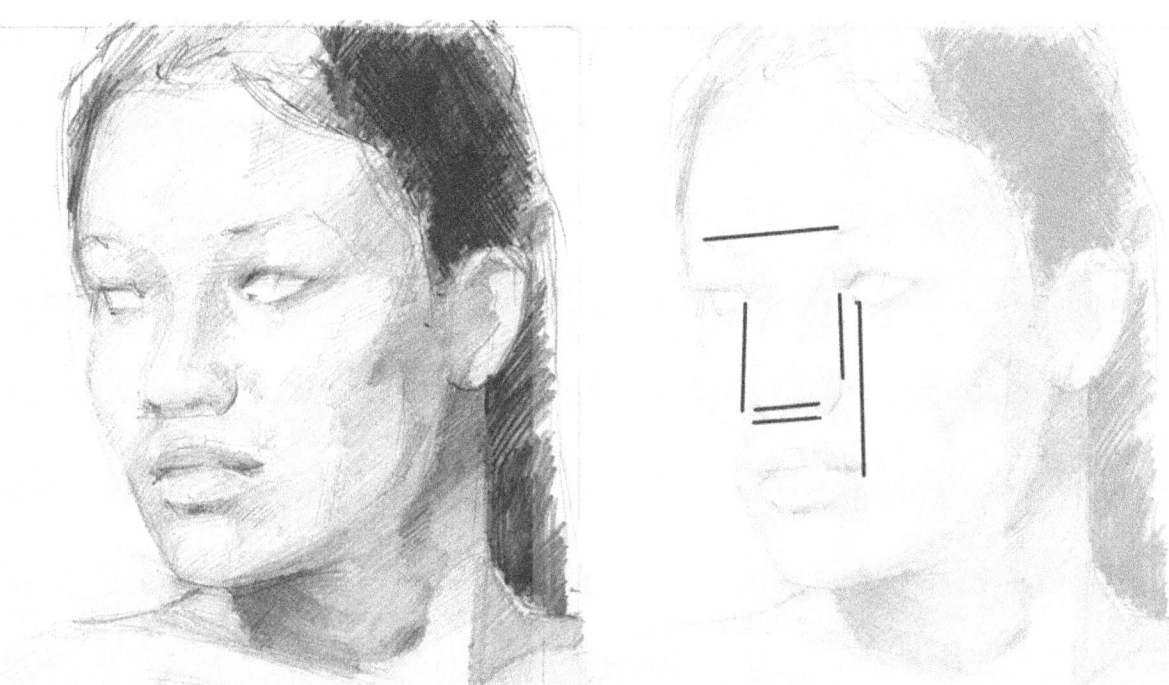

I place more light "alignment lines" all along the face (you can see slight remnants of them in the larger picture of Step Two). The eyebrows need to be aligned correctly. Do the inner edges of the eyes (on both sides) line up in the correct spot (at the edge or side of the nostrils)? The underside of the nose needs to be aligned accurately as well.

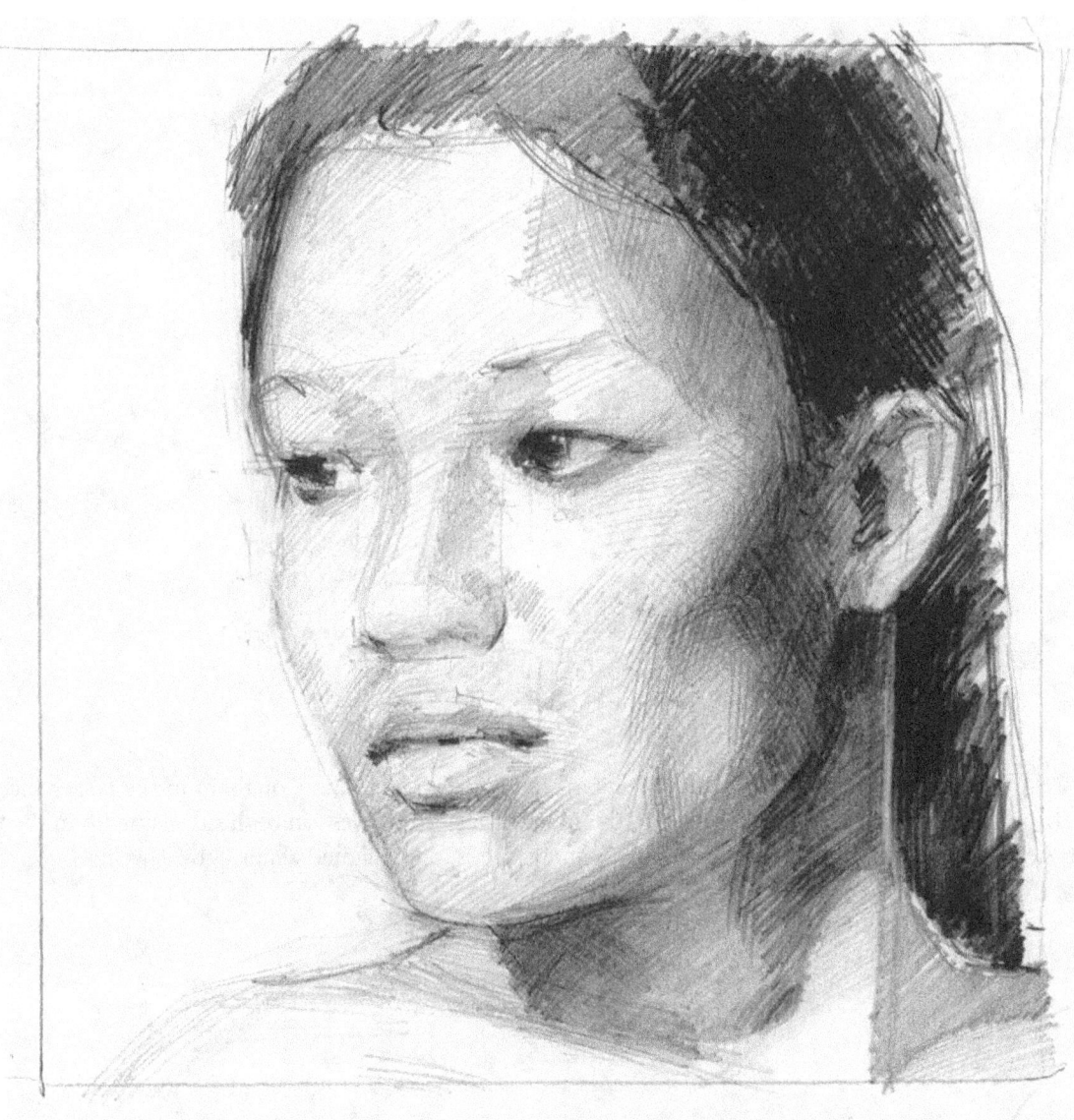

STEP THREE: I continue to add darker values. Finally, I am brave enough to darken the irises of the eyes—I feel they are in the right location now. More details and refinements are put to other parts of the head. I see some areas that trouble me, and I correct them before putting in additional darker tones. I consciously try to make my pencil strokes smoother and more delicate at this stage, but some of this is a losing battle, as my tendency to work enthusiastically and vigorously sometimes makes my hatch lines look vigorous too!

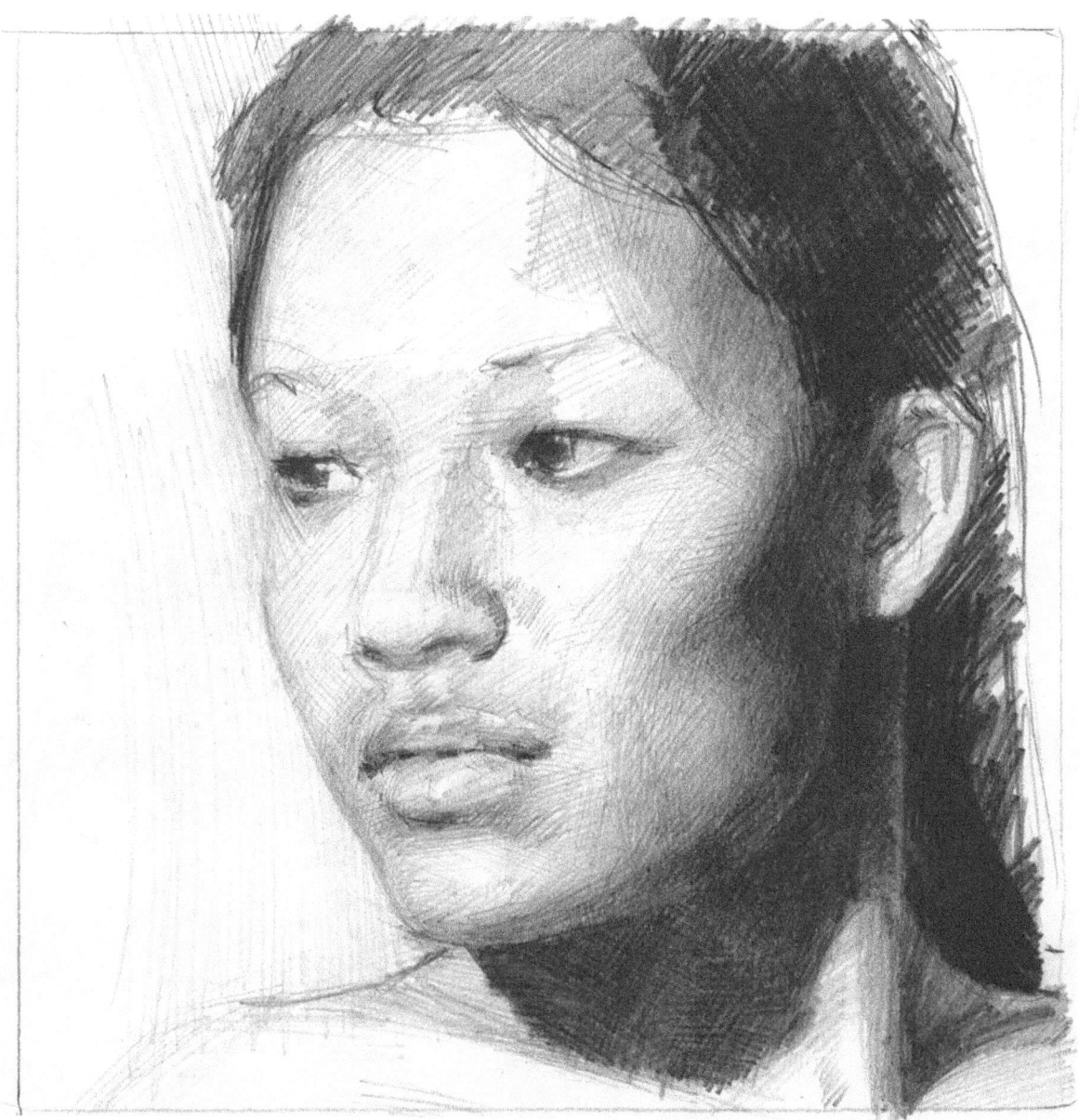

STEP FOUR: Much more effort and work is done to the darker values. I struggle with the mouth; something is not right there. I take a white rubber eraser and fiddle with her mouth and erase some of the pencil marks in order to bring out highlights. The shadowed side of the jaw and neck need a lot more attention. The forehead is a trouble area as well. The crosshatching there is too coarse. I need to slow down and work a little more meticulously. I use a regular wooden pencil with a 6B lead (very soft and dark) in order to darken the value in the hair and make it pure black. Trying to cover that much black with a HB or 2B pencil lead (which doesn't make as strong of a line as a 6B) is frustrating. I start to add some looser hatching to the background.

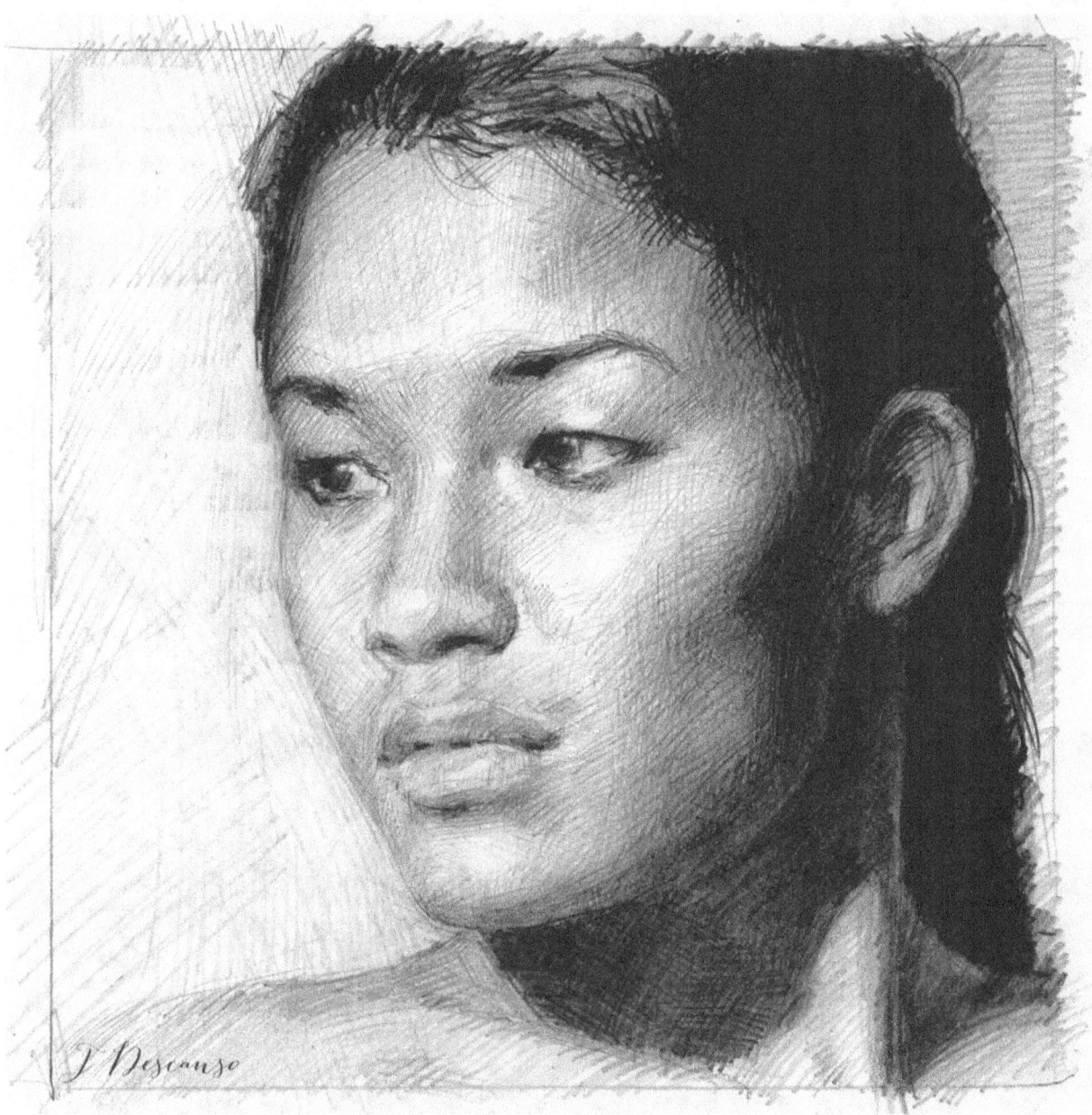

STEP FIVE: Finished! Now the picture is enlarged so it's printed bigger than its modest 4x4-inch size.

I re-worked the mouth and refined the area around the nostrils. I cannot lie; there are a few areas that still aren't quite the way I'd like them. (Most artists will admit this about a lot of their finished work.) But as they say in my neck of the woods, "Put a fork in it, it is done!"

A lot of attention was needed on the eyes. Some loose crosshatching was put over the background, but I decided that on the left side, in particular, the crosshatching was too dark and distracting. I used the edge of a white rubber eraser and pulled it horizontally across the background in a purposeful manner to lighten up some of the strokes but not completely remove them.

ADDITIONAL NOTES:

I have been teaching the crosshatch technique throughout this book. I hope I have demonstrated its versatility, and its suitability for both quick sketches and more detailed drawings. Crosshatching isn't taught nearly as often as I think it should be, so I hope this book has helped rectify that, at least a little.

We all are probably aware of an increasingly popular drawing technique, which is blending pencil strokes with the help of a blending stump or tortillion. I have avoided teaching this method, in part because it is not my preference, and also because so many books already cover it.

If you are interested in learning more about blending, I strongly recommend the book *Lifelike Heads: Discover Your "Inner Artist" as You Learn to Draw Portraits in Graphite* by Lance Richlin. It is available in both ebook and paperback format through Walter Foster publishing.

Richlin says in this book that he respects crosshatching, and I can wholeheartedly say the same about blending—when artists like him are using the technique! One of the first things you'll notice about his artwork is how strikingly crisp and detailed his portraits are, and how all the values are captured (with only small areas of the drawing left white). Richlin also is a strong advocate of working from life—another reason I admire and recommend his book!

CHAPTER TEN: FAQS FOR BEGINNER ARTISTS

Now that you're on your way to becoming an accomplished portrait artist, here are some commonly asked questions that many new artists may ask:

WHEN CAN I CALL MYSELF AN "ARTIST"?

A person who takes a lot of photographs will be called a "photographer" by those who know him or her. Someone who is always in the kitchen preparing food and trying out new recipes will be considered a "cook." Anyone who devotes hours each day to playing the piano will get the title of "musician." They won't always be assumed to be a professional photographer, professional cook, or professional musician, of course. It's the passion for working and creating that earns such people these titles, not whether they are doing it for a living.

When you have devoted a lot of time to making art, when it's gotten under your skin and you know you love it, you should call yourself an artist. If you feel self-conscious and worry that you could be saying this too soon, then go ahead and refer to yourself as a "budding artist" or a "student artist" for a while. But never forget: the act of creating art is what makes you an artist.

"YOU'RE NOT A TRUE ARTIST IF…"

There are people who will say things like, "Real artists don't do…" (and then they'll mention some practice, technique or style that they don't like). Most of the time, I don't buy into that.

Just like everyone else on this planet, I have strong opinions about what kind of art I like, and what artistic styles and techniques I respect and admire. Because of this, I may consider someone else a "bad" artist or a "lazy" artist if they do things in a way that I don't like. But, I will never deny that they are still an artist.

However, I believe that artists must actually make art. They make *something*. They don't just talk about how they are planning on doing it, they *do* it!

HOW DO I FIND MY "STYLE"? "BUT THAT'S MY STYLE!"

"I've decided that this particular technique is going to be part of my style." "I need to find a style!" Be careful before you utter these words! This is not something that should be a concern for you.

Your style happens when you're busy making art. More often, someone else will identify your style for you!

Style just happens. It shouldn't be forced or planned out ahead of time.

Granted, to some extent you can decide that your "style" is to do a lot of drawings of dogs, or to specialize in seascapes. But many aspects of style should happen without your even being aware.

I had no real conscious plan for what my style would be when I was a student. I don't know when it developed, but it did. I found out that I had a style when people started saying to me, "I could tell that you drew that! It's your style!" I thought, "Oh! I hadn't realized!"

The statement, "But that's my style!" can be a cop-out, a retort used when someone criticizes one's work. Yes, there are times when it's necessary to say that. If someone is wondering why you always draw dogs, then of course it's fair to say that favoring dogs as subjects is part of your style. If I am asked why I use the crosshatch technique, that's firmly in the style category as well.

Unfortunately, citing one's style is sometimes used as an excuse. A few years ago, I encountered an artist who was doing portraits of her favorite celebrity. Her goal was to draw a faithful likeness, but instead, her portraits were misshapen and never looked a bit like the actor. She refused to consider learning new techniques to improve her work. Instead, she wanted to keep on doing what she was doing (to stay within her comfort zone) and attribute all the lopsidedness and nonexistent likenesses to "style." But that's not how it works. Style is not meant to be a cover for an absence of skill or other technical errors.

WHEN CAN I START SELLING MY ARTWORK?

This question comes up often. The obvious answer would be when others are interested in buying it! When people start asking you if you could draw a portrait of [them, their spouse, their child, their parents], then congratulations, you're ready to sell!

I caution you, however, to not underprice your work because you believe that new artists don't "deserve" to earn more than a certain amount. It's not about how long you've been drawing, it's about the quality of your work.

If you are not sure of how much to charge, look at what other artists (doing a similar style of work and with the same approximate skill level) are earning for each piece, and price your work in the same range.

Stick to your guns if you are confident that your prices are "reasonable" (which often means on the low side). Some would-be buyers simply don't value any artist's work and won't be satisfied until we all give our work away for nothing.

It's better to price a little too low (then raise prices as demand for your work grows) than to price your work too high and be forced to lower the prices later in order to sell anything. Always remember: Your prices should go up, but NEVER down, at least not if you can avoid it!

There are a lot of ways to sell your art these days. You can only do local shows, or you can only sell online, or you can do a combination of both. Try them all and see what suits you the best.

SHOULD I START WORKING WITH COLOR?

If you have some particular reason for not wanting to work in color, that's okay. There are always going to be those artists who prefer to stick to a monochromatic style.

Assuming you have no objection to color, though, I'd advise you to get started fairly soon. Give yourself a little more time to become comfortable with drawing, but don't procrastinate. The longer you wait, the more you could regret the delay.

I've encountered some pencil artists who have become masters at their craft. When they reach such a high level in pencil, many people will naturally assume that they can paint, too. To have everyone expecting that they can paint—when they can't—can be aggravating to such an artist, especially when there isn't any real reason why they haven't already learned. That's why I advise you to learn color sooner rather than later.

WHAT COLOR MEDIUMS SHOULD I USE?

That is entirely up to you. Often, beginner artists are more comfortable with colored pencil, watercolors, or acrylics. The colored pencils are in their comfort zone because they're still pencils. (There's nothing wrong with that! I love colored pencils too!) Watercolors and acrylics are water-based, which can also be more comfortable as many of us used some sort of water-based paints in school.

I recommend that you try out various mediums and see what you like. However, I'll personally confess a bias in favor of oils. A lot of artists find oils intimidating because they require the use of special oil mixtures and solvents (like mineral spirits). I think a lot of these concerns and worries are overblown. There's no reason why a beginner artist can't try oils, assuming they do some research on it (which can be easily found online and in most beginning oil painting books).

If you think that you may want to sell your artwork in the future, be advised that works on paper (colored pencil, graphite, charcoal, watercolor, and so forth) don't fetch as high a price. A watercolor painting will not earn as much (on average) as an oil or acrylic painting of the same size. It also appears that oil painters usually earn slightly more than acrylic painters. None of these things are about what's "fair" or what's "better", it just seems to be what *is*. Use this information as you will. But, I discourage you from choosing a medium only because you believe it will make you more money. Always go with the medium that you love the best.

SHOULD I TAKE ART LESSONS AND/OR GO TO ART SCHOOL?

When a beginner artist gets bitten by the art bug, they might start to wonder if they should pursue a formal education. The answer will depend on the artist's budget and their goals.

There are some wonderful art schools that will give you excellent training. The secret is, find which schools are excellent. (Not all of them are.) Find a school that will help you fulfill your dreams. Find a school that you can afford without going into terrible debt.

Assuming you can accomplish these things, then art school (or a university with an excellent art department) is a wonderful thing.

But, never think that the absence of this type of art education means that you can't be a "real" artist. Furthermore, never believe that someone else is a good artist merely because they got a degree at XYZ university. Always judge an artist by the artwork they make, not by where they went to school.

Another route to consider is an atelier. An atelier is a small, private art school that is usually not accredited (so you won't get a degree), but it is far more affordable than many colleges. It will teach you the "old-fashioned" traditional skills that have (unfortunately) fallen out of favor in many mainstream colleges. Sadly, with many regular colleges, you'll get a degree but not much in the way of art skills. With an atelier, you'll get the skills, but not the degree.

To get more information, visit artrenewal.org and look for their page on approved ateliers.

If you decide not to pursue a college degree (and an atelier is not an option), then you can always take some figure drawing and painting classes at the local community college, community center, or other facility that offers classes for adults. I got some wonderful training from my first figure drawing teacher at a community college. Many times, an artist in your town will hold workshops or private lessons. If you like the local artist's work, then by all means, inquire about taking lessons!

There's nothing wrong with being self-taught, and you should feel no shame about it. You can still be an excellent artist even if you never attended an art class or workshop. But, I would never encourage anyone to deliberately avoid getting any sort of guidance or lessons, if the quality of the education is good.

One final note: I know of several artists who were introduced to drawing in their 50s, 60s, or beyond. I know one man who had never attempted anything with art until he was in his 50s. He is now in his 70s, and is giving painting lessons as well as winning major awards in art shows. NEVER say, "I'm too old to start learning this." If you are not too old to follow the instructions in this book, then you're not too old!

FINAL WORDS

Now that you've become a portrait-drawing veteran (of sorts), and have built several valuable skills along the way, you are ready to set out on your own wonderful journey of art.

Every seasoned artist will tell you—there are ups and downs. But when there is love for your craft, it will pay off for you. That pay-off may not be monetary (though it often can be) but it will still give you great value.

Remember that the love for art comes from within, and it must not be dependent on the approval or praise of others. While it's wonderful to have your artwork appreciated, if you don't love art for its own sake, then all the approval and encouragement in the world won't compensate. You MUST love it because only that love will get you through the inevitable failures and frustrations that come along the way. You *have* to feel that love. Those who don't feel it strongly enough are the ones who give up and say it's "too hard." It's NOT that it's too hard. It just requires more work and love before it will blossom and bear fruit for you.

Not everyone is destined to become a full-time artist, and that's okay. It doesn't make you less of an artist and it doesn't mean that your love is smaller. Whatever role art has in your life, it will make your life all the better.

Don't be discouraged if you have starts and stops and you question yourself sometimes—that's normal. Keep on working and see where things lead you. Don't let your age, your art background (or lack thereof) or anything else hold you back. The only thing that can keep you from moving forward is YOU.

I wish you many wonderful hours (and weeks, years!) of lasting fulfillment with your art.

If you enjoyed this book, please be sure to leave a review on the online store where you bought this book! And, be sure to visit my website at http://yellowcatstudio.com and sign up for the mailing list.

BOOK RECOMMENDATIONS:

Betty Edwards, *Drawing on the Right Side of the Brain*

Bert Dodson, *Keys to Drawing*

Andrew Loomis, *Drawing the Head & Hands*

Lance Richlin, *Lifelike Heads: Discover Your "Inner Artist" as You Learn to Draw Portraits in Graphite*

ABOUT THE AUTHOR

I am a native of Southern California, and attended Otis College of Art & Design in Los Angeles, where I focused on drawing, color theory, and anatomy.

Currently I run a small art studio where I paint in oils (and sometimes acrylics) and occasionally give private lessons to students interested in drawing and painting.

www.ingramcontent.com/pod-product-compliance
Lightning Source LLC
Chambersburg PA
CBHW080816180526
45168CB00006B/2468